Praise for
Special Children, Challenged Parents
Revised Edition

"This book engages the reader at many levels, both touching your heart and teaching your mind. Dr. Naseef refuses to engage in simplistic answers. He is able to embrace the paradox and ambivalence of experiences that include joy and sorrow, tragedy and blessing, and loss and gift. Just as he talks about what he learned from his son, Tariq, I would invite families, professionals, and friends of families and people with disabilities to spend a little 'floor time' with this book. It will help anyone involved."

— **Bill Gaventa, M.Div.**
Assistant Professor of Pediatrics
Community and Congregational Supports
Co-Editor, *Journal of Religion, Disability, and Health*
The Boggs Center on Developmental Disabilities
Robert Wood Johnson Medical School-UMDNJ

"Writing with the wisdom of a mental health professional and the compassion of a loving father, Dr. Naseef has given us a book that will instruct and inspire us all."

— **Rabbi Harold Kushner**
Author of *When Bad Things Happen to Good People*

"A very special book for parents with special children. Beautifully written with love and compassion, it is so much more than a resource guide. Parents will not feel so alone; clinicians and educators will gain better insight. Dr. Naseef clearly understands the complex range of issues that parents face because he has experienced these concerns firsthand."

— **Nancy D. Wiseman**
Founder and President, First Signs, Inc.

"A touching and insightful portrayal of the heartbreaking problems which confront parents of a special child. Dr. Naseef's account of the phases of grief, anger, bewilderment to final acceptance and peace of mind which the families (and Naseef) experience is eloquent. Professionals, parents, siblings, and anyone involved in the field of special needs should read this book."

— **Virginia Walker Sperry, M.A.**
Author of *Fragile Success: Ten Autistic Children, Childhood to Adulthood*

"*Special Children, Challenged Parents* is a compelling journey that speaks to the heart and soul of all who are touched by children with special needs. Bob Naseef is an expert in addressing despair, sorrow, and grieving, while offering us uplifting skills to achieve courage, hope, and joyful acceptance. This book is truly inspirational; you will never feel alone again."

— **Jody Swarbrick**
Parenting Special Needs, About.com

"A landmark book for parents and professionals. Beautifully written, this up-to-date book describes the complex challenges families face as the author integrates his personal growth as a father with his terrific professional empathy and expertise. You will find yourself reaching for this book again and again as an important resource for understanding families, for intervention strategies, and for inspiration."

— **Nancy Miller, Ph.D., M.S.W.**
UCLA Department of Psychiatry
Author of *Nobody's Perfect* and *Everybody's Different*

"Robert Naseef's book, based on his personal experience as a parent, and as a guide and mentor to other parents, provides a welcome beacon of light, information and inspiration to the beleaguered families searching for help and hope. This book will become a valued friend. Highly recommended."

— **Bernard Rimland, Ph.D.**
Director, Autism Research Institute
Founder, Autism Society of America
Editor, *Autism Research Review International*

Critical Acclaim for the First Edition

"A compelling account of his family's journey that is also a valuable resource for families and those who interact with them. Dr. Naseef is a patient and persistent guide. He does not back away from showing both the painful realities and the process he uses to maintain his course in the face of obstacles."

— *The Philadelphia Inquirer*

"Too good to put down." — *Stickler Involved People Newsletter*

"*Special Children, Challenged Parents* has the mysterious power to move its readers. The honesty and details allowed me to reflect on my own emotions as the father of a special son over the last seven years."

— **James H. Myers**
President, Congenital Heart Anomalies Support, Education, and Research

"As a father and a psychotherapist, Dr. Naseef provides a very well written discussion of the powerful issues faced by parents of children with disabilities or special health care needs in their day-to-day lives—a fine book for parents and professionals."

—**Stanley D. Klein, Ph.D.**
Special Needs Expert at Parents.com
Co-Founder, former Editor in Chief, *Exceptional Parent Magazine*

"Dr. Naseef is able to convey the personal journey of parenting a severely disabled child in a way that gives the reader the belief that within tragedy, there lies reason. *Special Children, Challenged Parents* is able to straddle that fine line between popular psychology and academic scholarship."

—**Jed Yalof, Psy.D.**
The Independent Practitioner, American Psychological Association

"This book represents the intersection of the heart and soul of the parent with the insight and knowledge of the therapist. By opening up his own personal journal, Dr. Naseef sheds a bright light on the emotional pain and victories of raising children with disabilities."

—*Focus on Autism and Other Developmental Disabilities*

"An extremely moving personal documentary. The professional work and detailed clinical work he describes are enriched by his own vivid experiences, thus making his suggestions more meaningful and practical. "

—*The Journal of Developmental and Learning Disorders*

"His book, like a good friend, made me feel less alone."

—**Jennifer Graham**
ACTION, Pennsylvania Council for Exceptional Children

"As you journey through the book, you follow Dr. Naseef as he reaches out to others to tell them what he has learned. You could say he has 'been there, done that' and each of us can gain much from *Special Children, Challenged Parents.*"

—*Hypothyroidism Newsletter*

"This powerful and moving book will serve as an invaluable guide for millions of families with children with special needs."

—*Vision Enhancement*

"A must for all parents of special needs kids, and possibly a sensitive guide for all of us coming to terms with the challenging emotions of caregiving."

—*Take Care!,* National Family Caregivers Association

"Each child is an individual unto themselves and a special gift unlike no other. Anyone whose life has been touched by someone with special needs will be inspired by Dr. Naseef's journey on the road to coming to terms with his son's disability."

—Columbia Parent

"Although each family's circumstances may be unique, Dr. Naseef has suggested a universal process for negotiating a challenging terrain."

—Breaking Ground
Tennessee Developmental Disabilities Council

"Taking the reader, whether it be the parent of or a person with a disability, on a journey of exploration of our emotions and how they work to make us healthy. Masterfully interweaves his own experiences as a parent and those of the parents he counsels."

—Horizons: News by and for People with Disabilities

"Written in a simple straightforward way with the authority of a professional and the tenderness of a father."

—National PKU News: News and Information about Phenylketonuria

"An especially moving book with a healing quality, and regardless of your child's age, a little more healing always helps when special parenting."

—The Myelin Messenger

"Poignant and well written, and especially helpful to fathers."

—National Lymphedema Network Newsletter

"My hands picked up *another* book about parenting children with disabilities. This time I had struck gold! With compassion, empathy, and vulnerability, Dr. Naseef shares his own heart through his experience along with anecdotes of those who he has counseled."

—Parent to Parent Newsletter, Summit County, Ohio

"Sound, authoritative advice with true insight to problems parents face. Good reading for medical professionals as well as parents."

—American Celiac Society

"I have been involved in and around special education for over 25 years, and this book is by far the most significant work I have encountered. I congratulate Dr. Naseef for taking the risk of writing about his experiences and feelings and for his modeling as a therapist and as a father."

—Thomas C. Flamboe
The Family Journal

Special CHILDREN
Challenged PARENTS

Special CHILDREN Challenged PARENTS

The Struggles
and Rewards of
Raising a Child
with a Disability

REVISED EDITION

by Robert A. Naseef, Ph.D.

·P A U L·H·
BROOKES
PUBLISHING C°®

Baltimore • London • Sydney

·P A U L · H·
BROOKES
PUBLISHING C°®

Paul H. Brookes Publishing Co.
Post Office Box 10624
Baltimore, Maryland 21285-0624

www.brookespublishing.com

"Paul H. Brookes Publishing Co." is a registered trademark of
Paul H. Brookes Publishing Co., Inc.

Typeset by Barton Matheson Willse & Worthington,
Baltimore, Maryland.
Manufactured in the United States of America by
Versa Press, East Peoria, Illinois.

First printing of revised edition: July 2001
10   9   8   7   6   5   4   3

DAY IS DONE, by Peter Yarrow. © 1969 Pepamar Music Corp.
All rights reserved. Used by permission. WARNER BROS.
PUBLICATIONS U.S. INC. Miami, FL. 33014

Library of Congress Cataloging-in-Publication Data

Naseef, Robert A.
    Special children, challenged parents : the struggles and rewards
of raising a child with a disability / by Robert A. Naseef.
        p.   cm.
Includes bibliographical references and index.
    ISBN-13: 1-978-55766-535-5
    ISBN-10: 1-55766-535-4
    1. Parents of handicapped children—United States—
Psychology.   2. Parents of handicapped children—United
States—Attitudes.   3. Handicapped children—United States—
Family relationships.   4. Handicapped children—United States—
Psychology.   I. Title.

HQ759.913 .N37 2001
649'.151—dc21   2001034530

British Library Cataloguing in Publication data are available from
the British Library.

To my future,
Tariq
Antoinette
Kara
and
Zoë

Contents

1
A Father Is Born
My Story........................ *1*

2
Feeling the Impact
Lost Dreams and Growth................ 15

3
The Other Side of Sorrow
Working Through the Grief................ 37

4
Day by Day
Tuning in to Your Special Child 63

5
How to Stop Spinning
Understanding and Guiding Your Child's Behavior....... 89

6
A Circle of Fathers

7
Keeping the Boat Afloat

8
Differing Views of the Mountain

9
The Trouble with Elephants

10
A Perilous Partnership

11
When the Miracle Never Comes

About the Author

Robert A. Naseef, Ph.D., along with his wife, Cindy N. Ariel, Ph.D., has a full-time independent practice in psychology specializing in working with families of children with special needs. He has "a foot in each world" because he himself is the father of a child with autism. He is a family consultant at Specare Pediatric Center (http://www.specare. com), which provides a medical home for children with special health care needs in the Delaware Valley, and serves as a consultant to school districts, special education parent groups, and human services organizations. He maintains a busy web site at http://www.specialfamilies.com and also writes regular columns at http://www.specialchild.com, http://www.parentsdirect.net, and http://www.specialchildren. about.com.

Dr. Naseef, a native of Philadelphia who received his doctoral degree in psychological studies from Temple University, has a broad background of experience in both education and psychology. He has a special interest and expertise in the psychology of men and fatherhood. He was instrumental in developing a training package to foster parent–professional collaboration for the New Jersey Department of Education, Division of Special Education, and taught graduate courses at Antioch University Philadelphia and Rider University in Lawrenceville, New Jersey. He held clinical privileges in psychology at the Pennsylvania Hospital's Department of Psychiatry and serves on the board of directors of the Center for Autistic Children, the professional advisory board of the Pathway School, and the parent steering committee of the Interdisciplinary Council on Learning and Developmental Disorders.

Special Children, Challenged Parents: The Struggles and Rewards of Raising a Child with a Disability has received local and national recognition, and Dr. Naseef has had speaking engagements from coast to coast.

Dr. Naseef lives in the Philadelphia area with his wife, Cindy, and his two daughters, Kara and Zoë. His oldest daughter, Antoinette, also lives and works in the Philadelphia area. His son, Tariq, graduated from the Devereux Foundation in June 2001. Dr. Naseef is an avid photographer and enjoys his leisure hours exploring trails and roads on his mountain bike and watching the sunflowers grow in his yard.

Dr. Naseef welcomes reactions to this book and is available to make presentations to parent and professional groups. He can be contacted at 514 South 4th Street, Philadelphia, PA, 19147, through http://www.specialfamilies.com, or through rnaseef@alternativechoices.com.

Foreword

Raising children is difficult and formidable work. Raising children with special health care or developmental needs is uniquely so. At times, the challenges seem overwhelming and even oppressive. But out of the struggles come victories, wisdom, and understanding. Having personally lived with a chronic illness for most of my life, I have learned remarkable lessons about patience, perseverance, and the power of the human spirit.

As the director of a national program for fathers and their families, I have witnessed ordinary people being shaped by extraordinary circumstances. For all parents, a child's birth is a time of great joy and optimism. "Your child has a disability" is among the most crushing statements that one can ever hear. For a time dreams are destroyed. Perhaps the easy choice would be to turn away, abandon expectations, and fatalistically accept life's injustices. For Robert Naseef that simply would not do. With eloquence he unabashedly shares with us the connections he creates with his son: the tears and depression, the fears and pain, and, ultimately, the love and care grounded in their extraordinary relationship.

Special Children, Challenged Parents evokes potent feelings in me. I find myself twisting and turning at the raw emotions that hit so very close to the bone. Bob's words resonate deep, fundamental truths. There is an authenticity here that simply cannot be denied.

Ultimately, families of children with special needs teach us about courage—what M. Scott Peck, in *The Road Less Traveled*, defined as "the making of action in spite of fear." New dreams take shape, grounded in the power of hope. Our children become our teachers as we learn to focus on what is possible rather than what will never be. In doing so, we are reborn.

James May, M.A., M.Ed.
Director, The National Fathers Network

xi

Acknowledgments

This book is the product of a journey in which one person has been indispensable. She is my best friend, my colleague, my lover, my co-parent, and my wife, Cindy N. Ariel. She is my first editor who always knows what I am trying to say and helps me shape it for others to understand.

My love for books began on my mother's lap as she read me one enchanting story after another. My father nurtured my passion by taking me and my siblings to the library every Saturday morning to borrow new and exciting books. I never dreamed I would write one.

For the gift of many hours of their time, listening, reading, and providing feedback, I am particularly grateful to Sam Osherson and Bert Ruttenberg for their assistance with the first edition. Many friends and colleagues, especially James May and Stan Klein, kindly gave their time and support. I am also indebted to Margaret Wolf, my editor at Carol Publishing.

The Center for Autistic Children loved Tariq and helped me learn to love and accept him just as he is, always believing that he would make progress. For more than 13 years, the Devereux Foundation has provided an around-the-clock commitment to Tariq's safety and happiness. Their unflinching vigilance provided me with the time and space to reflect and write.

The parents who have sought my counsel and their lovely children are due my humblest gratitude. Their confidence in my ability to guide them has sustained my efforts to continue writing and to keep this book alive. The readers and reviewers of the first edition have given me the encouragement to persevere and have made this revised edition possible. To Heather Shrestha, Deb Mills, and the team at Paul H. Brookes Publishing Co., I appreciate your belief in the enduring value of this book. And lastly, thanks goes to Kara and Zoë for their love and patience in awaiting their turn at our home computer.

God grant me the Serenity
  to accept the things
  I cannot change,
Courage to change the things
  I can, and the
Wisdom to know the difference.

Living one day at a time;
Enjoying one moment at a time;
Accepting hardship as the
  pathway to peace.

—Reinhold Niebuhr

Your joy is your sorrow unmasked . . .
The deeper that sorrow carves into your being,
the more joy you can contain.
                    —*Kahlil Gibran, 1968, p. 29*

Winter, 1993

Dear Tariq,

I'll never forget the night that you were born. It was more
than incredible; indeed, it was magical. It had been a long
labor—more than 24 hours. When you came out of your
mother's belly, you seemed to look all around the delivery
room, even before your body was completely out. Without
thinking about it, I jumped from my position behind the delivery table and wound up right there beside the doctor—my
knees wobbling and my heart pounding with excitement. The
doctor, an older man who had delivered many babies, commented on how alert you looked.

Right away I could tell that your head was the same shape
as mine. The skin on my face tightened as I beamed at you. I
counted your fingers and your toes and breathed easier knowing that everything was okay. While I eagerly watched, the
nurse cleaned you up and wrapped you in a flannel blanket.
You looked so cute—a perfect newborn. I had dreamed of having a boy, and I love retelling this story. I love reliving those
moments filled with ecstasy. It's one of my warmest memories.

When the nurse put you in my arms, I felt the electricity
of that instant. You felt so soft and delicate to my fingertips. I
cradled you next to my heart. Our eyes met and locked on to
each other's for the first time. Your eyes looked so big and
round. It was one of the most exciting moments of my life.
From then on I have looked at the world differently.

Ever since then, I have held a special respect for a woman's ability to give birth—for every woman's special partnership in the miracle of life. I thought of my mother, who gave

xvii

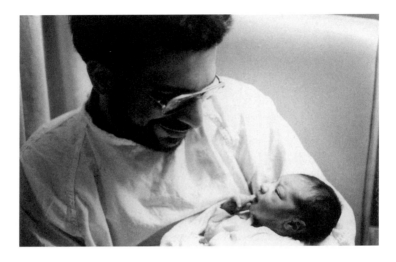

Our eyes met and locked.

birth to eight healthy children. That was a new beginning in my consciousness. Through you, the wonder of life began to be revealed to me in a way that I could have never imagined. Now I know firsthand what author Kahlil Gibran means about how inextricably woven together are our moments of joy and sorrow!

You were born in the wee hours of the morning on November 29, 1979. Jimmy Carter was the president; American hostages were being held in Tehran; Frank Rizzo was the mayor of Philadelphia. I saved the newspaper from that day for you to have when you were older to read about what was happening in the world on the day that you got here. You were born at the Medical College of Pennsylvania, formerly Women's Medical College, the first medical school for women in our country, high on the banks of the Schuylkill River in Philadelphia.

When I left you and your mom in the hospital that night, I looked up at the sky. The stars were shining brightly. There were a few clouds, but they didn't stop the nearly full moon from casting a warm glow over the earth near the river. It was a perfect moment frozen in time, in my memory, and in my heart. The cool night air filled my lungs and refreshed me, and even though it was winter, it reminded me of the words of a poem by Robert Browning that I had learned in grade school:

> *The year's at the spring,*
> *And day's at the morn;*
> *Morning's at seven;*
> *The hillside's dew-pearled;*
> *The lark's on the wing:*
> *The snail's on the thorn;*
> *God's in his heaven—*
> *All's right with the world.*

Telling people about you was so exciting. You were the second grandchild and the first grandson that my parents had. I remember my dad saying how lucky I was to live when fathers could be present at birth. He never saw any of his children being born, and listening to his reaction to your birth brought me closer to him, knowing the excitement that he, too, must have felt and hearing his wish to have been more involved.

I wish you could read this someday, Tariq. I wish you could know what you have meant to me. If anyone had told me when you were born that you would never read, never write, or never carry on a normal conversation, I wouldn't have been able to handle it. Truthfully, I was crushed for a long, long time when I found out that you have autism. It was as if a house had collapsed on me, but I stayed alive at the bottom of the heap of rubble. I have fought through it, and over time, the weight has lessened.

I want you to know that you have never lost your place in my heart. I still save that yellowed newspaper from November 29, 1979. Some of my greatest joys and some of my deepest sorrows have been in the moments that you and I have shared. In many respects, your life is limited. But, your life is priceless to me and even to the world beyond us.

Pearl S. Buck, the famous writer and humanitarian, had only one biological child and that child had mental retardation. Buck wrote a book about her daughter called *The Child Who Never Grew*. The title reminds me of how you will always be a little boy inside. Buck concluded that we can learn as much from illness as from health, that disability can have as much meaning as ability and sometimes even more, when we learn to find the treasures there.

There is one thing that you have done and continue to do uniquely for me. Without speaking a word, you have taught the little boy in me to speak. In this way you are with me at every moment. You have all of the positive emotions as well as the negative. You taught me to see them readily. When you feel good, you show interest and excitement. You show pride when you accomplish something you set out to do, and you have a refreshing sense of humor. When you're startled, you let me know by raising your eyebrows, opening your eyes wide, and opening your mouth.

Because of you, I have learned how to tune into the signals I used to miss. You don't recognize danger and you seldom sense fear, so I have to be extra vigilant. When you're in distress, you let people know it although it's often hard to tell what's bothering you. Because you can't connect with others, we can only use empathy to try to understand you . . . but what power lies there! In a world that has valued reason and intellect above emotion, nonverbal children like you teach us to look inside of ourselves.

Nature gave me a fair amount of intelligence and ability, but I was a shy child. Before you came, I didn't know much about my feelings or what they meant. When someone would ask me how I felt, I usually went blank. There was a confusing numbness deep inside my soul and a sense of frustration and inadequacy when I could not answer.

Unable to connect my thoughts and feelings, my abilities were locked in. Now I know the shades and colors of all of the emotions in my inner life—both positive and negative. You have revealed this great treasure to me. The need to translate our experiences together has made me more articulate about feelings, and I've been able to help others as a psychologist.

I've been keeping journals about you and our experiences for many years, and now I've made a book from them, Tariq. I am going to share what you have meant to me because there are millions of other children like you—some who have more ability, some who have less. These "imperfect" children are usually born to loving parents who struggle to rise from disappointment to find a stronger love—an unconditional love that lies on the other side of sorrow.

Not long ago, Tariq, I bought an old Peter, Paul, and Mary tape at a flea market for 50 cents. On it is a beautiful song called "Day is Done." As I was listening, Cindy, your stepmom, called my attention to a particular verse. She said it was about you.

> *Tell me why you're crying my son,*
> *I know you're frightened like everyone.*
> *Is it the thunder in the distance you fear?*
> *Will it help if I stay very near?*
> *I am here . . .*
>
> *And if you take my hand my son,*
> *All will be well when the day is done . . .*
>
> *Tell me why you're smiling my son.*
> *Is there a secret you can tell everyone?*
> *Do you know more than men who are wise?*
> *Do you see what we all must disguise,*
> *With your loving eyes?*

Of course you do, son. That's why the song speaks so directly to me. I think we have a lot to share with people about the meaning of our lives together, Tariq. It can be so full and rich amidst all of the difficulties. It will never fit completely in any book. It's a matter of the heart.

Take my hand . . . I am near . . . I love you,

Dad

Special
CHILDREN
Challenged
PARENTS

1

A Father Is Born

My Story

*W*hen you are a parent of a child who is developing more slowly than typical children, you may feel alone, but you are not. Knowing that you are not alone is a big part of the cure for the worry and pain. Parents whose children are not developing typically can greatly benefit from understanding the similarities between themselves and others. A lot of healing occurs when you exchange stories with others in similar circumstances, which is why I am including some of the details of my son's early days to explain more about the life I've led. You'll relate to the material in this book better once you know my story. My viewpoint results from a journey through the grief of broken dreams. It is a passage that redefines the meaning of life for all who must travel through it. The recovery is guided by hope and leads to deeper love for your child and the other people in your life. This book is the key to a way of thinking that has evolved from my personal life, my education, and my experiences as a professional guide to others.

More than 20 years ago, my only son and my oldest child, Tariq, was a seemingly typical happy toddler. He was all that I had imagined him to be and more. There was something new in our life every day. When he was 4 months old, for example, he began to lift his head and look around. I took a picture of him that I still prize. There was an amazing resemblance to an old picture of me that my mother had taken at the same age.

A month or so later he began to crawl. It was so much fun to see and feel his excitement. There was a gleam in his eye as he motored himself at will around the house, pulling himself along with the help of furniture and walls to get where he wanted. His explorations prompted more care to keep him safe, such as steering him away from the steps or the fireplace.

By his eighth month, he could pull himself up to a standing position, beaming with pride. He would glance around smiling and planning his route to whatever looked like fun. A few weeks later, he began to "cruise," holding onto furniture and getting around whenever he could. Frequently, I would hold his hands above his head and walk behind him, full of anticipation for his next achievement.

Before long it was his first birthday; he also took his first baby steps on that big day. I recall his look of apprehension and then the thrill of achievement expressed with a smile as he took his first awkward, wobbly steps. I was so proud of him. What an amazing accomplishment! I was cheering him on. That is still one of my most vivid memories of him—when he was "normal."

By 18 months, he was just beginning to speak and had a small but useful vocabulary. He had been reaching all of the usual developmental milestones, and I imagined that before long he would play little league baseball. In my mind's eye, I beamed with pride and cheered as he fielded a ball or swiftly ran the bases. I would be there watching as my father had watched me. Down the road, I imagined having philosophical discussions with him as a young man. Our relationship would be close and warm; he would come to me comfortably whenever he wanted. I would give him space when he needed or wanted it. In these ways and others I planned on being the perfect dad.

Tariq raises his head on time.

At this time, however, Tariq was treated for an ear infection, and our whole life changed. Tariq became frustrated
and withdrawn. He cried a lot and didn't sleep well at night. I
worried, especially at night, when I was awake with him. My
daughter, Antoinette, had recently arrived on the scene, and
at first, the pediatrician thought it could be an emotional response to no longer being an only child. I hoped that the doctor was right, but I was scared of what it would mean if he was
wrong. I began to wonder if my dreams for Tariq would ever
materialize.

Soon, Tariq stopped talking and stopped playing with the
toys that he had received for his birthday—like the little workbench with its nuts and bolts and tools that my parents had
given him; it was just like a workbench that I had when I was

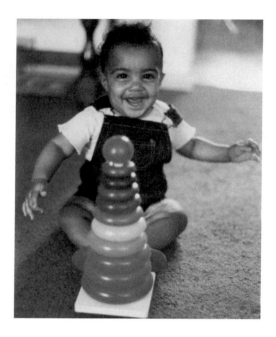

Tariq is proud of himself and is sharing his joy.

a little boy. Tariq began playing with a transparent rattle with brightly colored beads inside. He seemed fascinated by this toy and played with it for days and weeks on end while ignoring virtually everything else around him, including his baby sister. He became very agitated and upset if the rattle was taken away. My sweet toddler was gone.

When Antoinette was born, I was thrilled to have a daughter. I thought then that I had a perfect family—one beautiful boy and one beautiful girl. Life seemed complete; I felt lucky, but that feeling didn't last for long. I became tense and anxious, and though I kept telling myself that everything would be okay, I wondered if I or his mother had done anything to cause his condition.

The awakening was rude. That exciting time when every day brought a new accomplishment was gone. His life, which had been a great joy to me, became a worry that preoccupied what seemed like my every moment. I was glad to see him when I got home from work, but the fun of playing with him was gone. Because he still liked being touched and cuddled, even though now he always turned his face away from me, I clung desperately to the hope that Tariq would become "normal"—that he would talk again.

When he was 2 years old, I spent the summer with him while on vacation from my teaching position. The pediatrician had said that he might just need time. I worked hard to get his attention—to establish eye contact and a connection. I would put him on the swing in the backyard and stand in front as I pushed him. At the same time, I tried to catch his gaze for a fraction of a second. He would turn his eyes to the side on purpose; he was a master at avoiding contact. It felt like a personal rejection. It was especially frustrating because even though I was skilled at helping children with learning problems, all of my efforts with my own son were fruitless. It wasn't until he was diagnosed with autism a few years later that I learned that he was easily overwhelmed by stimuli and that I had to back off.

As his third birthday approached, it was clear that Tariq could not attend regular preschool. His lack of speech alone indicated that he was developmentally far behind other children his age, but that was very hard to face. His mother and I took him to a preschool that took children with special needs, but he didn't even fit there. The psychologist at the preschool thought that he might have a hearing impairment. On his advice, I went on a tour of a school for young children with hearing impairments. As I write these words, I can sense my insides shaking as I remember my worry that my child would be walking around with two hearing aids like the children I saw there.

I wondered what his life would be like. He would be different, I told myself, just different. Little did I know what was really in store for us. Then began the trips to numerous specialists and special schools. There were many sleepless nights waiting for test results and no answers to the mystery of why Tariq had stopped speaking.

A specialist found fluid in his ears that blocked his hearing, and he was treated for this condition with medication. My hopes rose—because it seemed like such a simple solution to Tariq's problems. Tests of his brain stem indicated that his ears worked, but it was impossible to tell if his brain comprehended words. The fluid cleared up, but as before, he expressed himself only with grunts and babbling and crying—no words— and he constantly twisted and turned to get away from physical contact. Still, I dreamed at night that the babbling would turn into words; after all, that's what babbling leads to for the typical child.

Tariq was in an early intervention program by his third birthday, and he was the most difficult child in the school to manage. He required one-to-one attention at all times. He couldn't or wouldn't stay in his seat for more than a few seconds when he was left unattended. Whenever I wasn't teaching, I spent the day with him in school, helping the teachers.

Eventually, my son was diagnosed with a "pervasive developmental delay," a broad diagnostic category that includes autism. The condition is found in 1 of every 500 children according to current estimates. The team of professionals that evaluated Tariq at the hospital where he was born used the words *autistic like* and *retarded* in their diagnosis. I went numb and then became livid with rage at them. Although the anger subsided long ago, the tears are never far. The professionals seemed to have no hope for my son. "Has anyone told you that your son is retarded?" With these words, the social worker broke the news. What a way to tell a parent something of this nature! How could they make such a diagnosis? Their words sliced through me like a knife. How could I give up on Tariq?

As I remember it now, I withdrew inside myself as I learned about the disorder. It was painful to read that autism is a severely incapacitating and lifelong disability. It was hard to comprehend that my child's brain cannot process what he hears, sees, or touches. The information that he takes in is distorted or fragmented, making it incomplete or confusing. I was told that communication with others would be extremely difficult for him.

I couldn't talk about it. I wanted to, but the words just wouldn't come out. They stuck in my throat, especially the word *autism*. Once in a while, I would blurt out my worry that my son still wasn't talking even though he was more than 3 years old, and at night I cried and cried. There was no comfort. Professionals, relatives, and friends rarely seemed to know what to say or how to say it.

Like many parents in similar situations, I spared no expense in the quest to find a cure for Tariq. We tried to help him with speech and movement therapies and even vitamins and a special diet. For many years, the burden of the debts from these treatments was in itself a constant reminder of my hope for a cure. My dreams died a slow death as I ran out of treatments to try. As I became strong enough to face it, the reality that Tariq's condition was lifelong slowly came into focus.

Unfortunately, I didn't get any help from within my marriage. I felt the most alone at home. To put it simply and kindly, the strain of Tariq's disability added to our other stresses and led to divorce. After years of trying to go through it together, it was easier to try it alone. As a single parent, I faced a life that had changed permanently and profoundly—something I had not planned nor allowed myself to imagine. But now I was comprehending what had transpired.

Every minute of every waking hour was affected—the list of Tariq's special needs seemed endless, and the amount of care required was overwhelming. Because he rarely slept through the night, I was constantly exhausted. This stage lasted for more than 7 years, and the feeling stayed in my body even longer. I never knew what would happen next. He was perpetually in motion, and it was hard to tell what you would find as you followed or chased him from room to room. The entire house had to be "childproofed," lest there be danger to my child or to my possessions. Even the refrigerator had to be locked.

As a child who knows no danger, my son was in constant danger of running into traffic, burning his hand, or stepping over the edge of the pool into the deep water. The only part of my original dream that came true was that Tariq became a fast runner, but unfortunately this made for few relaxing moments.

Once, Tariq got out of my apartment in the middle of the night. I was terrified at the thought of how I might find him as I ran looking for him. My heart pounded so hard that I thought my chest would burst. Even though I found him playing happily in the playground a few blocks and a few busy streets away, my heart kept pounding for what seemed like hours. His death would be the only thing that I could imagine that would be more difficult than his life.

I decided to enter psychotherapy, and this certainly helped me to keep going. It was one of the best things that I ever did for myself. I come from a family that doesn't often express feelings verbally or directly. This was something that I desperately needed to do to survive. It was like finding water in the desert. My therapist helped me to express my feelings, but it was hard to make sense of them—to reconcile them to the reality that I was experiencing. I was being flooded and overwhelmed with emotion, and it felt crazy at times.

Why couldn't I calm down? The constant emphasis on doing more for Tariq that came from many professionals was not helping me with my guilt or with the "acceptance" that I was supposed to reach. I felt like I must have some defect that kept me from accepting my son as he was. Was I a bad person?

At that point, more than 15 years ago, Cindy, a colleague and close friend, showed me an article in the *Journal of Counseling and Development* that talked about the grief experienced by the parents of children with disabilities. It was written by Dr. Milton Seligman, who is a professor at the University of Pittsburgh and, as I would later learn, is also the parent of an adult child with a disability. As I read sentence after sentence, I came to a deeper awareness of myself. Suddenly, many disconnected feelings and thoughts began to make sense. When I completed the article, I leaned back in my desk chair, took a few slow deep breaths, and thought, "So, that is what Tariq's life is all about to me; I am a bereaved parent."

From that day onward, my life began to change for the better. I had a new lens with which to analyze my experience. My new self-knowledge helped me in the process of learning to cope with the many problems associated with having a child with a disability. It took time and help from others. I understood my thoughts and feelings better. As I look back, I believe that the failure of my therapy in this regard was partially a failure of my therapist and partially a general lack of understanding in the field about the grief experienced by parents of children with disabilities.

I still struggled through some horribly dark moments, but I began to reclaim my life. Cindy helped me by encouraging me to talk and by listening to everything that I had to say without any judgment or expectation. By the end of this story, Cindy and I are married. Life did indeed go on with new dreams.

I had entered a doctoral program before knowing for sure that my son had a lifelong disability. Because I was doing everything possible for Tariq, I concluded that delaying my own development would serve no purpose. I knew in my heart that he would want me to do it. It was trying at times, but my professors and my boss at work were very supportive. There were things to look forward to once again—both personally and professionally.

When my daughter, Antoinette, learned to read, I was very, very thankful. Every time she learned a new word it let me know that her brain was normal. It was unbelievably exciting to live through this period with her—not to mention the great relief to know that she was "all there" and could learn in the typical ways. I could literally breathe easier and have done so ever since.

By this time I understood "normal" human development as the miracle it really is. As I daily observed her breaking the code to read, the intense joy I felt brought tears to my eyes. Antoinette has a special talent in art and writing that fills me with pride and gratitude, especially when she gives me a drawing or a painting or shows me something she has written. There is little that I take for granted anymore. Life is truly very fragile at times. You never know when something might break and what that will do to your heart.

For my doctoral dissertation, I researched the qualities of the families who coped successfully with having a child with a disability. It was a way of focusing on the positive. In addition to the obvious interest that I had in knowing as much as possible for myself, I hoped that what I learned might be of use to others. Actually, this research process led me to further integrate the thoughts, feelings, and experiences that I had begun analyzing both in therapy and on my own. I hoped to help bridge the gap of understanding that frequently exists between the families of children with special needs and the professionals whose job it is to assist them.

This dream came true as I spoke to countless groups of parents and professionals in various communities about my life and my work. Although these presentations are often draining, they also inspire me. I became more effective helping people connect across the chasm that too often divides parents and professionals. My reputation got around. I was asked to help develop a training package for the New Jersey Department of Education to foster parent–professional collaboration, which was implemented throughout the state.

Subsequently, I became a full-time trainer for the Division of Special Education in the New Jersey Department of Education. It was a tremendous boost to my self-esteem to know that my superiors there believed in me and in my ability to focus on the professional issues while drawing on my background of life experience. I spoke in that capacity to thousands of parents and professionals in countless preschool programs for children with disabilities and at numerous professional conferences. It was a way that I kept Tariq with me and derived meaning from life.

In 1991, the *Journal of Counseling and Development* that had been so helpful to me earlier published my article, "Lost Dreams, New Hopes," about my experiences and their impact on my professional life. I still get letters and telephone calls from people who have read that article. It has been extremely rewarding to hear from college professors who use it as a handout in counseling and special education classes.

Also in 1991, my third and our [Cindy and me] first child, Kara, was born. Watching her grow and develop has provided a living testimony to the vitality of our relationship. In 1992, another dream came true. My independent practice as a psychologist grew to the point where I was able to leave my full-time position with the New Jersey state government. My goal of being self-employed had been realized. I now specialize in working with parents of children with disabilities. Cindy is also a psychologist, and we share an office in the South Street section of Philadelphia near the historic district. We alternate the times that we work so that one of us is always home with Kara and Zoë, our second child who was born in 1993—it's a life that we enjoy together.

In addition, I serve as a consulting psychologist to numerous schools, agencies, hospitals, and parent groups. I make a living doing what I enjoy doing while being home with the children an average of 2 days each week. It's a special treat, and one that I am proud of.

I have come a long way. My son's disability helped me to develop more than I thought myself capable of. Tariq gave me the opportunity to do something special. The knowledge and wisdom that I acquired through losing my dream of a typical child are helping me to be all that I can. His disability was so severe that he needed 24-hour care by the time he was 8 years old and had to be placed in a residential program. Putting him into residential treatment was the hardest decision that I ever had to make.

As much as it has hurt and continues to hurt, Tariq has made me aware of the value of life. He is so innocent and generally happy. Tariq is such a gentle soul that he has always been a staff favorite wherever he has been in school. These thoughts alone bring a calming stillness to my heart and a smile to my face.

As difficult as it has been, I have been able to adjust and live a relatively normal, happy, and rewarding life. I am experiencing more fulfillment than I ever knew existed. I feel whole and loved and loving. I have learned so much from the other parents that I have met who are working through the many aspects of grief and then emerging hopeful, strong, sensitive, and proud. Sometimes I'm not sure if I deserve such a full life. I feel like a plane crash survivor with devastation all around me—particularly in the hearts of those parents in earlier stages of recovery than I. Every time I walk into an early intervention program, I feel like that. Every time a couple struggling with this kind of grief is referred to my practice, I revisit my own pain. Then, I am inevitably reminded as I listen to their story that I deserve to feel good sometimes—for I have paid my dues.

The process of grieving, coping, and "going on with your life" is the focus of this book. I am able to speak from a voice that integrates my personal experiences, my clinical expertise as a psychologist who specializes in helping the families of children with disabilities, and my research and knowledge in the field. Included are accounts of lives with children with various chronic conditions and disabilities. Regardless of the nature of the child's disability, parents have many similar experiences as they learn to survive and cope. It is the challenge of a lifetime to do everything possible to help your child and to maintain hope and fight off despair while striving to live as normal a life as possible. Trying to be realistic but hopeful is quite a paradox.

I trust that you as readers will be able to learn to help yourselves by understanding your own experiences and those of others that you will be reading about. Also, you will be aided as I am by current psychological perspectives on the many issues facing the parents of children with disabilities and special needs.

The various chapters that follow in this book trace the parents' journey—some of the mountains to be climbed, not one at a time necessarily or in any particular sequence, but a little of this one and a little of that one, until eventually you are healed enough to feel whole again. Chapter 2 describes that flood of emotion and the frantic thoughts that you experience when you realize that there is something wrong with your child. Making sense of these emotions is vitally important. Chapter 3 explores the somewhat predictable stages of working through grief and attempts to understand what "acceptance" might mean when your child is alive but is not who you expected.

Every day, one of the most trying challenges is accepting and just being with a child who has a disability or special need. The behavior of children with limited ability, understanding, or language can be very perplexing. Parents often experience a great deal of embarrassment when their child acts "weird" in front of others. Chapters 4 and 5 focus on bonding with your child and applying the principles of child guidance. Most books on parenting do not apply these concepts to children with special needs.

Chapter 6 shifts focus to the experience of fathers of a child with a disability. Because men don't speak much about emotional experiences, let alone grief, this chapter fills a need that I have not seen adequately addressed for fathers.

Chapter 7 focuses on the state of your marriage while this grief process is going on and the differences between men and women as they apply to this situation. It is another topic rarely addressed adequately in an area where guidance is sorely needed.

Parents worry about what happens to their other children and how to "be there" for them. Sibling rivalry takes somewhat different forms with the profound difference in the family structure that disability carries with it. Chapter 8 is devoted to this theme and asks you to look at your own sibling experiences as a model for what to do and what to avoid.

Chapter 9 deals with suggestions for getting support through relatives, friends, groups, or informal networks with other parents in similar situations. There is such a healing power to opening up and confiding in each other. This essay seeks to unlock that power.

Chapter 10 concerns dealing effectively with the professionals involved in your child's daily life. We want these professionals to rescue us and fix our child. We get angry when we can't get the services that we want and need. At times, we have to confront them. At others, we have to learn to work together.

All along this journey, whatever the sequence might be for each individual, we gain wisdom, develop a philosophy, and derive a meaning from our experiences that sustains us. Chapter 11 addresses this; then the book closes with an epilogue of letters to my son.

It has been quite a trek. I look back now with confidence born from my survival and recovery. I can look forward to the joys and challenges of my marriage and family life. My work feels like a success every time I can empower another parent by helping him or her understand his or her thoughts and feelings, find humor at times in his or her situation, and learn to cope with his or her problems. I hope this book does some of that for you. I feel good about how far I've come, but the cost has been great . . . my only wish is that I could have done it another way.

2

Feeling the Impact

Lost Dreams and Growth

*I*n 1964, when Japanese writer Kenzaburo Oe was 29 years old, his first child was born with brain damage. He named his baby boy "Pooh" and described their very close bond in a story called *Teach Us to Outgrow Our Madness*. Oe and his fragile child became so close that Oe said that he would die when Pooh died. Oe was convinced that he and his son shared sensations so completely that he directly felt the physical manifestations of his child's pain. Oe perceived his child's force on his dreams as that of a nuclear explosion—a personal holocaust. Coming from a man who grew up in Japan in the aftermath of Hiroshima and Nagasaki, this is an especially powerful metaphor to describe the change in his personal world. His novel, *A Personal Matter,* written the year Pooh was born, was the first of a series whose central character is the young father of a child with brain damage. Oe wrote of his connection to his child and of his quest to survive the personal devastation he felt. He won the Nobel Prize for literature in 1994.

The dream of a perfect child can die a painful death. If you have a child with a disability, you certainly want compassionate words. But moreover, you just want it all to go away; and it won't. Dr. Elliott Lube says in *The Bereaved Parent,* "When your parent dies you have lost your past—when your child dies you have lost your future" (p. 23). The purpose of this chapter is to help you understand the natural and normal feeling processes that are triggered by worries over a child's development, the troubling observations of a child, and the diagnosis of a disability or chronic illness.

Let's start with pregnancy, when expectant parents the world over worry that something could go wrong with their baby during the pregnancy or birth process. They are routinely told to calm down and that everything will be all right. When a child's early development is slower than expected or when a parent intuitively senses that something is wrong, medical professionals generally, and often wisely, urge parents to be patient because there is a wide range of "normal" development. Unfortunately, patience is not always rewarded.

Every year, approximately 10% of all children born have or develop a disability or chronic illness in their early years. The impairments may be "mild," such as a learning disability that will be diagnosed after the child starts school, or more "severe," such as deafness, blindness, cerebral palsy, heart disease, mental illness, juvenile diabetes, and others. I have put quotation marks around *mild* and *severe* because when a parent learns that a child isn't normal, it usually knocks that parent over for a period of time, whatever the severity of the disability. There are different incidences or odds for each disability, but when it happens to you, it's always 100%. You are totally surrounded by your fate, as the father played by Nick Nolte in the movie *Lorenzo's Oil* highlighted when he said that he felt like "a loser in the genetic lottery."

Every expectant parent has a lot of dreams—the kind you have when you're awake. Will the child be a boy or a girl? Who will he look like? What kind of personality will he have? What will he be when he grows up? What kind of things will you enjoy doing together? What new and exciting places will you go? How your life will be different! In all these ways and more, children are very important to parents. They can be a source of great joy—and devastating sorrow.

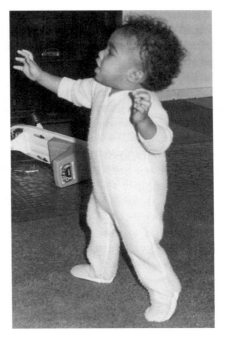

Tariq taking his first steps on his first birthday. He has had to be watched ever since.

Although people have children for different reasons, most couples look forward to having children as the fulfillment of their marriage. Because parents take great pride in and have great hopes for their children, when something is wrong the impact is profound. All of the positive feelings are deflated, and the wonderful pride and hope that filled life so naturally are difficult to recover. The dreams for a healthy child evaporate, and the real child cannot live up to the original expectations. There is often a profound sense of failure for bringing a "defective" child into the world and often a horrible guilt for feeling so disappointed in your own child.

As a child, I was very shy and reserved, so I expected my son to be dynamic and articulate—to give voice to my life through his existence. Like so many parents, I wanted to re-create myself and come out better. I gave my son the middle name Donato, the Italian equivalent of Donald and my grand-father's first name that means "gift." His first name, Tariq, is the name of a star and of a famous Arab general from the 10th century. The Rock of Gibraltar is literally "Tariq's rock," named for where that general crossed over from Morocco to Spain.

I had big dreams for my son. I guess I wanted him to do things that I hadn't—to be the man I hadn't yet become. These dreams set the scene for Tariq to enter my life, but it was to be otherwise. He would teach me to live myself and not through my children, as his disability has opened me to the world of my inner life of dreams, hopes, disappointments, and joys. This process also includes understanding the meaning of each feeling. At times, it hurts so much that I want to block them out. The feelings, however, are messages from the inner self about what is going on, and they serve as needed guideposts of the inner journey.

As John Bradshaw often says in his lectures on public television, "You can't heal what you can't feel." This seems simple, but generations have been taught to ignore or mute painful feelings. For this reason, these particularly powerful and spontaneous feelings are socially unacceptable. The idea that feelings interfere with thinking discredits people who seem to be emotionally involved in whatever bothers them.

ONE FAMILY'S JOURNEY BEGINS

The Warrens stand out in my memory from my doctoral research because they were highly articulate about their feelings. Through their willingness to share their experiences, they helped numerous families of other children with hearing impairments. They are a warm, friendly family of moderate means who live in a rowhouse neighborhood in Baltimore. My first interview was with Linda, a tall, slender, redheaded woman who told her story with intensity and fervor. At the time, Ben, who has a severe hearing impairment, was 10 years old, and his sister, Anna, was 12 years old.

According to Linda, she and her husband, Bill, noticed that something was different about Ben when he was about 9 months old and had not begun to vocalize as Anna had done at that age. But when they clapped their hands when Ben was sleeping, he woke up and they concluded that he was not deaf.

When Ben was a year old, they told the pediatrician that they didn't believe he was hearing properly. Although she knew that something was wrong, Linda had a hard time convincing the doctor. The doctor stood behind the infant and clapped. Ben blinked, and the doctor said there was nothing wrong. Linda was still concerned because her infant had not begun to babble. At the time of the next checkup, the doctor clapped his hands again, and this time (luckily, according to Bill and Linda) Ben did not blink, so a referral was finally made to an ear specialist.

The ear specialist diagnosed fluid in Ben's ear when he was 17 months old. The fluid was drained with tubes, and there was slight improvement; Ben began to babble, but he did not talk. Linda became very alarmed, but when she told the doctor, he responded, "Why do you worry so much? You must be a worry wart."

Intuitively, like so many mothers, Linda knew that something was wrong. Ben didn't act anything like his sister had acted. Bill had confidence and trust in Linda, and he had observed on his own that something wasn't right with their son. Bill and Linda kept pushing, so the doctor ordered a brain stem test. Both parents waited anxiously for the results. Eventually, Ben was diagnosed with a severe to profound hearing loss. Linda and Bill told me that they were both devastated. Even though they had suspected that something was wrong, they were numb. They couldn't believe what they were being told. They recalled being worried, angry, and sad.

They went to another hospital to get a second opinion. This time they were told that their child had a mild to severe hearing loss with some hearing in the upper range. Linda hoped that this meant her son could develop typically. She could not really believe otherwise; Bill hoped she was right. Together they clung to their dreams for their little boy.

The Warrens' experience can be generalized to many other families. Frequently, parents, especially mothers, who usually spend the most time with the child, get a sense that something is wrong with their child's development. Others, including doctors, try to calm the anxious parent. Doctors, too, can be subject to denial. It's hard to give bad news. The doctor doesn't want it to be true either. Denial on the part of a professional frequently makes things worse. When a doctor is in denial regarding a child's disability, a parent's anxiety may increase in response; "If the doctor thinks my child is okay, I must be crazy."

At times when she was "really down," Linda turned to her husband. She realized that their son was different and that she could not change that. Allowing herself to cry helped. She also tried to be "good to herself" by not worrying about housework. At times, she slept a lot to get through the day. She was not ready to reach out, and being alone helped her to grieve and heal.

Bill told me that his emotional reaction was not as intense as Linda's, although at one time he had cried unexpectedly while telling one of his best friends about Ben's disability. As he told me this, I reflected yet again on how hard it is for most men to allow tears or admit sadness.

Ben's disability was tough for this family, but they survived and even flourished. They loved one another deeply and enjoyed life. As Bill put it, "Once you accept the fact that life is not a level playing field, you can learn to deal with things." Their acceptance gave me hope.

GETTING IN TOUCH
WITH YOUR INNER SELF

When Tariq was 6 years old, I thought that I was ready to help other parents understand their feelings about children with disabilities. I quickly discovered that I was only a novice. I would stand in front of a group, talk about some of my experiences, and then ask the people about how they felt about their children's disabilities. An uneasy silence would ensue. Someone might ask a question and I would answer. It was difficult to get people to open up about their feelings. At this point in my training, I was in supervision with a senior psychologist, Dr. Bert Kauffman, a retired professor in independent practice in Philadelphia. Bert methodically taught me how to help people develop a vocabulary for their emotions. He patiently pointed out how asking people if they were angry might not help them to discover if they actually were. His way of teaching would be to ask if I was slightly annoyed or troubled about something. If so, he would ask me to explain it to him. From this experience, I learned quickly how to have this kind of dialogue with an individual. Combining Bert's instruction with what I was learning at Temple University about group process, I was able to apply these techniques to working with groups. I developed the Feelings Checklist as a way to help people explore their responses to their child's impairment (see Figure 2.1).

I have used the checklist with numerous groups of parents and professionals to facilitate talking about natural feelings that commonly arise. If you are a parent, imagine a typical day with your child. Likewise, if you have a brother or sister with a disability, imagine a typical day. If you are a relative or friend, do the same. If you are a professional, imagine some of the children you have worked with and developed strong feelings for, or imagine that you have a child with a disability.

Now, whatever your relationship may be with the child, look at the checklist and circle those adjectives that describe any of the unpleasant or negative feelings that are hard to deal with in a typical day with a child with special needs. When you have finished, take a few moments to look over the list. Then, discuss your responses with someone close to you.

Feelings Checklist

Shocked	Anxious	Unhappy	Fuming	Remorseful
Numb	Worried	Sad	Furious	Regretful
Dazed	Jittery	Blue	Disturbed	Tainted
Uneasy	Restless	Negative	Grouchy	Unworthy
Indifferent	Fretful	Crushed	Annoyed	Embarrassed
Sluggish	Nervous	Dejected	Uptight	Victimized
Emotionless	Afraid	Disheartened	Touchy	Unholy
Half-hearted	Pained	Gloomy	Distraught	Culpable
Dull	Tormented	Hopeless	Agitated	Penitent
Confused	Distressed	Discouraged	Troubled	Guilty
Apathetic	Worked up	Melancholy	Grumpy	Ashamed
Bewildered	Tense	Hollow	Upset	Mortified

Figure 2.1.   The Feelings Checklist is a way to help people explore their emotional responses to their child.

TYPICAL RESPONSES

The language of feelings is crucial in helping parents express themselves. I have met with one group in Philadelphia many times since 1989. They are all parents of children with visual impairments, and many of the children also have chronic medical conditions, learning disabilities, and mental retardation. As a part of their education, some of the children receive mobility instruction with canes; specialized computer technology, in addition to braille, is used to facilitate reading and writing. The parents, too, are groping in the darkness and the shadows of their inner lives. One purpose of the support group is to provide parents with a way to navigate through their feelings, just as their children are learning to navigate through the physical world.

One Saturday afternoon, after the 20 or so parents sitting in a circle had completed the checklist, I asked if they noticed any patterns as they were looking it over. I suggested that we go around the circle and share whatever felt comfortable for each individual.

"I checked off almost everything; I've felt all these ways," blurted out a woman sitting across from me. Her response is a frequent one when parents participate in this activity.

Then another woman spoke up, "The last column has to do with being mad, but I've been just thinking that all these words are negative. Where are the positive ones? When do we get to that?" I knew that she spoke for the group in wanting to turn away from these feelings. The time for that would come soon enough.

Indeed, these are very uncomfortable feelings, but all of them are normal and natural and need to be faced. Sometimes it's helpful to just say they're real. Let's take a look at how they make sense and how they might lead us to hope and other pleasant feelings. Denial, anxiety, fear, guilt, shame, depression, and anger are feeling states that are evoked by grief. Although it may be difficult to recognize or admit to these feelings, acknowledging them is the gateway to recovery and the renewal of hope.

The man to her left spoke next. His voice cracked as he remarked, "I don't know what I'm supposed to say, but I'm very frustrated. I've got a lump in my throat. That's what I kept thinking about after I read the word *disheartened*. I don't think I've ever admitted this even to myself."

A small, thin woman with a worried look spoke next. "I keep wondering what I did wrong—if I did something wrong. I have a lot of these feelings, but that is what I keep thinking about." The lines on her face seemed to tell the story of her worry.

"I just wanted to make one big *X* and be done with it. This is so hard to think about. I'm with everyone else," remarked a woman with very thick glasses whom I had noticed earlier because she had to hold the paper barely an inch from her glasses to read it. She showed admirable courage in choosing to live her life fully by parenting children despite her own disability.

"It makes me feel better to hear you say that," responded the next man. "I always feel bad—like I'm feeling sorry for myself that my son is blind—and like I shouldn't do that."

How wonderfully comforting it can be to discover that we're not alone. As one person after another disclosed his or her feelings, the comfort level increased. People spoke more and more freely—as is usually the case when they feel understood.

"I get so furious every time my child has to go into the hospital," countered the next woman in the circle. "My son has a brain shunt, and they're always telling me not to worry. How can you be calm when your child has to be hospitalized every 6 months? These doctors make me so mad when they say that."

Anger frequently bubbles to the surface in these kinds of meetings, as evidenced this time by the father who spoke next. A small man with a bushy head of dark hair, his face bursting with emotion, he blurted out, "My wife and I have been through so much. Our daughter was born without eyes—her optic nerves have just a little pea-sized undeveloped eye. It's not fair . . ." His voice trailed off, and his eyes filled with tears.

A hush came over the group. Sometimes a calming feeling comes when those deep feelings are articulated. We waited for the next person to respond.

After a few moments, the next woman spoke. "I was never much of a worrier. I always told myself that I would be different from my mom. Now all I do is worry. What will it be like for my daughter when she grows up? She's only seven now, but can she ever be independent? Nobody can tell me. If she can't, who will take care of her when my husband and I are too old? That whole second column in the list was about being worried."

"You're right," said the next woman, "these words go together in groups; I'm not sure why." She had sensed, as others often do, that these words in the second column are synonyms for various feelings associated with the grief process.

"The first column is how I felt in the beginning right after my son was born. I couldn't believe it. He had water on the brain, and his skull was enlarged. I couldn't feel anything. It was like this was happening to someone else—like in a movie." She was describing the numbness that comes when we first sense or are told that there is something wrong with our child.

"I never say anything, but I want to say something today," said the next man in the circle. "That column that starts with *unhappy*—that's me. I'm quiet because I'm crushed. People ask me how I feel, and that's it. I'll never play football with my son; I'll never do so many things. He's making progress. I can see it, but I'm so discouraged. I feel bad about that. Why can't I just be excited for him? Why can't I just accept this?"

His wife spoke next. "Well, I talk a lot—maybe I talk for the two of us. I wish Bill would talk more, but I can't tell you how glad I am that he spoke today. That third column hits me. A lot of my friends had babies the same time. Every time they talk about their kids, I'm speechless. My son will never do the things they're talking about. I want to crawl under a rock."

This woman's description of shame precipitated an uneasy silence in the group. Many parents of children with special needs have felt this way at various times in their lives. When our natural excitement or interest in our child is deflated, we may want to hide, and that makes us feel shame. This can occur whenever our child's growth isn't as exciting as that of other people's "normal" or more typical children.

This group activity helps people to recognize and make sense of their feelings about their child. I developed the lists of synonyms rather simply from a thesaurus. Just as there are many shades of every color on the spectrum, there are different intensities of these feelings. Each feeling resonates some-what differently based on individual temperament and past experiences. It is not possible to pass through grief without ex-periencing each of these feelings in a manner particular to each individual.

Such intense and complex feelings occur at other times in life. The people in the group were able to readily identify these times:

- When someone dies who is really close to us
- At the end of an important relationship
- When an injury limits us from activities that we really enjoyed
- Losing a job that we really liked or needed
- Moving from a community that meant a lot to us
- With failure to achieve a goal that we really worked for
- After a miscarriage
- When there is disappointment in a typical child who turns out different from what we had planned
- During and after a separation or divorce
- When a chronic illness takes hold in a friend, family member, or self

The woman whose child was born without eyes spoke up, "I was thinking, who died? I never thought this way before, but I think we've lost all of our dreams for a normal child. Now I know why I've cried so much—it makes sense. I almost didn't come today because I didn't want to get upset. I can see what I've been going through. I'm not crazy. None of us are." It does seem crazy, however, when your feelings don't make sense or when they seem out of sync with reality.

"I think I agree with Mary," responded the woman whose child was born with hydrocephalus (i.e., water on the brain). "It seems so simple now, but it's been so complicated and re-ally difficult."

"Do you ever get over this stuff?" asked the man who had earlier mentioned his sadness. "How long will I feel this way?"

Although grief is painful, it does subside over time. This process is spontaneous and unlearned—it has a natural course. Holding back the feelings can lengthen the amount of time it takes to process the loss.

At times, a parent may feel the need to talk to someone close. If you are unable to resolve your feelings in this way or feel "stuck," it is wise to consult a professional psychologist, psychiatrist, counselor, social worker, or pastoral counselor who has training and experience in helping people with grief and loss.

With my group on that Saturday afternoon, I tried to impart an understanding that acknowledging all feelings, both pleasant and unpleasant, is essential to psychological health. All feelings motivate people to behave in ways that nature intended and that help them meet many of life's challenges, including, of course, the challenges parents must meet to survive and to help their children.

DENIAL

An initial reaction to any loss is shock and disbelief. The parent of a child with a disability may respond, "Not me, not my child!" Other people may find it hard to understand the denial. There is pressure to "face reality." I constantly told myself that my son Tariq would be okay. He would talk again and catch up.

Denial serves an important role in everyone's personality structure. If we thought constantly of all of the terrible things that could ever happen, how could we live? How could we manage to go out the door? To prepare for all of the bad things that could happen, we couldn't have a life. What parents would want to have a child if they thought of nothing but what could possibly go wrong?

According to psychologist Dr. Ken Moses, in his video *Lost Dreams and Growth*, denial buys us time to discover the inner strength to handle a problem. He based his theory on his own experience as the child of Holocaust survivors and as the parent of a child with a disability. In addition, external support is necessary. Which relatives can be relied on? Which friends will understand? Denial provides the time to find out and keeps people from falling apart while they are doing this.

Denial makes the amount of pain bearable. We may deny our feelings and maintain that we are not upset. We may deny the permanence of the disability and believe that our child will grow out of it. We may admit the disability but deny the impact by reasoning that this problem won't change our lives. Denial is necessary until we find the inner strength and the external support necessary to face painful reality.

ANXIETY AND FEAR

When a parent is upset, others usually want to calm him or her down. He or she is uncomfortable to be around, so his or her uneasiness is treated as a problem. But anxiety by itself is not a problem—it is a feeling state that serves an important purpose.

It doesn't help when someone says, "Calm down—things are not as bad as you think." People can't calm down just because someone wants them to or because they would like to. The psychological system is mobilizing energy for the tasks ahead. This arousal is the effect of anxiety, and it fills a vital need. The feeling can range from a relatively light sense of insecurity to a panic attack.

Although extreme anxiety can be debilitating and needs treatment with psychotherapy and sometimes medication, a moderate amount is necessary for everyday functioning. When your child isn't developing typically, it is necessary to mobilize even more energy in order to make the efforts necessary to cope. I was constantly on edge for years, concerned about Tariq's safety, and my anxiety helped me to anticipate problems that he might have and to solve them *before* Tariq faced certain dangers. This process often required enormous energy to face the tasks of problem solving. Denial and anxiety together help to prepare for these tasks.

Although anxiety is general, fear is specific. Although it's common to be afraid of the changes that are coming when we experience a loss, it is wise to remember Franklin Delano Roosevelt's saying, "There is nothing to fear but fear itself," and to concentrate on doing what you can to keep your child safe. The unfortunate reality is that when your child isn't typical, *there is something to be afraid of:* Coping with a child with a disability or chronic illness is tough. Fear is a healthy response that mobilizes energy. Parents who have a child with a disability are also often afraid to have another child. Even when the problem is not genetic, some parents cannot even discuss the possibility of trying again. When you have faced the odds without fear and lost, the possibility that something could go wrong becomes very real.

Years after Tariq's diagnosis and my divorce and remarriage, when Cindy and I were expecting Kara, I felt more nervous than the average parent. Having faced the tragedy of disability before, the worry was based in reality. Parents can have more than one child with disabilities. We'd been told that our daughter was fine, but what if the genetic counselor was wrong? I remembered the discussions about birth defects in the childbirth classes. Everyone was silent. The instructor, who was a parent herself, quickly moved on to the next topic. I didn't blame the other parents-to-be. I wished that I could tell them about my pain and that my worries would not go away until I was sure this infant was healthy.

Cindy and I faced our fears together, and fortunately we had a healthy infant. Kara has been a source of great joy every day, especially as she learned to roll over, creep, crawl, walk, talk, and let us know what she wants and likes. Her development helps to reassure me that I am a vibrant person who can survive tragedy and maybe come out even better for it. I didn't worry so much when we were expecting our next daughter, Zoë, and fortunately, her development has delighted us all along the way.

While I was writing this chapter, I heard a news report that a 6-year-old boy with autism had gotten out of his family's apartment and been run over and killed by an early morning commuter train. I got an especially queasy feeling in my stomach when I heard that the accident had taken place near the train station that is only two blocks from our house. I shook internally as I remembered how I had lived with the same fear that Tariq might get out of the house and wander onto those same tracks, and my heart filled with grief for the boy's family and with relief that my son has the all-day supervision that he needs. A few weeks later, I found out from members of the Autism Society that the bereaved family had recently moved to the United States from Korea in order to get the more advanced care that is available here for children with autism.

GUILT

It is not unusual for parents to blame themselves for something that they did or did not do prior to their child's birth that caused their child's impairment. The very process of diagnosis often exacerbates the feelings of guilt. Every time we take our child for help somewhere, we hear a line of questions something like this:

- When did you first notice something was wrong?
- What was your pregnancy like?
- What was your mental state during the pregnancy?
- If you were working, when did you stop?
- Are there any similar problems in your family?

These questions can be particularly painful for mothers, who are led to wonder what they might have done wrong during pregnancy. Fathers may doubt that they took good enough care of their spouses. No matter what their religious background, somewhere in the back of many parents' heads comes the question: Is this a fair punishment for something I have done—or even thought?

Because it is commonly believed that good things happen to good people, it follows logically that bad things happen to bad people. Why do some people have children with impairments while others have children without impairments? This is a gut-wrenching question when a child has been diagnosed with a disability. A parent feels terrible if he or she believes that he or she has caused this tragedy. I recall how I blamed myself and wondered if the conflicts between me and Tariq's mother had caused or contributed to his condition.

When Bad Things Happen to Good People by Harold Kushner is the book I recommend most frequently to grieving parents to deal with feelings of guilt. I reread it myself every few years. It is a common belief that God is just. When people try to deal with guilt, they often come to the conclusion that they deserve what they got and somehow their misfortunes come as a punishment for sins. As a rabbi and as the parent of a chronically ill child who died, Kushner speaks to the unfair and uncontrollable distribution of suffering.

Whatever the reason, the world is not as orderly and understandable as we might like it to be. Guilt helps precipitate a long, drawn-out thought process that we can use to determine the meaning of other feelings, thoughts, beliefs, and actions. As difficult as this process may be, it always make people laugh when I remind them that people without a natural sense of guilt often find themselves in prison.

The resolution of guilt is an individual matter. Quite naturally, but painfully, parents wish that they could have done something to avoid the tragedy. They are able to move on with their lives after settling for themselves what their responsibilities actually are toward the child. Learning that autism is caused by defects in the neurological system, for example, helped me realize that marital conflict and divorce could not have caused it and helped me to move on. It is a tremendous relief when you no longer believe that you did something to cause this terrible thing to happen.

SHAME

Guilt and shame are often confused. Whereas *guilt* refers to the uncomfortable feeling attached to violating an inner standard or taboo, *shame,* however, is much broader and involves a failure to live up to one's inner ideals. Shame makes us feel small, powerless, and inadequate. There is a way out of guilt because a person can make up for things done wrong. Shame leaves us wanting to hide, with no easy way out.

According to psychiatrist Donald Nathanson, the antidote to shame is pride. When your child isn't typical, there are countless occasions in which you may feel a shame response and far fewer opportunities to experience pride in your child's accomplishments. This fact has another negative impact: It is more difficult for you and your child to have a mutually satisfying relationship—the kind that reinforces the pride of the parent as well as the child.

Shame affects the daily lives of parents and children when there is a disability in the family. Nathanson developed a construct called the "Compass of Shame" that delineates the four basic responses: withdrawal, attacking the self, attacking others, or avoidance or denial of the feeling. All of these reactions are expressed clearly in the comments of the group members as well as by countless parents I have met, talked to, and counseled. Still, they kept searching for a way to feel good. Being able to find pride in yourself and in your child is the only way to relieve the pain. This can only happen as parents redefine who they are and what is possible for them and their children.

DEPRESSION

Depression has been called the common cold of the mind. This feeling state can be brought on by a loss or disappointment of some kind. No one is a stranger to the experience of feeling down or "blue." It is a natural reaction to stress or tension.

For a time after a child's condition is clear, a parent may feel physically or mentally drained and may be unable or unwilling to perform even routine tasks. There may be little interest in activities that previously brought pleasure; there may be aches, pains, fatigue, poor digestion, or too much or too little sleep. When these symptoms are severe or prolonged, the parent may be experiencing *clinical depression*—a disorder of mood that calls for professional help in the form of intensive psychotherapy and quite possibly medication.

To feel okay, a parent must feel valuable, competent, capable, and worthwhile. When a child isn't typical, a parent's sense of self can be violated—evoking feelings of incompetence, weakness, worthlessness, and so forth. I certainly encountered this when I couldn't help my son in the way that I wanted to by fixing the problem.

Most of us spontaneously want to cheer up people who are depressed. Professionals too frequently respond by saying, "You're not worthless," but discouraging feelings of sadness does not alleviate these feelings; it does not cheer people up. What does help, however, is to accept parents' sad feelings and acknowledge that losses are hard for all of us.

Similar to the other feelings that cluster together in the grief process, depression serves a vital role in helping redefine our sense of self. Struggling against sadness helps us to explore and come up with new ways of feeling competent, valuable, and worthwhile.

ANGER

Anger, one of the most intense and least understood human emotions, is probably the scariest and most socially unacceptable feeling to own up to. It often arises with the thought, "Why me? Why did this have to happen to me?" Losing something precious hurts and seems unfair. Parents want someone or something to blame. It might be themselves, each other, the doctor, toxic waste, or in the case of adoptive parents, the birth parents.

Angry parents in this situation are trying to make sense of what has happened: "If we are decent people, how could this happen to us?" Parents need loved ones and friends to allow them to experience anger, to cry, and to scream. Indeed, what has happened is terrible and makes no sense. Trying to be patient by holding in the anger only prolongs the pain.

There are people who neglect and mistreat their children horribly and yet they have perfectly healthy offspring. Sometimes parents of children with disabilities resent people who have healthy children, a common but uncomfortable reaction. If the universe is unfair, it sometimes seems reasonable to become embittered and chronically angry. But most parents don't want to go through life this way, so a new sense of what is fair is needed. As Rabbi Harold Kushner speaks to this age-old question about justice that appears in the Bible, he reminds us that, "Anguish and heartbreak may not be distributed evenly throughout the world, but they are distributed very widely. Everyone gets his share" (p. 112).

It's hard to accept that some things happen for no reason. More than 100,000 children are born with disabilities each year in the United States of America, distributed virtually randomly among classes and ethnic groups. No expectant family is exempt from the possibility that their child might be a part of this "statistic."

Resolving anger depends on coming up with a new definition of fairness in the universe. If you believe that the universe is fundamentally unfair, you will remain chronically angry and embittered—walking around "with a chip on your shoulder." Yet, many parents have been able to use their anger to activate and energize themselves in the struggle to get the best possible services and education for their child's special needs. In this way, parents can actually make the world behave more fairly toward their child.

HOPE

The spontaneous feelings of denial, anxiety, fear, guilt, shame, depression, and anger eventually give rise to hope—as all of these feelings are shared and validated with supportive people. There is a particular way that each person acknowledges the loss and focuses on the future. Parents eventually come to think about their child with less pain, believing that no matter how difficult life may get, they can pull through. A sense of relief and normalcy is restored when hope is resurrected.

There is relief, too, in acknowledging and resolving your negative feelings. Some adjectives that describe this emerging emotional state are

- Reassured
- Upbeat

- Positive
- Optimistic
- Heartened
- Gladdened
- Secure
- Confident
- Encouraged
- Strong
- Proud
- Steady
- Peaceful

These positive feelings are missing from Figure 2.1. As emotional wounds heal, these new feelings arise. How individuals experience them varies widely. Although denial and anxiety are common initial reactions to learning of your child's disability, the other feelings occur in no particular order and may re-occur throughout the life of the child. Each person brings a different set of thoughts and beliefs to his or her relationship with the child, and there are no rules for how to grieve.

Some people, most of whom don't have a child with a disability, say that, "God gives special children to special people." I myself find no particular comfort in the statement and I usually resent it. It's fine for those who can truly believe it because those people will feel no pain, but I can't believe that God or any higher power would do such a thing. I do believe that my experiences with my son have transformed me and made me somewhat special. I only wish that there was another, easier way to have accomplished this. The German philosopher Friedrich Nietzsche believed that life does indeed break us at times, but when we heal, we heal stronger where the break occurred.

Because grief, especially prolonged grief, is painful and not acceptable to talk about, most of us try to make it "go away." Unfortunately, this doesn't work. There is no joy without pain. The steep price for actually avoiding grief would be to live without compassion or love for others. As long as we are alive and continue to live, love, dream, and strive for things that we want, we will experience loss.

We grieve spontaneously after losses. It's as natural as losing a seed to form the sprout or the transformation of the bud to a flower. Every loss sets the stage for future growth, however reluctantly we may face it. As the Lebanese philosopher Kahlil Gibran wrote, "Your pain is the breaking of the shell that encloses your understanding" (p. 52).

3

The Other Side of Sorrow

Working Through the Grief

"*G*rief can drive you places you never expected to go" (p. 167). In *The Broken Cord*, Michael Dorris tells his moving story as an adoptive parent of a boy who is eventually diagnosed with fetal alcohol syndrome after years of slow development, learning problems, and seizures. As Dorris pointed out, "When you decide to have a child, you are hostage to an uncertain future" (p. 198).

So where does grief take you, and when does the pain of the lost dream end? When will you feel better? Is it ever possible to actually "accept" what has happened? Sigmund Freud said that mourning is a kind of work that you have to do in order to move on, and that those who don't do the work will stay in a state of melancholy. Part of our basic human condition is that we spontaneously ponder our experiences and try to make sense of our myriad and sometimes confusing feelings and thoughts.

Probably one of the best ways that I can explain the sequence of grief is to share some of my own visions. My dreams changed as I went through an inner transformation. At first, when I knew that something was wrong with Tariq but couldn't accept the severity of the problem, I would dream at night of my daily encounters working with Tariq doing things that the speech-language therapist showed me and things that I had read about. For instance, I would imitate his repetitive movements—I would flap my arms when he flapped his. When I would do this during the day, Tariq would usually notice me and stop what he was doing for a few moments. He would give me a little smile and then go back to what he was doing, lost in his little world.

By night, in my frequently recurring dream, Tariq would look at me intently, as he would in my waking life, and then slowly form a word or two. I would feel the excitement in my chest as my heart beat faster. The sound of his voice forming words was a dream come true. I would rejoice, hug my son, and hold him next to my chest. In the morning I would wake up full of hope, believing that he *would* talk, and I kept working with him.

By day, the dream fueled my efforts and kept me going by renewing my hopes. I would tape record his grunts, groans, babblings, and whatever noises would come out of his mouth and listen to them, searching for progress or meaning. At times, I thought I heard some. But no words came back after years of intense effort and after having the same dream over and over for so many nights.

Over time, I began to wake up exhausted and overwhelmed. It was hard to go on. My hopes were fading. While writing this chapter, I retrieved one of the tapes from a dusty box in our basement. Listening for just a few moments brought back the feeling as if it had all happened yesterday. I heard myself patiently trying to coax meaningful sounds out of my son. Soon, I couldn't listen any longer. I realized that Tariq still makes the same vocalizations; the only difference now is that his voice has undergone transformation to a deeper tone.

Speech can be delayed, but when a child is not speaking by age 5 there is little chance that typical speech will ever develop. Still, I continued to hope and to be very disappointed. All of my life, whenever I worked hard at something, I had

I had to give up the dream, but Tariq was still special.

gotten results—things had worked out. I could remember so many examples, such as developing from a child who was physically awkward to a competitive athlete in high school.

In the beginning of my relationship with Cindy, I had a daydream that our love could heal Tariq. In my fantasy, I would see us sitting in a grassy spot under the willow trees in the park near my apartment. Tariq would come running to us with a daisy in his hand saying, "Look at the flower!" I would hug Cindy, and we would both hug Tariq in a romantic tableau image of love healing the hurt and the disability.

It was so hard to admit to myself that it was not to be. Fortunately, I got some help from my unconscious. Somewhere around Tariq's eighth birthday, I had a somewhat different dream. In this dream, my son spoke to me in sentences, and I was amazed, relieved, and overjoyed. I ran to share the news with Cindy, who was in the other room. As the dream continued, however, I woke up within the dream and knew that I was dreaming and that Tariq had not spoken.

When I actually woke up, I felt a deep relief, a sense that I could just live with things the way that they were. I didn't have to keep pushing myself. If a miracle came, I'd accept it, but Tariq's inability to speak was just a fact. Now I could be a whole person despite his silence. In my sleep, my mind had let me know that having a typical son was an unreachable dream.

That dream repeated over 3 or 4 years, and then I had a new dream. This time, Tariq talked to me again. Looking at me intently with his big brown eyes, he told me that he loved me, that he felt my love for him, and that he knew that I had done everything possible for him. He told me that he was happy in his own way and that he wanted me to be happy. Then he went back into his everyday state of autism—playing with his tongue, making unintelligible noises, and sometimes being unaware of my presence for long periods of time unless he wanted something. I felt sorrow and longing for what could have been if only he could have continued talking.

Waking up from this dream is harder to describe, but there was a definite sense that I had moved a little further on my journey. Tariq was a part of me—not all of me. I was a whole person—not just the wound from the loss. I had not bled to death, nor had I drowned in my grief as I had often feared. Instead, by inviting the feelings in, accepting the lost dream, living with it, and incorporating it, I had grown.

STAGES OF GRIEF: WORKING THROUGH IT

Dr. Elizabeth Kübler-Ross brought death and dying out of the closet in 1969 in *On Death and Dying*, her book based on her work with terminal cancer patients. She did for the subject of death what Freud had done for sexuality. It has become far easier to talk about loss, and in this respect alone her work is monumental. Kübler-Ross conceptualized five stages that characterize reactions that people experience to impending death: 1) denial, 2) anger, 3) bargaining, 4) depression, and 5) acceptance. It is now commonplace to hear people casually talking about these stages and wondering where they might be in dealing with a particular loss.

These stages have been adapted by numerous writers to fit the parents and family members of children with disabilities. As discussed previously, the birth of an infant with special needs sometimes feels like the death of the expected typical, healthy child. When I present workshops to groups of parents, I often ask them what stages they have been through. The group can usually identify stages very similar to those in the theory, which validates the model. (Of course, not everyone goes through the same stages in the same order, and they may overlap or repeat.)

This subject brings to mind the myth of Procrustes, the innkeeper who believed that people should fit exactly in their beds. All of the beds in his inn were the same length, and when travelers stopped, Procrustes would stretch those who were too short and cut down those who were too big to fit the beds exactly. Procrustes was the mythical forerunner of inflexible thinking. People should not be stretched or cut down to fit the psychological theory. With this in mind, let's see how a parent might work through the heartaches without taking the Kübler-Ross stages too literally.

There is little disagreement among anyone I've read or talked to that some form of denial comes first. Denial creates a necessary buffer zone because it takes time to learn to deal with a new reality. The thought, "Not me, it cannot be true," is a virtually universal response to loss. Although people may say, "Face reality," the initial reaction of disbelief is perfectly normal and healthy.

Because it is hard to believe what has happened, parents may resist recommendations from professionals who bear the bad news. Some people try to push their child beyond his or her abilities or delay enrolling their child in a special program. Others may delay beginning prescribed medications while they "shop around" trying to get a more hopeful or less serious diagnosis. It is not uncommon, for example, for the parents of a child who needs a hearing aid to at first keep the child from using it because they cannot accept the seriousness of the problem and the implication that their child cannot hear adequately without the device.

Parents may fantasize about a miracle cure or refuse to believe that the disability is severe. Sometimes doctors *are* wrong, and on first diagnosis it is nearly impossible to predict how far a given child can develop. And it's true that many parents, through hard work, hope, and love, have helped their child develop far beyond the expected potential. Each person must find his or her own blend of hope and reality.

In an award-winning film, *My Left Foot,* based on Christy Brown's true story, we see that Brown is unable to walk or speak because he has cerebral palsy. Everyone but his mother, who always believed in him, thought he had severe mental retardation. Eventually, Christy was able to begin expressing himself by writing on the floor with a piece of chalk held between the toes of his left foot. He had long understood his surroundings, but he had been locked inside his own body until then. Once Christy began to communicate in this unique way, his mother found a special program for him. He was able to learn to talk and become proficient enough with his left foot to express himself further through art and writing. His autobiography became the basis for the movie, and his life story became a gift to the world.

Many parents share the attitude of Christy's mother. She saw her child's potential despite the obvious, and she didn't let the negative assessments of others blind her. Despite her child's obvious disability, she developed a strong bond with him, as recommended by such authorities as renowned pediatrician T. Berry Brazelton of Boston Children's Hospital. Parents like Christy's mother help many children with serious impairments to eventually astound the "experts." What resembles denial may instead be unconditional love and hope that results not in a cure, perhaps, but in tremendous progress for the child.

In 1995, I was fortunate to meet Kathy Buckley, the first comedian who is deaf on the "hearing" circuit. She provided the evening entertainment at a statewide conference for the families of children in early intervention programs from across Pennsylvania. I was a presenter at the gathering, and my wife and I had the opportunity to eat at the same table with Kathy at the banquet. Kathy was articulate, impassioned, and funny.

During her presentation, she related how she had spent 3 years in a school for people with mental retardation because no one knew that she was hard of hearing. Could such a waste of human potential be funny? "They thought *I* was slow!" she quipped, bringing laughter and tears to the hundreds of parents in the audience, many or most of whom had experienced the gloomy predictions of experts.

People who don't understand why parents might deny aspects of their child's problem can seem condescending and impatient. It might even seem that those parents are being irrational, but grief cannot be understood simply as a cognitive phenomenon. It is a complex and compound feeling process. Although some parents get stuck in denial, most move on—when they are ready. As the Jewish Talmud so wisely states, "The sun will not set before its time."

If we look at the loss of a healthy child in terms of psychological trauma, then an extended period of healing is necessary to bring the parent back to a state of psychological well-being. As in the case of posttraumatic stress disorder, the individual tends to keep reliving the incident, and he or she has the tendency to expect the worst after such a sudden and terrible shock. The numbness is an emotional anesthetic. The sufferer may even feel that he or she is watching his or her own life from a distance or even that it is someone else's story. This split between affect and cognition keeps him or her from being overwhelmed and it is helpful in gaining perspective and integrating emotions.

During my doctoral studies, I met Phyllis Morgan. She was a teaching assistant and fellow student. Her husband had one of the first kidney transplants, and they had been coping with his condition for many years. She had trained many doctors and nurses in helping people to deal with loss. Morgan, as everyone called her, was spontaneously warm and supportive. She related how numbness often allowed her to get up in the morning and function. The scary part, she pointed out, was knowing that the numbness was going to end—you were going to eventually feel its source.

Psychologist William Worden calls working through denial the first task of grief work and labels this stage *accepting the
reality of the loss.* Part of the acceptance of reality is to believe
that your child will never be typical but at the same time
knowing that he or she is loving and lovable; this can take a
considerable amount of time.

When a disability is detected at birth, it is, of course, trau-
matic and devastating, but parents in this situation have told me
that they experienced very little denial of the reality. "Invisible"
disabilities, such as autism, learning disabilities, attention-deficit/
hyperactivity disorder, and emotional disorders that are diagnosed well after birth, are often much more difficult to accept.

CRYING OUT IN PAIN

Significant loss always causes mental torment, but when a
parent "loses" a living child, there is no obvious right or capacity to grieve. People often don't want to hear about it, and
because the loss of the dream cannot be openly acknowledged
and publicly mourned, the resulting grief is "disenfranchised."
Sometimes, people deny the pain even though they may accept the reality of the loss. They often feel pressured to move
on. Of course, they want the anguish to end.

The words of the great Russian novelist Leo Tolstoy can be
comforting in this regard: "Only people who are capable of loving strongly can also suffer great sorrow; but this same necessity of loving serves to counteract their grief and heals them."

As denial has been worked through, parents begin to get
angry that their child's condition will not improve signifi-
cantly. This anger may be the first outward expression of pain.
It often takes form in the questions, "Why me?" and "Why
my child?" Intense rage and resentment may arise at the apparent unfairness. I remember resenting the cosmic injustice
of my son's condition when so many healthy children were
born to parents who abused or neglected them. I would lie
awake with the same thought repeating over and over until
my head would throb.

Yet, great energy and vitality can come from this anger, and the resultant action can be rewarding. It gave me the drive, for example, to work with my son every day. Passive acceptance of his condition would not do this. Many parents want to work personally with their children because they know this kind of "homework" can make a difference. Wanting to prove the experts wrong spawned the ambition in me to make more money to pay for my son's therapies. Many parents have told me that they didn't know what they would do, who they would be, or how they would function without the anger.

The anger stage is when we look for a source to point the finger of blame. Many people even experience a crisis of religious belief because the God they thought to be just now seems unjust. In the June 3, 1985, edition of *People* magazine, Sylvester Stallone stated that when his son was diagnosed with autism, he went out into his backyard, looked up at the sky, and cursed God. A mother who sought my professional counsel told me that she no longer believed in hell since finding out that her only child had autism—according to her, she was living it here and now.

The feelings of anger may be spewed out and displaced in all directions, making it difficult to cope for all who are involved—including professionals. Sometimes, this kind of anger leads to isolation. It often seems that no one can possibly understand how you feel. You may feel guilty for being angry, especially if the depth of your anger is frightening. If you sometimes hold your child accountable for putting you through such a horrible tragedy, you will probably feel guilty for blaming such an innocent soul.

In my case, Tariq was 5 years old before I was able to admit to myself that I was angry at him. He was simply not who I wanted him to be. Even now, I am uncomfortable acknowledging this. It feels like a defect in me, a flaw that I would rather hide if I could. Isn't a parent's love for a child supposed to be unconditional? I first realized my anger on one of those many nights when he woke up and I heard him making noises and playing in his room. It took me a few minutes to wake myself fully in order to get up and try to rock him back to sleep. I was quick but not quick enough this time. As he had on other occasions at home and in school, he had a bowel movement and started playing with it and smearing it all over himself, the walls, and the furniture. I have since heard other parents in groups that I have led call this *diaper art.*

I was so furious at him for doing this to *me*—for making me go through this when most other 5-year-olds, even with disabilities, knew better—I wanted to throw him out that window in his room; I really did. I didn't touch him, however, except to lead him to the bathtub and start cleaning him up with warm, soapy water and a washcloth.

I felt the rage within me boiling, ready to erupt, and I was terrified of what that might make me do if I couldn't control it. Do you remember the television show, *The Incredible Hulk?* In each episode, David Banner would tell someone, "Don't make me angry! You won't like me when I'm angry!" If he did get angry, the civilized, mild-mannered Banner turned into an out-of-control monster. I took a few slow, deep breaths. As I washed Tariq and put clean pajamas on him, I thought once again about those abusive parents with healthy kids. Now that I knew my own anger, I wasn't mad at *them* anymore. I hugged my child. I understood. This was an example of what William Faulkner, in his Nobel Prize acceptance speech, had called the human heart in conflict with itself. It's part of the agony and sweat of the human spirit—not that I didn't still long for that dream of pure untainted love for my child devoid of anger. I was able to realize from understanding my own passionate anger that I was capable of controlling it. I now had empathy for people who lose control—they need help learning to manage their emotions. What a fine line divides us!

LET'S MAKE A DEAL

Wishing for a remedy may help fight off the overwhelming feelings of sadness. Parents may imagine a miracle cure. Perhaps by working extra hard, the child's condition will improve. Having been unable to face the sad facts in the first stage and having been angry at people and God in the second stage, perhaps now some kind of "deal" can postpone the inevitable.

The professional literature often refers to this phase as *shopping* for a diagnosis, hoping that there is a way out. If the right program or the right teacher will make this problem go away, then life can go back to the way it was before. To the outside observer, whether professional or not, it may seem that the parent is grasping at straws.

Parents frequently complain to me that their pediatricians are particularly impatient with them when they want other opinions and other less established treatments. I advise them to calmly ask their child's physician for an extended consultation at a time when he or she isn't rushed. Many times, the physician will respond quite differently when approached in this way and when the parents come prepared with questions and information. Given more time to discuss things, the physician may be more supportive of an alternative treatment and more understanding of the parents' wish to try another approach. If not, then the family might choose a new pediatrician.

Bargaining is another way of buying some time. Usually, the bargain is with God or our "higher power." Tariq graduated from the early intervention program at 4½ years of age and was due to start public school in the fall. He wore a little cap and gown with his classmates and squirmed through the ceremony in my arms. I just couldn't accept that he needed to go into a special education class like the ones being recommended.

At the time, the choices were a self-contained classroom for children with multiple disabilities or a specialized program for children with autism. I thought that these places would make him worse because he would not have any typical peers as role models. I couldn't imagine that his condition would be permanent. I couldn't find a nursery school that would take him to give him that extra year that I hoped would help him catch up.

I put an advertisement in the newspaper and found a small Montessori school that would accept him and give him extra help for an increased fee. I took on extra teaching and therapy cases to make the money. After trying extremely hard for more

Tariq playing at his early intervention program.

than a year, it was clear that Tariq wasn't improving. The teachers couldn't manage him and give enough attention to the other children at the same time. The parents of the other children, who had at first been patient, were now concerned and were complaining.

I took Tariq to the Center for Autistic Children, a specialized program that I had visited a year before. At that time, it had looked cold and pessimistic—therapists working one-to-one with children who couldn't benefit from group activities. I had sworn to myself at the time that I would keep my son out of such a place at all costs. But now I had spent more than one third of my gross salary on private school and therapies with no visible results, and I was going through a divorce. My parents, grandparents, and siblings had lent me money hoping, along with me, to find a cure.

This time, the center looked different: It appeared that one-to-one therapy was a realistic place to begin with my son. The social worker, the therapists, and the psychiatrist were warm, caring people who loved children like Tariq, knew how to work with them, and helped me feel comfortable with my decision to accept their help that I had previously refused. What a difference a year made!

FROM ALL WALKS OF LIFE

Isolation is a major effect of this kind of grief for a lost dream, so it helps to know that people from all walks of life react in similar ways. Rich, poor, or in between; African American, Caucasian, Hispanic, or Asian; you have to go through the same stages. Parental grief is a normal reaction that aids in attaining an inner peace and serenity. My research into how families coped successfully with disability was planned to help me grow while I completed the requirements for my doctorate. (I will always be grateful to my examining committee of Dr. Mel Silberman, Dr. Susan Whelan, and Dr. Emil Soucar for believing in me and supporting my efforts.)

One of the most articulate families that I've ever met came from the inner city of Philadelphia. The Greens are African American, and their son, Walter, who was 8 years old at the time, has cerebral palsy. Their oldest child, Nick, was 18 years old and had just gone away to college, majoring in special education. Sean, the youngest, had just turned 2 years old. Their story is included here because they can serve as role models for the collective experience of many families.

When I first went to their home, Charley Green was at work at his job with the transit system, so I began talking to his wife, Shirley. She had a lot to say and hoped that it might help others to hear it. She began by recalling Walter's premature birth after 6 months of pregnancy. Soon after his birth, the doctors told the Greens that their son would be a "vegetable." The doctor thought that Walter was probably deaf and blind and would never talk. Hospital officials asked the Greens if they could use the infant to try experimental drugs because he was not expected to live.

Charley and Shirley were vehemently opposed to experimental treatment. They were overwhelmed with worry and short on hope. Shirley recalled that every time the incubator was opened, their son would fight hard. He would grasp the opening until the nurse removed his tiny hand. As Shirley remarked, "Do you think God would give him the ability to fight like that if he was going to die?" Charley's attitude was, "Good, bad, or indifferent, he's my son, and he comes home with us."

Walter spent the first several months of his life in an incubator, but as soon as possible his parents brought him home. Because they were so upset with the negative prognosis that they received in the hospital, they changed to a private pediatrician. The new doctor thought Walter had developmental delays because of the premature birth but predicted that he would "catch up." (How many parents have heard similar reassurances and kept their hopes up?)

Despite the more positive prognosis, Walter's first year was extremely hard for the family. He was hospitalized for pneumonia four times within those 12 months, and each time, Charley and Shirley were worried that their son might die. At 6 months, there was still no diagnosis, so the Greens took Walter for a developmental evaluation. He was diagnosed with cerebral palsy.

Shirley told me she cried uncontrollably on the spot when they were told, and for weeks afterward she cried profusely almost every time she was alone. She looked for someone to blame. She had worked as a secretary until shortly before Walter was born and at first she blamed herself. She wondered what would have happened if she had not been working. The doubts lessened, but they would not go away.

When Charley got home, he told me his perspective. He was a big man who spoke softly but with great intensity. He took out a few record albums from his jazz collection and put one on as we began to talk. The sounds of John Coltrane and Miles Davis formed the background for our dialogue. Charley said, "I'm a believer, and I don't believe it's over until it's over. If I had followed the doctor's advice, I wouldn't even know my son now." He described his shock, "I see all his fingers, all his toes, and so on, and then I hear he's going to be a vegetable. It was too much. I was in hell. "

After Walter was diagnosed with cerebral palsy, Charley found himself drinking too much and picking fights with his wife. He was resentful, and he blamed himself. He wondered if he had done everything he could do—maybe he should have spent more time with his wife, and maybe he should have gone with her to the prenatal appointments. He found himself lashing out at others. He wondered if his seed was bad.

Shirley had told me earlier that Walter had ultimately strengthened their marriage. He became the catalyst for her and Charley to really talk to each other. Up until his birth, their marriage had been "up and down," and they had separated whenever they weren't getting along. After Walter was born, the couple focused on their marriage and how to make it work. Shirley tried to understand her husband better and appreciate his sensitivities.

Walter helped Charley, too. Charley described himself as a man who doesn't show much emotion except when he is angry. "Shirley could see what was going on," he recounted, "and said that I was holding it in and that I had to let it out." As Charley and Shirley learned to express themselves to each other, they argued less. They solved problems together.

As life went on, and Walter grew and did well in school, their pride in his progress eased their shame about his physical disability. They stopped blaming and attacking each other. When describing his son's progress in keeping up to grade level academically, Charley beamed and told me, "That's my main man."

Shirley and Charley did not plan to have another child. Shirley's new pregnancy was not discovered right away because Shirley was on a diet and was losing weight. When she found out that she was pregnant, she worried that something would go wrong, but it was too late for an abortion. Amniocentesis showed possible complications. Shirley and Charley were sick with worry.

Fortunately, fate was kind. The new infant was delivered by cesarean section, and both parents were relieved when she had no birth defects. Betsy's first year went smoothly. When she took her first steps, Shirley finally stopped blaming herself for Walter's disability. "Betsy's first steps told the whole story," she told me. Shirley believed that Betsy was "like the string who pulled the whole package together." The Greens had gained a new sense of who they were as a family.

REDEFINING WHO YOU ARE

When reality can no longer be denied, when angry energy does not change the child's condition, and when there are no more deals to be made, a sense of depression sets in. Sadness grips the heart as a reality that must be dealt with. The truth is extremely painful and often overwhelming. During this period, parents may question the meaning of life and their value as human beings. Because of the intense grief and shame, they may avoid others with typical children.

The depression that accompanies a loss varies from person to person just like the entire grief response. It can be deep and compelling as described by William Styron in the personal account of his own battle with depression, *Darkness Visible: A Memoir of Madness*. It is a pain that can be unimaginable to those who have not suffered it, and as Styron recounted, it can "frighten the soul to its marrow" (p. 21). If your child's diagnosis is made a relatively long time after birth, your grief reaction may be more intense because your hope for the typical child lived longer. Your bond with your child is stronger, too. Whatever its intensity, sorrow is the natural response that has been waiting in the wings while we go through the other stages.

It's hard to feel like you're a good parent when your child isn't "normal." Energy and hope are in short supply. Many people report a feeling of hollowness, headaches, difficulty with sleep, eating problems, and other physical symptoms. Your self-confidence may be shot. It helps to consider that there is a task involved. Worden called this task adjusting to an environment in which the loved one is missing, but in this case it is the typical child that is absent.

When someone dies, people often become more aware of the roles played by the deceased loved one, which can lead to the realization of how much or how little the loved one actually meant to them. Similarly, when the loss is the dream of a healthy child, parents are not aware of all of the facets of that dream. As opposed to the dreams about life with a typical child, experiencing life with a child with a disability demonstrates exactly what is missing.

The task of adjustment requires adapting to the demands of everyday life with the child who has special needs. New coping skills must be developed. Parents may have to give an injection to a child with diabetes, develop new skills, or learn sign language.

A lot of fear can be involved in moving on. In our culture, people tend to minimize this reality. Often, we hear clichés such as "cheer up, things will work out." These are not comforting when reality is teaching us otherwise. Things don't always work out, and when they don't it hurts horribly. For instance, when a relationship fails, it can be very hard to fall in love anew. When we are redefining ourselves, we fear being hurt again, rationalizing during this phase of grief that if we refuse to dream again and love again, then we can't be hurt again.

For parents who have lost a dream, the dilemma is how to adjust to the child that we actually have. We need to formulate new dreams and goals based on our child's real abilities. Doing this is a part of healing and growth, and it takes time. How much? As long as you need.

Alexandra Bricklin, whose daughter Rebecca has a pervasive developmental disorder, talks about how her tears operated during this period of grief. She expressed it in the following poem:

FROZEN RAGE

As I grieve frozen rage,
I remember my child's birth.
Her newborn skin so tender
pushed against my harshness.
I felt frosty burning,
then warm tears.

Something is wrong.
I was born open
but mamma built me walls. . .

As I grieve frozen rage,
My icy heart drips.
Warm tears
melt anger away.

GIANT STEPS

The Green family has more to teach us about how to come out of the feeling of sadness. Shirley described to me the periodic bouts that she experienced with overwhelming sadness. As Walter was developing in his early years, it was particularly painful for her to watch him try to do things that he just could not do. One example that she recounted was Walter learning how to crawl without the use of his legs by just dragging himself around with his arms.

Her sense of guilt was intertwined with her pain because she was still blaming herself for Walter's condition. One way that Shirley coped was allowing herself some time each day just to be down in the dumps and not fight the feeling. She would give herself a time limit and then get back to whatever she had to do. By accepting how low she felt and just letting it wash over her, she was able to rebound and feel refreshed.

When Walter was 2 years old, he was placed in a special preschool. He was diagnosed with mild mental retardation and cerebral palsy. After 3 years there, he was re-evaluated by a new school psychologist who determined that Walter had been misdiagnosed and did not have mental retardation. Shirley and Charley jumped for joy. Things were nowhere near as bleak as originally predicted.

Not long before I had met Charley and Shirley, Walter had been hospitalized for 8 months. He had an operation to straighten his legs and took part in intensive physical therapy to begin to use his legs with the help of braces. Shortly before leaving the hospital, Walter was able to walk with the aid of braces and a walker. When the time came for Walter's discharge, the nurses, the physical therapists, and the orthopedic surgeon all shed tears of joy along with Shirley and Charley.

Shirley told me how she could feel the weight of sadness lifting from her heart. She began to envision more successes for her son. Charley had been greatly disappointed that he couldn't play sports with his only son, but nonetheless, he told me that when he saw his son walk with those braces, after years of therapy and surgery, it was more exciting than the Super Bowl. Charley called this his proudest moment.

Walter, who still uses a wheelchair, faces life with great vigor. He takes weekly horseback riding lessons and goes deep-sea fishing with his dad. A measure of hope has returned to this family. As Charley and I finished talking, we sat back and listened to the last side of the albums that he had selected when we began. It was the soprano saxophone of John Coltrane with his exciting rendition of "My Favorite Things." It reflected his loving acceptance of his child, and it was a fitting conclusion to our dialogue.

A certain warmth and closeness comes from having shared each other's stories. Renewed interest in others can signal growth and a movement out of self-pity. Charley and Shirley show how parents can redefine themselves when something is wrong with their child. Going through such an experience in a loving relationship can help to prove that life is still worth living after a serious loss.

ACCEPTANCE

Many people question how the acceptance stage can apply to parents of children with special needs or disabilities. The very term *acceptance* seems to imply that a completion has occurred. Instead, because the child lives, the grieving experienced by parents is in some ways more complex. Helen Featherstone, a parent, poses a striking comparison between the death of a child and life with a child with disabilities in *A Difference in the Family: Life with a Disabled Child:*

> *The most important difference between mourning a death and mourning a disability is that the child in question is not dead at all. Instead of an aching hole, the empty bed, the now useless baby clothes, parents face the insistent demands of a child who needs even more care than an ordinary infant would. They must shoulder the heavy responsibility of leading this child into life, and love him as though he embodied all their dreams. Although death provides a moment's respite from ordinary demands, disability generates new tasks and necessities.* (1980, p. 234)

Although it may take a considerable amount of time, feelings of depression and anger eventually subside. Kübler-Ross stressed that this is not a "happy" stage. For a dying person, the pain is gone and the struggle is over. For the parents of children with disabilities and chronic illnesses, the pain has lessened but the hard work is beginning. On the plus side, we have become stronger and more able to deal with the everyday challenges of parenting a child with extraordinary needs.

Acceptance might be thought of as "going on with your life" and reworking the dreams for your child. It is a time to focus outward and make realistic plans for your child's care. Having worked through feelings of anger and guilt, it becomes possible to feel better and begin to trust yourself again. Then, parents can trust others and ask for help when needed from family, friends, and professionals. You now have a realistic hope that the family will survive the crisis. There are rough times ahead, but the disability is real and can be accommodated and worked into everyday life.

The task of acceptance involves withdrawing emotionally from the dream of the typical child and using the resultant energy to form new dreams and new relationships. It can be very difficult to withdraw this energy from old dreams. It may seem like withdrawing love from the child if parents stop hoping for a cure and move on to making the best of the situation.

In some respects, acceptance is the most difficult task of all. There may be a fear that new dreams will only be crushed if they arise. No one wants to be hurt again. Learning to love the actual child as opposed to the child of your dreams involves making new goals and hoping to achieve them. If we regard the completion of this task in this way, it actually lessens the burden. The "down" periods are less severe and people bounce back sooner.

People respond to a crisis from within the context of their own individual lives and from within the collective lives of their families. Although the model discussed here explains much about the experience of having a child with a disability, each person will experience each stage differently. The length of time each stage will last, the sequence of stages, and how they may overlap or repeat will vary. If grieving previous losses was arrested or blocked, those old feelings will no doubt come up and complicate the current loss.

In 1995, I received a telephone call from a woman in great distress. Carol had been referred to me by a close friend of hers who knew about my specialty in psychotherapy. Her 7-year-old son had asthma, and her 4-year-old son was extremely active. She seemed stressed to her limit. During her initial consultation, Carol blurted out all of her frustrations, including how horrible she felt to be admitting that she was having a hard time raising two very bright children.

She impressed me as an extremely articulate and intelligent woman as she vividly described her daily life as a full-time caregiver. Her face was drawn tight and her speech seemed pressured. Her oldest was easily upset and had a hard time sleeping because he worried so much. The youngest was so active that he would walk away whenever he had the opportunity and sometimes turn up as a lost child at the supermarket or shopping mall. As tough as all this sounded, I got the feeling that there was something else going on with Carol.

I asked her if she had experienced any major losses recently. Sure enough, both of her parents had died in the past 10 years. Her father had died suddenly from a major heart attack. Her mother, who had lived somewhat longer, had died from cancer while Carol was engaged to be married. Neither of her parents lived to see her get married. Carol had always imagined that her parents would be fine grandparents. They would have helped and supported her in many ways. She especially missed her mother because she had imagined that her mother would have guided her through the pregnancies and the transition to parenthood.

As we talked, it was clear to Carol that her parents' deaths had compounded the loss of her dream for perfect children. She imagined that her parents might be disappointed because of their grandchildren's emotional and behavior problems. Only with these considerations in the open and in perspective could therapy proceed. Carol said it was a relief to "unload her story."

CHRONIC GRIEF

On every occasion that I have spoken to parents about the stages of mourning, people have found the ideas extremely helpful. It never fails, however, that someone immediately responds, "When do you get over this? It happens to me over and over." In fact, this is true for most parents in this situation. We tend to revisit the grief as the child grows and matures, so there is no simple solution or resolution. It's just there.

Paul Monette described this problem so well in *Borrowed Time*, a memoir of his relationship with a friend who died from AIDS. He wrote that his cup is neither half full nor half empty. It's just half. Although you may cry when you revisit the loss of your dream, over time it becomes a land beyond tears. Life is now about survival and meeting the challenge.

One of the little things that remains difficult for me is passing a little league baseball game on a summer's night. When I hear the crack of the bat, I want to stop and watch and see my son there. I want to cheer him on, and then I'll get a tear in the corner of my eye or a lump in my throat. It *never* doesn't hurt.

I have been fortunate—I have survived, and time and people have been kind to me. I have gotten over isolating myself from people with typical children. I can't describe how good it is to enjoy hearing and sharing the joys that a father experiences when he beams with pride about his child. It's a normal part of life that lets me know I'm whole.

So, living with and raising a child with special needs is not something that you merely accept once and get over. The impact on daily life extends through the entire family—mother, father, child, and siblings. The experiences of the Smith family illustrate the chronic nature of grief and how families might cope with this unavoidable reality—this glass of hope that sometimes evaporates slowly over the years. The Smiths live in a rowhouse in a small town in New Jersey. Jim Smith works as an electrician, and Mary had been a full-time homemaker until she began working as a secretary. Jimmy, the middle child of three, seemed typical at birth but gradually lost both his sight and his hearing.

When Jimmy was about a year old and Mary was feeding him, she noticed a little flickering in his eye. She told her husband, but Jim did not see it. She lived alone with her worry. By the time Jimmy was 2 years old, his father eventually saw the flickering. The family doctor had believed that it was nothing serious.

When Jimmy was 3½ years old, Mary took him to a pediatrician because his eyes were jumping all of the time. The pediatrician referred the Smiths to a neurologist, who diagnosed a strabismus—the inability of one eye to focus with the other due to an imbalance of the eye muscles. At age 4, an ophthalmologist examined Jimmy and found optic nerve damage that had probably begun at birth and had deteriorated.

Jim and Mary told me how devastated they were by the diagnosis. At the time, Jimmy had to sit closer to the television than his sister, Susan, who was about 18 months older, but in every other way he still seemed typical. He could hear and walk, and he even rode a tricycle around their neighborhood.

Jimmy was hospitalized for numerous tests. Doctors found no cause and could make no prognosis. Mary was afraid of what the future would hold for her son. Her first thought was to shelter Jimmy and keep him inside to protect him. Jim countered that they should let their son do whatever he could and treat him as normally as possible. Mary agreed, and Jimmy continued to ride his bike and play with other children.

Jimmy went out for sports, and even though he could not see well enough to hit a baseball, the coaches let him run the bases. He was also in the cub scouts like most of the other children in the neighborhood. When the other cub scouts were climbing trees, his father would climb part way up with Jimmy, and Jimmy would then go as far up as he could on his own.

Around age 9, Jimmy began to lose his hearing. At first, his sisters and parents spoke loudly and then even shouted. As Jimmy's capacity for hearing diminished, he began to lose his speech. Eventually he had to learn sign language, and his family had to learn sign language to communicate with him; they had to make signs in the palm of his hand. Again, doctors could find no reason why Jimmy was losing his hearing.

Adjustment was a constant process for the whole Smith family as Jimmy's condition worsened. As a teenager, Jimmy began to have problems with his balance. At the time I met him, Jimmy was learning to use a cane but was having a very hard time accepting the progressive loss of his mobility. At times he has even refused to use the cane because of his feelings about it.

Jimmy and I discussed this on the telebraille device that allowed us to communicate. I would type on a keyboard and my message would be communicated to him in braille. He would type in braille, which would be transmitted into letters on a monitor. Before this technology, only those who knew braille could communicate with him. I felt fortunate and blessed to have met this young man.

Friends, neighbors, and relatives all wanted to communicate with Jimmy, so a sign language class was begun in the Smith home. Jimmy was the teacher, and every Friday night people gathered and had a good time learning. At the end of the year, Jimmy gave each of his students a report card—in braille. Both Jim and Mary look back on the sign language class, which lasted for 4 years, as some of the happiest times in their life with Jimmy. Jimmy has a good sense of humor, and most people enjoyed being around him, so the house was frequently full of friends and relatives.

One of the hardest times for Jimmy was adolescence. When he was little, he had friends in the neighborhood, but when they reached their teen years they no longer wanted to be around Jimmy, who by then couldn't see at all and had lost most of his hearing. In effect, the family became Jimmy's social group and they frequently went places together. At school, Jimmy did have one good friend who was deaf and had cerebral palsy. His friend could drive, and they went places together when Jimmy was on vacation. At age 22, he left home to attend a 2-year residential vocational training program as a young adult with deaf-blindness.

The constant adjustment to Jimmy's lessening ability to function independently has been especially trying. This is the main dilemma for the families of those who have a degenerative condition. There is one loss after another; it's not just revisiting the loss of the original dream. Jim and Mary are constantly faced with getting used to a new and more difficult level of functioning. They struggle and revive some hope based on their son's ability—they repeat this process again and again only to see components of that ability disappear. These folks are real survivors. They're always warm, friendly, and caring. We cross paths at least once or twice a year and they always ask how Tariq is doing. I know they don't expect him to be better. The way they ask lets me know they care.

AS LONG AS IT TAKES

The impact of the lost dream on the family is lifelong. Whether looking at feelings, stages, or tasks, working through this is a long-term process. Many factors affect how each individual and family responds. The nature and severity of the disability are, of course, major factors in how the loss is experienced. The ability to cope and deal with adversity is another major component.

Taking individual differences into account, most families display similar characteristics as they adapt to everyday life after experiencing grief over their lost dream. Once they have faced and dealt with the reality themselves, parents become able to discuss their child's disability with other people. Once parents have worked through their anger and no longer see professionals as the enemy, they are able to collaborate with them in making needed plans. They stop blaming them for not curing their child. Family members find themselves more able to pursue their own personal interests. Their lives are bigger than just the child with special needs; they are able to be loving but not overprotective toward the child.

In 1993, Eric Clapton won a Grammy for "Tears in Heaven," a song that is about his 3-year-old son who died in an accident. Clapton said in an interview that writing the song helped him to accept losing his son. I listen to the song frequently because I find comfort in Clapton's artistic expression of his journey to find peace. Clapton sings that time can bring you down, bend your knee, and break your heart, but nonetheless he finds peace "beyond the door" because "there are no more tears in heaven."

In other words, we have to keep living. The point of the song for me is that on the spiritual level, in the moments when we can transcend momentary experiences, all is at peace. My son knows my name. He holds my hand. Life is still hard, but Tariq and I are at peace—just as we are in my dream.

4

Day by Day

Tuning in to Your Special Child

I was the type of parent who, for a long time, refused to give up the hope that my child would be normal again, despite a good deal of evidence to the contrary. It was not because of lack of effort that my son did not turn out to be another Christy Brown. By doing all that I could do, I was able to look at myself in the mirror, hold my head up, respect myself, and go on with life. People who don't try everything that they think they should may live an existence haunted by guilt and doubt.

While writing this chapter, I talked at length with Dr. Bert Ruttenberg, who had been Tariq's psychiatrist for several years at the Center for Autistic Children. He believed and helped me to see that my efforts contributed to making Tariq pleasant and likeable to others. Tariq's personality engages people's interest and their wish to understand and help. He certainly needs a lot of help, and it is to his lifelong advantage that people like giving it to him.

As Dr. Ruttenberg so wisely taught me, the more a child is loved, the more loveable that child is. A child who is rejected, however, will tend to be angry, and others will tend to shy away or reject that child. It is comforting to know that Tariq's lovable personality is my legacy to him even after I am gone, and it will help him to get what he needs for the rest of his life. The acceptance of a child with special needs can challenge our ability to love as well as our notion of love between a parent and child. Giving everything and expecting nothing in return—no ballet recitals, no home runs, no A's on the report card—is the lesson that a child with a disability teaches and perhaps forces a family to learn. This unconditional love is a positive regard for who the child is in essence, not what he or she will achieve or acquire in life.

Unfortunately, it is not an easy lesson nor one that is eagerly embraced at the outset. When a child has a disability, grief and disappointment can cloud over and complicate everyday life. There is a constant process of reconciling the dreamed-for child with the actual child and restoring pride in the family, the child, and the self as we hope, watch, and help our special child grow. The key to reviving pride and hope is to build a mutually satisfying parent–child relationship. This chapter looks at how this is possible amid the stresses of everyday life, which begin with pregnancy and its buildup of hopes and worries.

Most women and men have some fear of having a child with a disability. The barrage of information about the impact of food, drugs, alcohol, tobacco, and pollution on the developing fetus serves to heighten the fears that universally haunt expectant parents. In *The Earliest Relationship: Parents, Infants, and the Drama of Early Attachment*, T. Berry Brazelton and Bertrand Cramer explained that these fears are counteracted by visualizing the infant as perfect. Positive wishes for the infant and wishes to be perfect parents increase through the pregnancy. This is a normal, natural defense that blocks out the worries that might otherwise predominate.

Men and women differ during this period in some general ways. Because men's bodies do not change during pregnancy, they are often able to put aside the worries. Yet, "morning sickness," fatigue, emotional lability, and the growth of the fetus inside of them are constant reminders to women that the pregnancy is real.

Some parents even imagine what they will do if they have an infant with mental retardation, cerebral palsy, or any of the disabilities that may have been present in the families that they came from. These scary dreams and fantasies explain why most expectant parents constantly want reassurance from their obstetrician the fetus is developing typically. They never tire of hearing over and over that the fetus is okay, and then when the infant is finally born, they want reassurances from the pediatrician that everything is developing typically. Even experienced parents may find themselves getting up in the middle of the night to check on the new infant's breathing, particularly if the infant hasn't made any noise for a while.

One major psychological adjustment to any newborn is the parents' need to feel better about themselves through bonding to the actual infant. In order to do this, they must mourn the perfect imaginary infant that got them through the pregnancy. The creation of this imaginary infant is a normal part of the parenting process and is identified as *image-making*, the first stage described in *The Six Stages of Parenthood* by Ellen Galinsky that focuses on how parents develop as their children grow and their personalities unfold. As mentioned previously, parents have mental pictures or dreams of how things are supposed to go when the child is born. Parents remember the child that they once were and then form images of how they would like to have been treated by their parents.

Galinsky saw parents as having myriad images that filter in and out of their thoughts, as opposed to one dream. Parenthood can, therefore, be seen as a journey of images failed and achieved. It is a sequence of stages that parents go through in response to their children's growth. After *image-making*, which occurs during pregnancy, comes *nurturing*, which extends from birth through the first couple of years. Next comes the *authority* stage, as small children begin to show independence and assert their wills, and parents have to learn to set limits. Then, the *interpretive* stage follows, when children reach the "age of reason" and parents explain the world and their values. The *in-*

terdependent stage follows when teenagers challenge authority, and finally, *departure* occurs when parents let go and take stock of their successes and failures as their children move out into the world.

The initial stage of bonding with the actual child and letting go of the image of the perfect child can be far more difficult when the infant presents with an actual disability or congenital disease. The gap between the real and the imaginary is much wider and harder to accept. The child is like a mirror to the parents of both their positive and negative traits. A visible "abnormality," such as a cleft lip, unconsciously stirs up an inner sense of inadequacy in parents. "What's wrong with us?" is the question raised. It is no wonder that having a child with a disability or chronic illness can create a trauma that wounds the parents' self-esteem. Having known this pain firsthand, it is something that I live in dread of happening again—indeed at times it has haunted me. At this point, I'll take a page out of my own life to show you what I mean.

FOUNTAIN TIME

Some times are harder than others as Michael Dorris pointed out in *The Broken Cord,* when he described his son Adam's birthdays—reminders of the pain and "the rage that he was not born whole" (p. 262). For me, the holidays that quickly follow Tariq's birthday on November 29 make for an especially difficult period. Images of warm, cozy family life fill our heads from Thanksgiving through Chanukah, Christmas, and the New Year. It's a time to be close, to give thanks, and to look forward. It's a time to celebrate the lives of children—a time that families get together and assess where they are, notice changes—and remember losses.

Cindy and I entered the 1993 holiday season looking forward to the birth of our second daughter. Zoë was due to arrive in late November, and in order to combat our fears we had amniocentesis performed as we had with our older daughter, Kara. Seeing the electron microscope "pictures" reminded me of my old biology textbooks, but these were exciting pictures of our infant's genes. It was a great relief to know that our infant had the right number of chromosomes, but it felt like we might be intruding into nature—looking too deep. How dare we! But we needed to be reassured. Now that we knew that the infant would be a girl, we began to imagine what her personality would be like and how she would fit with the rest of the family, with our toddler, Kara, in particular.

Since 1988, Tariq had lived and attended school at the Devereux Kanner Center in West Chester, Pennsylvania. With his need for vigilant around-the-clock care, he was safe and secure there and only an hour's drive from our home. So, although he was never far from our minds and hearts, Kara had never lived with Tariq, and Zöe was due to arrive any day.

We kept busy trying not to be too nervous waiting as the due date approached. On the Saturday after Thanksgiving, we took Kara and Antoinette to pick up Tariq to go shopping for Chanukah and Christmas gifts. As usual, Tariq was glad to see us when we picked him up, smiling broadly, grabbing me by the hand, and pulling me from the living room of his residential unit to our car. Even though he has no concept of the days of the week, he senses the increased activity and the excited mood around the holidays. He knows the general feeling, not the specific feelings attached to it. Somewhat fortunately, he is unaware of what he is missing, but I can't help but ponder what these holidays would be like with him if he were "normal."

As we approached the mall, I began to wonder what it would be like this time. Would it be upsetting being with Tariq? Would my eyes glass over? Would I get grumpy and irritable? How would I handle it? I began to focus on the anticipation of my two daughters and that helped my mood to lighten.

As we parked and got out of the car, 2½-year-old Kara got excited by the decorations and the sound of Christmas carols. At 2½, it was all new to her, and she could talk about it. It was exhilarating to be a part of her excitement. Antoinette wanted to shop on her own for some presents. At 12 years old, she was old enough now—it made her feel mature.

Another lost dream—Tariq playing sports.

Tariq had a look of wonder on his face. He clung to my hand and pulled me toward the mall entrance. Kara held Cindy's hand. She put her head next to Cindy's stomach and said, "Come out baby! Come see the toys. I want you to play with me."

We all laughed—it was a warm, memorable moment. Even Kara had a warm fantasy of the infant as a playmate. Tariq just kept walking happily, sharing the feeling of our family's humor even though he couldn't comprehend the words.

When Tariq was born, I had looked forward to shopping for toys as I envisioned having fun playing with him. Because he hasn't played "normally" with toys since he was 18 months old, this part of my life with him has been an unfulfilled dream. Images of holidays past danced through my mind. I recalled how for years, everywhere I went I tried to pick toys that Tariq might like, hoping that he might become interested and have fun or learn something.

Gradually, over a period of years, I had learned to let go of that image of playing with my son with exciting new toys, like cars and trucks, on Christmas morning. Because it was not a realistic image for Tariq, I tried to create a new image—a more workable one. On this day, I couldn't help wondering what I would be buying him if he was "normal." At first, my mind went blank. What are 14-year-olds into these days? I thought of one of my nephews who is a year younger and fairly typical to get a perspective. Baseball cards, sports equipment, CDs, computer games, and clothes came to mind.

Well, I could buy Tariq clothes, and I enjoy doing that. He's a good-looking kid; people always comment on that, so it feels good to pick the styles and colors that enhance his appearance. Teenagers enjoy getting new clothes for gifts. Tariq wouldn't notice the same way. He would get the positive feelings, however, from others seeing him in a colorful new sweater. Looking at it this way gave me pleasure in buying him some presents appropriate for his age. That helped me feel like a typical parent and got me out of the strong feelings that seem to cave in on me when I compare my son to a typical child his age.

We split our family up for a while because Tariq just liked walking, and it was difficult to actually shop with him. Antoinette was on her own, Cindy and Kara would shop together, and Tariq and I stayed together. We would meet again in an hour. We had learned various strategies like this to deal with the stress that could become strong enough to drive us apart if we didn't figure out how to manage it. I would miss the rest of the family, but I could have an enjoyable interaction with my son.

The mall was crowded with holiday shoppers whom Tariq didn't seem to notice. He did notice a vendor selling soft pretzels and pulled me over that way pointing to his mouth, signing that he wanted to eat. Then, he pointed to the center of his chest indicating "please." It was wonderful that he communicated; just this brief connection about a basic need gave me a

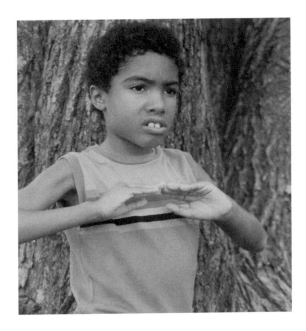

Tariq learned to sign the word for *more*.

warm feeling. That exchange of affect is the basic vehicle of the relationship that he and I have. Indeed, as I have learned, it is the basic vehicle for any human bond—affect is the bridge between people.

This approach of joining Tariq where he is at is something that I learned to do during his years at the Center for Autistic Children—the simple but profound contribution of child psychiatrist Bertram Ruttenberg who founded the Center more than 45 years ago. As opposed to wishing and pushing for a child to be typical, this technique encourages acceptance of the child where he or she is and encourages further development. Even more, the tactic fosters an enjoyable relationship for both parent and child. Learning how to tune in like this has been a vital part of my own healing process.

I bought a few pretzels and we sat down next to the fountain munching on them. It was pleasant to "go with the flow" and just be there—embodying a concept by child psychologist Stanley Greenspan called *floor time.* (A complete and systematic explanation of this concept is found in *The Child with Special Needs: Encouraging Intellectual and Emotional Growth* by Greenspan and his colleague, psychologist Serena Wieder.) Floor time is basically unstructured time when a parent follows the child's lead and the child's interests—the child is the director. With little children, you might get down on the floor on the child's level. With older children, you might be sitting, walking, or playing a board game or a sporting activity.

The main idea behind floor time is to build a warm, trusting relationship. A parent can't always just join a child where he or she is at, but the more the better. Greenspan recommended this for at least 30 minutes per day. This joining with a child establishes a communication loop on the child's level in which feelings can be passed back and forth. The warmth and trust provides the foundation, or platform, from which to face all of life's challenges with any child—not just a child with special needs.

The cascading fountain was hypnotic, and Tariq enjoyed it, giving us some rare time to just sit together. I knew he was enjoying it. I was enjoying that he was enjoying it. He knew that I was in tune with him and this filled me with a feeling of contentment, however momentary it might be. I knew he would be itching to walk again as soon as he finished his pretzel. I put my hand on his shoulder and squeezed tightly for a moment—he likes that kind of firm deep touch. My thoughts drifted as I recalled other peaceful moments in my life such as sitting by the ocean and listening to the sound of the waves.

Just then Tariq got up, yanking my arm and interrupting my reverie and, in essence, demanding something from me. It was back to the present. He had had enough sitting and he wanted to walk. That ended our stillness for a while. The good feeling I got from it fueled me, and being alone with him allowed me to just follow his impulses. If the whole family was together, I might have to hold him back, and he would protest—

stamping his feet and uttering sounds of frustration. That kind of tension breaks my heart. It deflates my spirit and drains my energy. I hate that reaction and work hard to prevent it.

Whenever possible, I try to go at Tariq's pace and on the level of intimacy that he can take. As long as I don't get exhausted, this makes our time pleasant. Over time, with any child, a parent can learn how to deal with the trouble spots that come up in the course of the day. This is the real art of parenting. This day it meant walking around the mall at a brisk pace. The walk itself was something I could enjoy with Tariq, although I would have preferred being outside if the weather was better. People must have noticed us—a tall, thin teenager smiling broadly, babbling like a very young child, holding his father by the hand, and leading him through the mall at a pace twice what everyone else was walking. Occasionally, Tariq would twirl his free hand near his head, making a contented but unusual sound for someone his age, or he would stick out his tongue, seeming to enjoy whatever sensation he got from that.

I wondered what people thought was wrong with Tariq. Long ago I accepted that most people, relatives included, probably preferred not to think about it—a natural response to an unpleasant reality. If they did think about it, I thought that they must realize that it was hard being his dad. I imagined that they knew how much I loved him. That was a pleasant projection. It had taken me years to understand and come to peace regarding Tariq as he actually is and to find and enjoy as many pleasant moments as possible.

This harmonious walk through the mall was one of the moments that told me that I was a good father. Tariq felt good, and I felt good that he felt good. Like every parent in a similar situation, I need as much of that as I can get. It wasn't what I would have thought of as a Hallmark or Kodak moment before I had my son but it is a valuable lesson about life and parenting even with typical children. Now, let's take a closer look at how to develop that type of relationship with a child who has a disability and who may be more difficult to nurture than a more typical child.

JULIE AND DAVID, HER BUSY CHILD

Julie has a very active 4-year-old son and sought my counsel to help her relationship with him. "He's my only child," she told me with tears in her eyes and her voice trembling. "He was born when I was 38. I waited for him my whole life and this is the way he is. You see it; everyone sees it—he isn't normal. That hurts to say; I'm not sure a good mother would say such a thing or would feel so very, very disappointed in her own child."

David was a bright-eyed, attractive child, but from the first time I observed him it was obvious that he was different. The new environment excited him. He fidgeted; he went from toy to toy never completing a play activity; and he didn't seem to listen to his mother. His mom told me that once he started crawling, he was never still for long. He got into everything around the house. In preschool he wouldn't sit in the circle.

Julie always felt like people were looking at her when she took him places. His difference made her feel different, defective—at times even ashamed. How often I had wished that Tariq had turned out normal and how often I had felt the way that Julie and so many other parents describe when they tell their stories. Indeed, how often I had wished that Tariq's disability was as "mild" as David's.

"Their eyes seem to say that I'm the mom of a bad kid," she blurted out. Certainly her eyes told me how painful that thought was as I observed a tear forming in the corner of one of them.

She told me how overwhelmed she felt just trying to keep up with David and keep him safe. He was very impulsive. If Julie wasn't totally vigilant, he would get out of the house and wander through the neighborhood. She cried as she related to me that he would never just sit and cuddle with her as other children his age did with their mothers. She never got that quiet time, and she longed for that. It was a part of her dream as a mother.

Recently, at the playgroup she brings her son to, the daughter of one of her friends sat on Julie's lap for a breather. It felt so good to her. As she soaked it in, Julie wanted those moments to last and last. Then she felt guilty for wishing for another child. She wondered why she couldn't just love David as he was at that moment, playing actively and happily with one toy after another. That was the real David. There was something so special in this young boy's zest for life.

What a bind for a parent to be in! Yet, understanding these complicated feelings is the door to the way out. It's the dilemma of every parent whose child isn't "normal"—working to help the child and yet simultaneously loving and accepting the child for who he or she is at the moment. It helps to remember that the child is not static but rather a dynamic evolving organism with tremendous potential for growth.

From the first moments of a child's life, parents hunger for responses from their newborns. Infants begin their social interactions with soothing body and eye contact and then later by smiling and making sounds. What expecting parent doesn't dream of a smiling infant who snuggles in his or her arms? So, Julie's disappointment that she cannot have this is quite normal but extremely uncomfortable for her.

Babies come into the world "wired" in ways to elicit responses from parents; they need this feedback loop to develop. The infant's responses, in turn, fuel the endless work of parenthood by encouraging a strong attachment, reassuring parents that their love is helping. The parents' enthusiasm, in turn, encourages and nurtures the child's development through stage after stage. The child is also fueled from within. Anticipation generates energy in the infant and a sense of mastery begins to develop early on. This propels the infant toward the next achievement along with the responses in the environment.

When a newborn breaks into the tiniest of smiles, for example, the adoring parent enjoys this and will smile back and often talk to the infant. The infant may coo or gurgle and wriggle in response. This, in turn, causes the parents to continue the interaction. As child psychiatrist Daniel Stern observed, the face of the mother and the face of the infant have a dialogue with each other. The infant is prewired to look at the parent's face because this is where the affective bridge first occurs. Thus, the infant is interactive from birth and an active partner in the relationship.

Stern's book, *The Interpersonal World of the Infant,* has a painting by artist Mary Cassatt. In it, the infant is focused on the mother's face and is reaching a hand up to it, demonstrating how the initial bond is built between the faces. The French sculptor, Auguste Rodin, conceptualized the face as the mirror of the soul, based on the premise that it is in the face that love is found. How common to see a new parent making silly faces in order to get an infant to smile and then to smile back in the quest for this most pleasant interaction.

As the infant gets older, the capacity increases for verbal interplay—and it is genuine fun for parent and child. Then, if an infant says "ooh," for example, parents may say, "That's good!" or say "ooh" in an encouraging way. Infants like to look at faces and can understand facial expressions and tone of voice, so the parents' natural response offers reinforcement for the infant who is then fueled to do more and develop further.

It used to be thought that parents had the primary influence in the parent–child interaction. Research, however, has shown how vital the child's response is to parents. In this early type of dialogue, each partner influences the other and sets up a response to the reaction of the other. Difficulties experienced by either partner can profoundly affect the relationship, as it did in the case of David and his mother.

When the infant's ability to respond to parental nurturing is impaired by some biological factor, the parents' expectations for the relationship are immediately violated. Their dreams are deflated, lessening their interest and causing their energy level to lessen. Quite naturally, this unpleasant feeling results in parents playing and talking less with an infant who doesn't respond, so the positive flow of affect is interrupted.

The infant, in turn, receives less response from the parent and thus loses some of this source of motivating energy, making interactions less rewarding. This may lead quickly to a withdrawn infant who slumps away from the parent instead of reaching toward the face. Studies by Brazelton and his colleagues showed that the parent, in turn, becomes withdrawn or even frightened or agitated and slumps away from the infant. Even a short gap in communication can leave parents feeling helpless and ineffectual.

Unfortunately, the infant who has trouble interacting and responding needs more—not less—help from his or her parents. He or she needs them to talk and play even more than they would if he or she were ideally responsive. Studies of infants with developmental disabilities have consistently shown that many of their behaviors, such as frequent and loud crying, difficulty in being comforted, and infrequent eye contact, have discouraged their caregivers from responding. Thus, the parental bond as well as the child's social and emotional development are put at risk for various problems. The infant may become withdrawn and his or her development slowed even more dramatically than the biological problem would seem to indicate.

Getting back to Julie, it is with good reason that she worried about her parenting. She had sensed that her interaction with her little boy was not helping him. Intuitively, she knew that a change in her could help her son. From birth, David had a generally positive mood and was easy to comfort when upset. This quality had kept her going even when she was discouraged by his dislike for physical contact. Now, he was becoming moody and disgruntled. Julie thought this was because she had to supervise and correct him so much of the time.

The tension between Julie and her son was living proof of a joint problem, but she experienced it as a maternal failure because she expected everything to come naturally and blamed herself that it hadn't. She needed professional guidance to help her be more comfortable with her son and to encourage his development despite his overactive nature and all of the practical challenges it created. Any child who has difficulty hearing, seeing, moving, or processing information will most likely have a similar effect on his or her parents. Now let's focus in more detail on how to bond more closely when it isn't happening easily, and then we will apply this information to Julie and David as well as other situations.

TUNING IN

Getting in tune with the actual child and letting go of the lost dream for the perfect child starts with the parents coming to an accurate understanding of who their child really is. Brazelton made an important contribution by first stressing the positive in each child, demonstrating those positive traits, and promoting bonding and then helping parents understand their infant's limitations. The child with a disability or illness is first of all a child; the disability is secondary. Often parents' fears turn out to be worse than a realistic perception of the "damage."

Everyone is born into the world with a set of temperamental traits. It is helpful to learn about these traits in order to be able to more objectively observe the child. It is a powerful intervention when the child's individual characteristics are observed and described by a skilled clinician, such as a pediatrician, a psychologist, a psychiatrist, or a social worker. Although this written explanation cannot approach substituting for that, it can be helpful. Each infant, with or without a disability, learns and grows at his or her own pace and with his or her own style. This section starts with a general overview and then applies this perspective in a way that can help a parent such as Julie and her son, David.

Very early in the first weeks of life, parents begin discovering what pleases their infant and what causes distress. How often the infant needs to sleep, eat, and be changed becomes clear, and routines are established. What stops the infant from crying and how the infant prefers to be held are recognized. Observant parents who learn how to respond to their infant's cues answer their own questions and reduce their anxieties about the infant's health and well-being.

Getting to know the actual child occurs through holding, touching, and caring for the infant. The discrepancy between the imagined and the real child can then be resolved. It is a process of sorting through dream images and settling on what is realistic, thereby strengthening the relationship. This kind of bonding foreshadows the entire course of parenthood for children with both typical and special needs.

Some babies are almost always cheerful, whereas others are cranky. Some like to be held, whereas others prefer less physical contact. Some go along with whatever their care-givers' preference may be, regardless of how fast or slow a child's development may be. To further complicate matters, the child's traits may be very different from the parents' traits. This can create what has been called a *temperamental mismatch* and can challenge the parents, who must learn to understand and respect innate rhythms or characteristics that may be much different than their own.

Child psychiatrist Stella Chess, a pioneer in this area, has identified several temperamental traits. Looking at these at-tributes one by one in the child as well as the parent can dra-matically improve their relationship, whether the child has a disability or not. This can be a powerful and healing revelation to parents to learn that in many areas nothing is wrong with them or their child—they are just different by temperament. Although it seems fairly simple, this material is unique and complex on an individual basis. It is the way in which skills and personalities unfold that makes each child's personality so unique.

Activity level may be the most obvious trait. Put simply, how much movement or bodily activity does a child prefer? Some children, such as David, never seem to stop for long except when something new catches their interest. On the other end, some children prefer a low level of physical activity. When par-ent and child prefer a similar level, it is easy for the relationship to be harmonious. A very active parent, for example, would probably regard an active child as typical. Yet, a parent with a low activity level may regard a child with an average level as overactive because the parent can't keep up without straining.

Biological rhythms as a temperamental trait can be regular or irregular and apply to sleeping, eating, and toileting. Some children never seem to nap, exhausting their parents, whereas others nap consistently, providing their parents with much needed breaks. Those who eat regularly make mealtimes easier, and those who eliminate regularly are far easier to toilet train. Although most would prefer children with regular rhythms, parents who have irregular patterns themselves tend to be more understanding of similar children. Children with irregular patterns may need extra care, with an emphasis on routine, to help them become more regular and function more easily within groups, such as those found in school.

Adaptability concerns how quickly a child can accept or get used to a change in routine. Some children react negatively to even small changes, such as being handed an unfamiliar cup at snack time, whereas others readily go with the flow. Children who have trouble adapting are not helped by avoiding new situations. They need to be prepared and then gradually introduced to new things and thus helped to adapt. These children tend to be less distractible. The down side of being very adaptable is that it is more difficult to understand that child's needs and wants. Children and adults with this quality may have their needs consistently compromised.

The *approach/withdrawal* reaction has to do with how children approach new situations. Some children will initially withdraw from a new person, toy, or food. They need time to observe and approach slowly, often with support and encouragement. Other children are drawn in right away by the novelty of a new situation. They may need help to avoid potentially dangerous situations because they automatically approach without thinking or observing.

The *physical sensitivity threshold* is another trait that varies widely in children. Some children are very easily upset by loud noises, bright lights, temperature changes, or differences in clothing. Others barely seem to notice all but the most extreme changes in their environment. Children who are easily upset may be regarded negatively when actually they are just more sensitive. Being able to understand this can be of great help in the child's development.

Distractibility refers to how easily a child can be diverted from eating or playing by an unexpected noise or another person. Some children can concentrate easily despite their surroundings, whereas others are distracted by the slightest noise. Either extreme can present difficulties to parents. The very distractible child often has trouble sitting still, whereas the child at the other end of the continuum resists switching attention easily to a new activity.

The *persistence/attention span* is a similar attribute. Some children continue an activity even when it is extremely difficult. Others give up right away. Those with greater persistence will be more likely to succeed in school, but they may also have problems switching attention when that is necessary. At its extreme, persistence after the job is done is known as *perseveration,* and it shuts the child out from making progressions to new or more complex activities.

Quality of mood is the final area in which children vary widely. Some children are pleasant and cheerful most of the time and are considered to have a "positive" mood. Others are fussy and cry easily representing a "negative" mood. Parents of those with a more positive mood may have difficulty knowing what bothers their children. The parents of those who cry easily, however, may fear that their children are essentially unhappy and believe that they are not "good enough" parents.

From looking at these traits, Chess and Thomas Alexander identified three major temperamental patterns. These patterns have been called *flexible* (or easy), *slow-to-warm-up,* and *feisty* (or difficult). There are advantages and disadvantages to each pattern, as well as strategies that are helpful with each temperament. Approximately 65%–70% of children fit into one of these categories, according to the researchers, with the remainder being a mixture of the patterns.

The *flexible* child has regular biological rhythms and is therefore easy to feed, toilet train, and take care of basic needs. Approximately 40% of all children fit into this category with these characteristics of a "perfect baby." Unfortunately, infants without these qualities are often considered "bad" because of a lack of understanding that these qualities are innate. Flexible children enjoy most new situations and adapt quickly. They seldom fuss and have a predominantly positive, cheerful mood. They have a low sensitivity to physical stimulation and a low intensity of emotional reaction. Flexible children have deep feelings, as do all children, but they express themselves quietly. For this reason, other children may take advantage of them, or they may become lost in the shuffle. They are easy to forget or take for granted when a busy parent has two or more children or when a teacher is trying to manage a large group.

The needs of flexible children are just as great as those of more vocal children. It helps to check on them regularly, observe them, and see if any particular help or attention is needed or wanted. Because they do not usually present a behavior problem, they rarely demand attention except in a crisis. It is vital to set aside special time so that flexible children receive the attention that they need and deserve. Zoë, our youngest child, tends to fit this profile. She is usually smiling and rarely upset although she can be shy and timid. When she does cry, it seems out of character and hard to figure out. Because it doesn't take much to make her happy, we feel bad when we miss giving her what she needs. In her quiet, agreeable manner, she provides new challenges and rewards for us as parents.

About 15% of all children fit the *slow-to-warm-up* pattern. They are often regarded as shy or timid and need ample time to warm up to new situations and people. Their biological rhythms may be regular or irregular. If pushed too hard, they tend to withdraw. They, too, express themselves quietly, sometimes nonverbally with their body posture or tone of voice. Kara, our older child, fits this pattern and has taught me firsthand how to respond to children like her. In fact, she has made me aware that I myself share some similar qualities. Despite their cautious nature, these children often become very attached to their parents and teachers. For example, once Kara has warmed up, she gets very upset and sobs when it is time to leave the home of someone she has become comfortable with. A trait that may initially prove challenging can, over time, become an endearing quality.

Cautious children need to feel close to their base of security. The key for them is to go slowly, step by step. In this way, they can be drawn into new activities and situations. The parent can then back off but remain available when needed or wanted. Consistency in the environment and the daily routine also helps fearful children by decreasing the feeling of newness and adding to their sense of security.

The last temperamental type is the *feisty* child, who, unlike the cautious child, seldom holds back. Feisty children tend to be very active, comprising about 10% of all children. They are intense and are often fun to be with. They live with zest while letting everyone know how they feel and what they want. Yet, feisty children can overwhelm their parents and caregivers because they are so intense, easily distracted, and often moody with irregular rhythms and intense reactions to various stimuli.

Feisty children need flexible parents who are sensitive to their feelings yet can set firm limits on unacceptable behavior. A parent who isn't flexible will be challenged to become so in order to have a satisfying relationship. The feisty child needs more time to experience his or her emotions before settling down. Only afterward can such a child be redirected to a new toy or activity when upset. Looking ahead in life, a child with these qualities may be more assertive than average and a real "go getter."

These intense children need peaceful, calm surroundings. By making the most of quiet moments, parents can strengthen their relationship as well as reinforce the child's more focused behavior. Feisty children also need many opportunities for active, vigorous play as well as more supervision to ensure their safety. The quiet moments often grow from periods during which the child has found something interesting on which to focus. It helps when a parent is energetic and participates enthusiastically in these kinds of activities. This is a form of approval that this type of child exalts in.

These were the strategies that I recommended to Julie for her son after observing him in my office and at the playground nearby. After conferring with his teacher, it was decided that the same strategies would be appropriate in school. When I met Howard, David's father, it was clear that his son's activity level was not adversely affecting their relationship. Although calm and thoughtful in demeanor, Howard had an easier time with their son than did Julie because he enjoyed the vigorous physical play that is often more characteristic of fathers' interactions with their children.

Howard did need, however, to look for and stretch out quiet times to aid his son's developing ability to prolong his attention and concentration. Because he had been unaware of the problem for so long, Howard and Julie experienced a good deal of dissonance whenever they discussed their perceptions of David. Under the guise of "boys will be boys," many children like David are not easily identified as needing help. Having an objective professional observer helped Julie and Howard to work together in their son's best interest.

Looking at the broad spectrum of these temperamental qualities in children is helpful in appreciating the uniqueness of each child. It gives insight into each child's behavior and needs. By tuning in and accepting these normal and natural traits, children get the message that they are good and worthwhile—they can feel loved and secure. Likewise, parents get the feeling that they, too, are really decent folks because they understand and love their child for who he or she is. It then becomes a building block in a relationship that feels good and is a source of pride to parent and child alike.

FLOOR TIME

Julie got a harmonious feeling when she was able to match her rhythms and behaviors to her son's. I saw this happen while observing them at the playground near my office for one of their sessions of floor time in action. The guiding principle is that healthy emotional development is the foundation for social and intellectual growth. The first step to helping Julie was *observing* the child in action. I noticed David's agility in climbing and the sparkle in his eye as he took obvious pride in demonstrating his prowess.

This was the same behavior that often exhausted, stressed, and even angered Julie at home when it was more than she could handle. In the environment of the playground, however, climbing could be embraced almost unconditionally. I pointed this out to Julie. The only limits, or rules, during floor time are that you can't break things or hurt anyone. This is because there must be a structure in which the child feels safe and secure. Julie was then able to relax. It was a relief not to have anything else to correct David about and he was able to play freely, which he did with great exuberance.

Next, I encouraged Julie to respond to David, which Greenspan called *opening the circle of communication.* The idea is to join the child in whatever he or she is doing while acknowledging the emotional tone, which in this case was excitement. Showing interest in what the child wants to do helps him or her to feel valued for who he or she is. In this case it was climbing, an application of gross motor skills.

"Wow! Look at my boy. You're really good at this," she remarked. In enjoying him and staying nearby in the playground, she entered his world and *followed his lead,* Greenspan's third step. This gave David the support to build his own drama and simultaneously, in this case, offered him an incentive to reach for his mother's slower-paced style. He paused for a moment and smiled back, clearly enjoying her enjoying him. Then, he quickly moved on to his next challenge. His mother's support encouraged him.

"Look at this!" he exclaimed as he slid down a pole to the ground, and he smiled as Julie arched her eyebrows in an approving glance and then moved on quickly once more. By continuing to actively express approval, both verbal and nonverbal, Julie had encouraged her son to *extend and expand his play,* Greenspan's next step in floor time. Julie took pride in her son, and David took pride in himself. It seemed contagious—what a boost to the sagging self-esteem of both parent and child! Complimenting David on what he already felt good about added to his sense of competence. On the other side of the equation, finding the opportunity to respond to her son in this way helped Julie feel like a good mother.

After about 20 minutes of vigorous play, David came over to the park bench, from which Julie and I were then watching, and sat on his mother's lap. The drama of our session in the playground had reached its conclusion. It was a fitting and welcome end to a vigorous performance. The child had *closed the circle of communication,* the last of the five basic steps in floor time. Each child-centered activity had received approving expressions, gestures, and words, and now David was reaching out to his mother in a tender, well-deserved moment.

David demonstrated that he enjoyed Julie's enjoyment of this time. The drama of their relationship was unfolding. Julie began to feel more fulfilled as a mother. David's basic nature would not change, but their relationship could change. In the moments of mutual comfort and acceptance there was great warmth. This kind of reciprocal relationship sustains the development of the child and bolsters and heals the injured self-esteem of the parent as well as the child. Julie had entered David's world as partner and facilitator, something that had become rare in everyday life where she was forced to struggle to contain and control his extremely active behavior. The child was able to feel more comfortable in his mother's love. This renewed relationship would facilitate effective behavioral strategies during the rest of the day and guide David in further social growth.

The video, *Around the Clock: Parenting the Delayed ADHD Child* with Joan Goodman and Susan Hoban, explored in detail the many challenges facing parents whose child has both attention-deficit/hyperactivity disorder and delays in areas such as language, coordination, and learning. Although the difficulties can seem insurmountable at times, when broken into smaller chunks, effective coping strategies can be developed. The video shows "behind-the-door" scenes of what it is really like for two families in their own words.

The same basic floor time philosophy that we have been discussing can be a guide for engaging with infants or young children at the other end of the activity spectrum as well. Young children who are slow to respond or whose development is delayed also crave mutually pleasurable interactions. Holding or gently touching such a child; talking or singing in a quiet, soothing voice; or rocking or swaying according to the child's preference can be quite pleasant and stimulating. Joining in the slower pace provides motivation for the child to join the parent at a somewhat faster pace—the inverse of what we described between Julie and her son.

These activities can be built into the daily routine of feeding, dressing, bathing, and diapering or toileting. Siblings, relatives, and friends who are comfortable with the child can all learn to participate in this way—making for a more cohesive family life and facilitating an interlocking web of relationships that can be beneficial to all involved.

Donald was a man I met at one of my workshops for fathers. His child fit the slower-paced rhythm, and he had trouble bonding early on for this reason. He told me how much he imagined having a son who would enjoy outdoor activities with him. He wanted to teach his son sports and enjoy the same kind of companionship that he had enjoyed growing up with his father. His son, Kevin, had been born blind and with mild cerebral palsy. Donald was devastated. He thought that all of his hopes and dreams had gone out the window because his first image of Kevin was that of a totally helpless child.

It took a period of several years for Donald to come to grips with his son's disability. As Donald became more and more involved with his son's development by playing with him at his own pace, he learned what Kevin could and couldn't do and realized that there was nothing holding his son back from fishing; this was one of the sports that he loved. It would not be easy, but virtually everything that he had imagined about fishing with his son was possible. That realization helped Donald to remake his dream—hunting might well be out, but fishing was in. Kevin would need help baiting his hook and a lot of coaching.

Within months of that realization, on a warm spring day, Donald was sitting with Kevin on a bridge over a stream near their home with their fishing rods in hand and lines dangling in the water. It was a dream come true for Donald. The quiet challenge, the fun, and the relaxation that fishermen love were all there. What he thought was out of the question at the time of his son's diagnosis was now firmly grasped in the bond between the father and the son.

Every child is constantly maturing, evolving, and becoming dynamic. There is an unfolding of temperamental qualities and positive and negative behaviors that are not apparent at birth. In this process, knowing and accepting your child's unique developmental skills is a key to relating in a mutually satisfying way. Expectations that are too high will be frustrating when they are not reached. Yet, expectations set too low provide for little challenge. There is a constant process of assessing the child's skills and joining where he or she actually is.

It is normal to wonder and not to know what is to come. The best antidote to the worry is to be able to find excitement and joy in the here and now. This positively energizes both parent and child to meet the main developmental challenges that lie ahead. As Gilbert Gaul, a Pulitzer Prize–winning journalist, observed in *Giant Steps: The Story of One Boy's Struggle to Walk,* "Life isn't made up of exclamations so much as a succession of small moments strung together like beads on a necklace. Where we go wrong is by expecting too much. Then disappointed and empty we have to find someone to blame" (p. 71). The resentment pales as we learn to live moment by moment and find those beads to string on our necklaces.

5

How to Stop Spinning

Understanding and Guiding Your Child's Behavior

"*S*imply imagine he's not your child. Everybody knows how to raise other people's children." Or so it seems. Whenever I address a group of parents about how to handle the behavior problems of children with disabilities, this statement never fails to evoke a round of hearty laughter. It's so much easier for all of us, even experts, to discuss other people's children. The balance between love and discipline is one of the toughest challenges of parenthood.

In the heat of the moment, it is difficult but vital to learn how to back off and look at your own life calmly and objectively. An important key to this approach is to seek support and insight from another adult—a spouse, a friend, or a professional with experience in the behavioral issues faced by parents of special children.

This chapter provides a framework to address behavior problems: First, get to know yourself and the deep inner feelings evoked by your child; second, understand the deeper meaning communicated by everyday problem behaviors; and third, learn to flexibly, yet firmly, apply behavioral strategies to implement change. Numerous other helpful books are available and some will be cited here, but personal professional guidance is often necessary. If you are spending more time telling your child what not to do than enjoying your child, then that may be the signal that it is time to seek help.

GETTING IN TOUCH WITH YOURSELF

The pressures of everyday life can push a parent to his or her wit's end. For many parents, not only is family life not like *Ozzie and Harriet*, it is also not like *Life Goes On* or *L.A. Law*, programs in which characters with disabilities have nothing but endearing traits. In real life, all people, including people with disabilities, can have many annoying behaviors and habits that can try the patience of others. Although a parent may have been sad holding and thinking about an infant or toddler with a disability, a preschooler's difficult behaviors may arouse anger that can be projected outward toward its source. This reaction, in turn, may produce guilt for not having been more understanding, resulting in a cycle that is not easy to break.

Not long ago, a father called me for an appointment. George, a well-dressed man of medium build in his early forties, seemed to have a lot going for him, but his outward appearance belied the inner turmoil that he told me about. His finely tailored suit was complemented by a blue textured shirt and a rich looking tie of contrasting colors. He was a partner in a leading management consulting firm and secure in his professional life. As he told me how he had looked forward to the birth of his son as the fulfillment of everything that he wanted in life, his eyes glazed over.

He said that the frustration building up inside of him was becoming unbearable. His body was reacting through colitis and a skin condition, and a concerned physician had recommended that he seek psychological help. He was obsessed with thoughts about his 4-year-old son, Billy, and he was becoming short-tempered with his wife. He was also grumpy with their 2-year-old daughter for no reason that he could identify.

His son Billy had Down syndrome and many developmental delays. Billy was not yet toilet trained and his speech was limited to a handful of words. George and his wife, Maureen, had heard me speak at a conference in Harrisburg, Pennsylvania; George had been part of a fathers' group that I had conducted there. He thought that I could understand him, but thinking that he should be able to handle things by himself, he had been delaying getting help.

There was no one in George's everyday life that he could turn to. Lately, he was likely to start crying unexpectedly whenever he was alone in the car. He was very close to his wife; they had been together for 10 years and they had always been able to talk about their problems. But now, when the subject of George's difficulties with Billy came up, they usually had to stop talking before it got tense and they became upset with each other. George told me that his wife felt that he was blaming her for giving birth to a child with Down syndrome and blaming their child for having the extra chromosome, the short forehead, and the slanting eyes. He didn't want his wife or either of his children to be the object of his grumpy moods, and he was worried that crying so much meant that he was a weak man.

At least in my office, his emotions were close to the surface, which is not very common among men. George triggered my own excitement about Tariq's birth. As I looked into my patient's eyes, I sensed that my own eyes were televising my empathy of his predicament—rooted and intertwined with my own sorrow. His words flowed smoothly as if he had prepared for this session.

"Sometimes I feel that my life is over, that I have no future; Maureen is afraid to try again for a normal son. Maybe this is all there is for us. When I'm thinking like that lately during the day in the office, then I don't want to go home. It's hard for me to face Maureen and Billy when I'm feeling like that. It's so disappointing that Billy can't run up and hug me and sit on my lap and tell me what he has been doing all day. That's my image of what should be happening. Other people are so excited talking about their little children. I'm not even enthused about my daughter, Dawn, and that's not fair to her. I find myself running from them and feeling guilty that I'm not excited to get home after work."

I commented on how well George was expressing himself.

"Well, as a consultant, I'm a professional communicator, so I was ready to tell you why I'm here. I've read up on this stuff, gone to workshops and support groups, and gone through what I've recognized as stages of grief, but I'm stuck. Other people think I have it together—that I'm a good father. I hate when people say that I am because I know it's not true, but I wouldn't want anyone to know."

"Where are you stuck?" I asked.

"It's like I've got a chip on my shoulder. I'd love to be a bad dad of a typical son. At least he'd play sports and do other things that I could brag about. And most of all, he'd bring grandchildren with my last name to see me even if I was a jerk. Again, I know this isn't fair to my daughter. So, I'm grumpy a lot. It feels like a contagious disease that is ruining my life and infecting my family."

In a situation like this, I try to get hold of some of the pressure points, or what child psychologist Saul Fisher calls *pivotal areas* of everyday life. So, I asked George to describe a typical day.

"What's so typical," he related, "is not sleeping through the night. Billy wakes up a lot around three or four in the morning; usually he wants to play. Maureen and I take turns getting up and getting him back to sleep. Lately, it's harder and harder for me. I get so worked up and I didn't used to. It's like that wakes him up even more and makes him stay awake longer. Then, I start yelling at him. That wakes up Maureen and then she gets mad at me. I can't blame her really. She doesn't get me up when it's her turn. I feel like a real jerk. Whether I get back to sleep or not my day starts out with me in a grumpy mood."

As we discussed the rest of a typical day, it was clear to me that George had a good feel of how to manage many situations that come up. He was sophisticated and knowledgeable as a parent. I couldn't help but imagine how well he might do with a typical son. By the end of the session, George commented that he was feeling a sense of relief that he was beginning to unload something very heavy. I asked him to reflect on his interactions with Billy in the middle of the night so that we could understand and modify how he dealt with this flashpoint.

When he came for his appointment the following week, George looked outwardly upset. He began telling me about his family history and why he had wanted a son so badly. His dad had spent a lot of time playing baseball with him and his older brother and taking them to Phillies' games. He wanted to do the same with his son and pass on the tradition. He related how he had begun sobbing lately every time he passed a little league baseball game. He wondered if that was "normal" in his situation; I assured him that it was.

"You know, I feel guilty at times like that. It's not Billy's fault. It feels wrong of me to be upset about baseball. He's such a peaceful child. Everyone who works with him tells us how well he is doing with his ability. He likes playing a little rough with me at night, and I like that. I feel really good in those moments."

I intervened and asked what he was thinking and feeling the last time he was up in the middle of the night with his son.

"Well, that was some tough homework you gave me to think about. I want to tell you the whole truth and get it off my chest. I wonder what you'll think of me after you hear this?"

George's voice started to shake. His neatly pressed suit couldn't disguise his distress. His face got pale, and his eyes widened. He leaned slightly toward me.

"When I got that angry way the other night, I wished that Billy would die and Maureen, too. Then I would be free of this burden—this horrible, ugly burden. Then I could go on with my own life . . . right now I'm stuck with the two of them."

Then the tears started to roll slowly down his cheeks. George leaned back and slumped down in his wing chair. He reached for a tissue and took a few deep breaths before wiping away the tears.

After waiting a few more moments, I asked him what the tears meant today.

"I feel such a sense of relief that I told someone. I've been having these thoughts for a while. How can you tell the woman you love that sometimes you wish she was dead? My tears feel like a release and not a sign of weakness. I'm not sure what you think of me, but your eyes still look at me kindly. I wonder if any of the other people in my support group have thoughts such as these. Has anybody else ever told you something like this? Can you tell me that?"

Now that George was strong enough to admit to these scary thoughts, he may soon have the courage to ask others what they're really thinking inside. It is relieving and healing to hear from other people you know personally. As for what I've heard—I've heard similar things many, many times—often with tears. The anger is part of the sorrow, as I pointed out previously. For many of us, the tears don't come so easily—not every man can cry like this—even though there are often tears on the inside. Admitting, accepting, and embracing your sorrow as normal but still uncomfortable is part of the healing process and the road to an inner peace.

Anger at the child causes the parent's image of him- or herself to come tumbling down. Feelings of inadequacy often arise around behavioral issues such as sleeping. These feelings can be especially frequent and intense because of the high stress level experienced by the parents of children with disabilities. It is necessary for parents to admit to these uncomfortable feelings in order to reconstruct an image of themselves as "good" parents and then to think clearly and "objectively" about how to handle their practical situation.

Initially, George wasn't ready to share his negative thoughts with his wife but he wanted to eventually. He told me that he thought he could handle Billy's waking up better now. I asked him to take careful mental notes of what transpires during these times. In the middle of the night, when his defenses were down, was when he had discovered the darker side of his personality, and times like these presented opportunity for growth. Having been there myself in the middle of many nights with Tariq, I remember all too clearly how horrible George could feel. I knew, too, that acknowledging such dark, frightening thoughts was the first step in breaking free of the shame of having them.

When I saw George the following week, there was a bounce in his step as he walked from the waiting room into my office. He looked at me intently and smiled. "I feel 20 pounds lighter," he began, "and less angry. I'm still short on sleep, and physically life is just as difficult, but I'm less angry about my situation. I don't feel my anger spilling out onto Maureen and Billy and Dawn. When it's my turn to be up with Billy, I've been a lot better getting him back to sleep. I am able to rock him and play lullabies and basically do what works without getting caught up in my anger, which had been making the situation even more difficult."

I commented that sometimes when we can change ourselves or the way we handle things as parents, it leads to a change in our child. Then I asked how things were going between him and Maureen.

"She thinks I'm handling things a lot better, so I told her what we talked about. She understood and she hugged me after I got done telling her. The amazing thing, to me, was that she said that she had been feeling like I wanted to get rid of her and Billy. She said that some days she felt like life wasn't worth living, and that's not her. I've never known her to feel like that. Even more, now that I have been able to admit this stuff, I feel even closer to Maureen. I feel like before long I will be able to tell her anything again."

Now this couple will be able to comfort each other and work out the problems that come up. They might need professional guidance from time to time if they get stumped. This can be the case for any parent as a child grows and develops. George's need for intensive psychotherapy, however, would probably be short term because his primary relationship—his marriage—could provide the emotional support he needed.

It was clear that George had to get in touch with his anger in order to understand himself and begin thinking clearly about how to handle a problem behavior. In another situation, it could be embarrassment about a child's behavior in public, guilt over a previous strict punishment, or inadequacy in understanding a child's needs. Whatever the case, understanding and embracing your inner reaction and discussing it with others is the key to acceptance and figuring out solutions.

UNDERSTANDING WHAT
YOUR CHILD'S BEHAVIOR MEANS

Once a child becomes mobile and develops an increasing ability to communicate needs and wants, questions of authority
assume heightened importance. Parents are faced with a set of
questions that will be with them for many years, such as the
following:

- When do I say yes?
- When do I say no?
- How do I enforce the rules?
- How do I know when I'm right?
- What is safe for my child?

From birth, the child and parent have learned to understand each other through smiles, eye contact, crying, and coo-
ing. As a child's mobility increases through rolling, creeping,
crawling, cruising, walking, and climbing, parents will have
more and more decisions to make about what to allow and
how to enforce it. Near the end of the first year and onward
into the second, what has been complex and subtle becomes
more direct and verbal. Included in the parent–child repertoire
of communication is the concept of *no* that can be conveyed
verbally or physically.

It is very uncomfortable to be angry at one's own child.
An angry parent can make a child feel unloved, humiliated,
and abandoned, and we remember these feelings from our
own childhood. As Galinsky mentioned in *The Six Stages of
Parenthood*—and I have found confirmation of it in my work
with groups of parents—an unmet expectation is usually at
the core of parental anger. The emotional turmoil is compounded by guilt in parents who are not aware of the source
of their anger and who feel bad about lashing out. When
George was up in the middle of the night with his son, Billy,
for example, he was confronted by his anger about the loss of
his dream for the perfect child.

The challenges faced by the parents of children with special needs are sometimes overwhelming. It can be extremely difficult to remain objective. Not all children with disabilities have these problems, but they do have an increased risk of developing troubling behavior patterns. Some children draw attention to themselves within the family and the community through intense emotional expressions, biting, kicking, or other physically forceful behaviors. They often have more than average difficulty moving from one activity to another and they have a lot of trouble separating from parents or significant others.

Their external displays also draw attention to their parents. When a child is having a tantrum in a supermarket, for example, other customers may wonder why the parent can't control that child. The parent is likely to be embarrassed and may think of him- or herself as inadequate in the eyes of others. The frustration and anger generated during such moments can be very toxic to the family.

It is common, as in other experiences that evoke shame, to want to disappear or to want the child to disappear. It is hard to think clearly when embarrassed, particularly when well-meaning people offer unsolicited advice about what to do based on what they did with their own children or what they've heard or read.

The more typical a child looks, the more unsolicited advice parents seem to get because there is no visible reason for the child's problem. Children who have attention-deficit/hyperactivity disorder, autism, and other neurological problems draw unsolicited attention, which can make life even harder for the child and for his or her parents. When a child's disability is visible, however, it is more likely that the parents will be viewed with compassion.

Child psychiatrist Rudolf Dreikurs developed a way of understanding and responding to children's misbehavior. His approach works with all children but is particularly valuable with young children and those with various disabilities that slow development or compromise the child's ability to communicate verbally. Dreikurs focuses on what the child is trying to communicate through the behavior that may be inappropriate. In this framework, all behavior—even what is frequently labeled *misbehavior*—falls into four categories: seeking attention, wanting power, displaying inadequacy, or plotting revenge.

First, all children need *attention;* meeting this need for infants and young children is a major part of parenting. Infants often cry in noticeably different ways when they are hungry or uncomfortable or need to be changed. Parents learn to recognize what their infant needs at the moment from the type of crying they hear. Likewise, it helps to think about what a young child might be asking for through his or her behavior. There are many possibilities; for example, the child may be

- Hungry
- Sleepy
- Scared
- Overstimulated
- Understimulated or bored
- Frustrated with not understanding
- Avoiding something
- Allergic
- Feeling sick

Some children have problems processing information received through their senses. These children have difficulty interpreting sights, sounds, and sensations from touch and movement. They may become unusually upset, for example, by bright lights or loud noises or by being touched or moved unexpectedly or in a certain way. They might also have problems using their muscles effectively, which might cause difficulty in learning to run, jump, or hop if groups of large muscles are involved (gross motor). If groups of small muscles are involved (fine motor), they might have difficulty with such activities as buttoning, zipping, cutting, or writing. If a child has difficulties rooted in the sensory system, then sensory integration therapy may be able to correct the problem. In *The Out-of-Sync Child: Recognizing and Coping with Sensory Integration Dys-*

function, Carol Stock Kranowitz helped parents understand and address these issues.

Young children who have limited verbal and nonverbal vocabularies must give their parents messages through their behavior. This is called *communicative intent,* and behavioral messages naturally stimulate parents to wonder what is on their child's mind. When these messages are misunderstood, especially when the child is using socially unacceptable behavior to express him- or herself, both parent and child can become intensely frustrated. Parents often understandably focus on what is considered unacceptable and try to stop it. Therefore, both parent and child can become intensely frustrated.

Tension for both parent and child heightens when the parent tries to stop the behavior without understanding its intended message and is heightened more when the child keeps doing the same thing. The unacceptable behavior may be the only way that the child can express his or her need or want. Trying to grasp the intent provides a starting point for parents to receive the child's message and then guide him or her toward expressing it in a more socially appropriate way.

When you can understand why your child is behaving the way he or she is, you can have empathy for his or her point of view. Empathizing doesn't mean agreeing or giving in, but *understanding.* Empathizing makes it a lot easier to work on changing a behavior that is a problem. For example, 3-year-old Joanne starts pushing her 5-year-old sister when she is tired of playing with blocks. Realizing that Joanne is bored enables her mother, Christine, to empathize with her child's limited language rather than just criticize her for being physically forceful. Joanne can then be asked to point to what she wants to do.

Sometimes children want more than attention; they need a sense of *power* and a feeling of control over their environment. At times, virtually every child wants to take over from the parent and be in charge. Doing so is an important step in gaining independence. Temper tantrums, are an example of power plays between parents and children. When they occur, parents typically feel provoked and angry; some tend to fight their children, some tend to give in. Fighting may encourage the child to intensify his or her protest or he or she may submit defiantly. When parents give in to tantrums, they are teaching children that having tantrums is a way to get what you want. All of these responses can intensify the child's desire to win and be in control.

Yet, withdrawing from conflict can help a child learn how to use power constructively. It can be difficult to observe objectively and notice the patterns, but by observing a child's tantrums, parents can often learn to avoid the situations that provoke him or her. Not long ago, a woman consulted me for help in dealing with her son's tantrums. She cried as she told me about her son. Josh was 3 years old and had been enrolled in a special education preschool program for the past few months. He had very little speech compared with other children his age, but Josh was making good progress in his program. He had tantrums that could last a half hour or more. These tantrums did not occur when her husband was at home, and that made her feel even more inadequate.

His mother was extremely frustrated and felt ineffectual as a parent. Her upset feelings often ruined most of the afternoon for the mother as well as the child. When I asked her when the outbursts occurred, she told me every day, specifically when her son got home from school and she was fixing his lunch. As is frequently the case for a frustrated, overwhelmed parent, she had never considered that there might be a pattern. I wondered aloud if Josh was hungry and did not understand that he had to wait for lunch. That made sense to his mom. I suggested that she could have his lunch prepared in advance so that he could eat as soon as he got home.

Josh's mother soon called to tell me that the tantrums after school had stopped and their afternoons together had become enjoyable. It seemed too good to be true. Instead of fighting over waiting for lunch to be ready, more play, floor time, and positive communication were occurring as the boy's language developed. Of course, not every problem such as this one can be solved so simply, but this example does illustrate one way to reduce tantrums by avoiding them and promoting mutually enjoyable interactions between parent and child.

Sometimes children get extremely discouraged and act out in order to *display inadequacy.* Of course, this occurs more frequently when children have learning difficulties. The child may want the parent to back off from expecting a new milestone, such as going from words to sentences, so the behavior can be an expression of helplessness. Despair and hopelessness may then be evoked in the parent, leading to passivity and a lack of response in the relationship. This is another negative communicative loop that reinforces the idea that nothing can be done and ensures that improvement will not occur.

An example of this behavior would be a child who is learning to eat with a fork and who cries and kicks the table whenever he or she drops food. Parents often don't want their child to feel frustrated so they back off expecting the child to use his or her utensils. The way to encourage adequacy, however, and thereby reduce frustration over the long term, is to focus on the child's assets and encourage all attempts and little successes, no matter how small, to use the fork. When the child drops something, respond by encouraging him or her to keep trying.

Breaking the challenge into small pieces, such as any successful use of the fork, enables the child to have a feeling of success. Learning to appreciate small increments of progress helps parents to avoid hopelessness and helps children to persist in their efforts. Of course, this principle applies to all children, but children with special needs need a lot more understanding in this regard because it takes them longer to learn and master tasks for which their disability may delay or inhibit learning.

I can still picture vividly how excited Tariq was when he learned to drink through a straw. He was 9 years old at the time. What was a small increment for other children was a big step for him. I was excited and happy for him. His big smile seemed to say that he was really proud of himself.

Finally, when children feel hurt, they may want *revenge,* displaying a tendency to retaliate in order to "get even." This kind of behavior often occurs during the preschool age range of 3–5 years. For example, a child who does not want to put his or her toys away before bedtime may kick or bite the parent who is asking him or her to do it. This is a form of communicating or connecting by hurting. This type of behavior is also frequently perceived as a lack of respect on the part of the child. The unprepared parent will frequently feel wounded and sometimes enraged by his or her child's behavior and may even be impelled to retaliate physically or verbally to get even. Such a response is likely to only intensify the child's attempts to strike back and to result in steadily escalating emotional and physical tension.

Behavior that has revenge as a goal may be the most difficult type to view objectively; teamwork with a spouse or another supportive adult is often necessary to control it. It can be extremely difficult for parents to overcome negative feelings in this case, but avoiding retaliation is the key to a helpful response. Using time-outs, described later in this chapter, while accepting and verbally acknowledging that the child feels hurt and angry can neutralize the hurt, often visibly relaxing the child, and help him or her to feel loved, which ultimately makes revenge unnecessary.

Understanding that children are always trying to tell us something and that all misbehavior has one of these four purposes often serves to defuse the buildup of tension between parent and child. Oftentimes, I have observed parents visibly relax when they start thinking this way about their child. Doing so makes it possible to look at how to change behaviors that are problems while acting as a guide and a positive role model.

STRATEGIES FOR CHANGE

Children with special needs are undergoing constant change just like their more typical peers. Styles of discipline that work today or tomorrow may not work next week or next month. Parents do better when they have a broad repertoire of positive strategies to deal with challenging behaviors. The goal of positive discipline is self-disciplined children who are responsible and cooperative at their own developmental level. An added value of using positive strategies to guide children's behavior is that it helps parents feel positive about themselves and their children. The techniques outlined here are all aimed at guiding children toward learning what is expected of them in various situations and at avoiding the ineffective punishments, including:

- Threats, which parents often don't carry out and therefore undermine parental authority
- Yelling, which often doesn't work and may teach children not to listen unless parents raise their voices
- Insults, name-calling, and negative comparisons to other children, which teach shame to the child
- Withdrawal of privileges that have no clear relationship to the problem behavior and creates resentment
- Spanking, which is most often a sign of frustration in adults and may teach children to become physically aggressive themselves or passive, timid, and afraid

Renowned child psychiatrist Haim Ginott believed that spanking teaches a child that when you're angry, you hit. Although spanking may decrease an undesirable behavior for a time, it does not teach an acceptable behavior. Spanking may also relieve a parent's anger, but most parents feel guilty afterward. Many children are able to use that guilt to acquire all sorts of privileges after a spanking. As Ginott said, "I've never known of a child who was spanked into becoming a more loving human being" (as cited in Lally, 1990, p. 73).

STRESSING THE POSITIVE

An ounce of prevention is worth a pound of cure. Positive reinforcement of desirable behavior is the best prevention for negative behavior. It is all too easy to spend a lot of time focusing on a child's problem behaviors, especially because any behavior that makes the child appear different is particularly unpleasant for parents. Reducing or eliminating that behavior may make the child appear and actually be more typical, which is one reason we often focus on the problems—and may overlook many of the child's strong points.

When a child consistently gets a lot of attention for a certain negative behavior, he or she learns that as a way of relating or belonging. Parents, however, often grow discouraged and feel guilty when they must constantly correct their children. Although setting limits is, of course, necessary, doing so can be balanced by noticing and praising positive behavior. This kind of effort results in a child getting more *yes* responses and fewer *no* responses and has been called *catching the child being good*, which feels better to parent and child alike.

Ellen Galinsky reported on an informal experiment in a child care center with the parents of typical children, which concluded that parents tend to overestimate the amount of time that their child is difficult to handle and to underestimate the time that he or she is cooperative. The "Four to One Rule," something that I learned from child psychologist Lawrence Shapiro, can be helpful in sustaining a positive attitude. According to this guideline, you have to notice and comment on four positive things before commenting on one negative or undesirable behavior.

Responding to the positive also builds a positive self-image and confidence in the child. It is especially beneficial to notice and comment on positive behavior as soon as possible after correcting a child for an undesirable behavior. Doing so reassures the child that he or she is still loved and valued even though he or she has just been corrected.

SETTING LIMITS

Children need both loving, positive attention and limits; a deficit in either area will inhibit growth. This is particularly true when the challenges are steep; children with special needs make more progress when reasonable expectations are made and held to by parents. Conversely, unrealistic expectations may be a blow to an already delicate sense of self-esteem. For parents, the inner struggle over setting limits and establishing who is in control is a struggle that continues until the child with or without a disability leaves home.

At the core of many conflicts between parent and child is the expectation that the child should be acting differently. Successful limit setting is based on realistic evaluations of the child's skills. Understanding a child's capabilities helps avoid setting unrealistic limits, and it is important to understand the effect of the child's disability on whatever limit is being considered. The child may not be able to do what is being expected or may not be developmentally ready. Reasonable expectations can be formulated with help from other parents, friends, teachers, therapists, and doctors who know your child, as well as from books.

Child psychiatrist Stanley Greenspan recommends increasing the amount of floor time whenever you increase the child's limits. The resultant empathy and warmth will help the child realize that you are trying to teach him or her through that pleasant connection as well as through limit setting. The parent in turn feels less guilty for restricting the child. Greenspan also recommends teaching one key issue at a time and using broad enforceable rules that are repeated frequently, calmly, and firmly.

When we begin to set and enforce rules for our children, there is virtually no way to avoid revisiting our own childhood. Most parents consciously aim not to repeat what hurt them as children. In this respect, we may be re-creating our own childhood in the hopes of trying to be the parent we wished for. People who grew up with inflexible, authoritarian parents strive to be flexible and empathetic and, therefore, find it hard to set and enforce limits. On the other end of the continuum, those who grew up with permissive parents may have longed for more structure and rules with the security that can come from firm direction. In either case, our techniques for dispensing authority will have to be reshaped over and over if we are to become successful parents who help our children achieve their full potential.

The language that we use in limit setting can be instrumental in helping the parent to remain firm and the child to cooperate. Positive, rather than negative, suggestions work best. For example, "Close the door gently," instead of "Don't slam the door"; or "Take little bites," as opposed to "Don't take big bites." It is also preferable to make pleasant requests such as, "Take a few more minutes and then we will go inside," instead of "Stop playing." Specific requests get better responses than general ones; for example, "Put the blocks here," rather than "Pick up the toys." These techniques help create an atmosphere that minimizes guilt and prevents the slow buildup of anger that can be so harmful to parent–child relationships.

REDIRECTING THE CHILD

Toddlers eagerly explore the world around them and often get into things that may be dangerous or inappropriate. Older children who are impulsive, who are overactive, or who are unaware of danger due to cognitive difficulties create similar concerns for parents. This difficulty is compounded because this behavior in a child whose peers are more developed in certain areas reminds parents of their lost dream. Parents can become physically stressed from the demands of extra supervision. Very frequently, however, this can become a pleasant, playful interaction by distracting and redirecting the child to a safe, acceptable alternative.

Distraction works well because it is a respectful approach to curiosity and short attention spans. An easy example would be a 6-month-old infant who begins pulling on a parent's hair and won't let go, causing discomfort to the adult. Simply giving the child something interesting to play with can quickly alter the situation. The child is thus distracted from the hair and redirected to something else that is enjoyable.

This technique was extremely helpful with my son, Tariq, who was very active. I think he was attracted to the gleam of a sharp kitchen knife because he would often get one and begin waving it around playfully. If I just pulled it away from him, a negative cycle would ensue as he got upset, cried, and stamped his feet. It could go on for an hour or more with him trying more and more desperately to get the knife back.

An hour of that kind of conflict can really give you "a bad head." Calling his name gently and offering to trade him something else that he liked, such as a koosh ball or a rubber snake, would usually work. It was like magic to watch him come over and agree to the exchange. He would become ab-

Tariq is self-stimulating but happy with a Snoopy toy.

sorbed in the exchange and forget about the knife. Then he could be easily steered to another part of the house, restructuring the environment to avoid the re-occurrence of the problem. Instead of feeling like I was ruining his fun or that he was getting the best of me, I felt like a competent, loving parent who knew and understood my child.

IGNORING INAPPROPRIATE BEHAVIOR

Although it may be far easier said than done, remember that behavior that is not recognized is not reinforced by attention. As we discussed previously, children frequently misbehave in order to get attention. It is far easier to encourage appropriate behavior when attention for misbehavior is avoided as much as possible. According to mountains of behavioral research with laboratory animals, children, and adults, behavior that is not reinforced tends to subside or to be extinguished.

This skill can be used to handle minor problems that are not destructive or dangerous, such as whining, sulking, mild crying, having temper tantrums, attempting to interrupt, insulting others, and so forth. Of course, these problems often feel "major" because they challenge the authority and self-concept of loving, good-natured parents. Consistently planning to ignore a child's whining, for example, will usually result in decreased whining. At first, however, there may be an increase in the rate, duration, and intensity of the undesirable behavior. This occurs because the child is trying to get the parent to respond in the old familiar way. It helps to be ready for this temporary increase that often precedes the gradual decrease.

Rick and Judy came to me overwhelmed with their son's whining and crying whenever it was time to go out and he was having a good time. Keith, who had limited speech at 4 years of age, would lay on the floor and refuse to cooperate. When I asked if the same problem occurred at school, Rick and Judy told me that their son's teacher handles him very well. I suggested that they ask the teacher what she did. They subsequently learned that his teacher just expected Keith to cooperate and get ready to go out or move on to the next planned activity. At times he protested but never as intensely as at home.

It was hard for Rick and Judy to ignore their child's whining and crying. They felt guilty and sad when he didn't want to stop what he was doing, yet giving in to this behavior was reinforcing it and giving Keith an unhealthy amount of power in the family. I suggested that they observe their son at school and see if he was unhappy when expected and required to cooperate. Both parents noted that when their son's whining was ignored, he quickly complied with his teacher's request and returned to a positive mood. By exploring their feelings and seeing this strategy in action, Rick and Judy were able to implement a plan that changed their son's behavior.

STRUCTURING THE ENVIRONMENT

Young children need to explore in order to learn. The down-side is the constant concern about what harm or damage can be caused by an inquisitive toddler getting into something. In order to help them to have as much of this vital experience as possible, it is up to parents to structure the environment so that children can grow and be safe. This strategy often goes by other names such as *childproofing* or *babyproofing*. By limiting the need to say no, a more positive atmosphere is created in the home. Parents have less need to invoke their authority and children can play happily.

As soon as infants can move around on their own, it is time to childproof the environment. It is important to have plenty of things that the child can handle freely, safely, and without distressing the parents. In the kitchen, for example, the lower cabinets can be fitted with childproof latches com-monly available. One cabinet can be left open and full of safe, nonbreakable items such as plastic containers and bowls so that the toddler or child can have fun while hanging out wait-ing for dinner.

Children with special needs require this kind of structure longer than their peers and sometimes indefinitely. This can be painful to accept for parents as they watch other children moving on and requiring less childproofing, which in turn makes parents feel more free in their homes. It is another image violated when you realize that you have to make child-proofing an ongoing part of life.

Setting predictable schedules and routines is another part of structuring a child's environment. Dressing may come be-fore breakfast, for example, and baths may come before bed-time. Children feel secure and their behavior is more consis-tent when they know what to expect. Tantrums that occur when a child does not want to switch activities can be mini-mized when the child understands that bath time comes be-fore bedtime, for instance, and therefore, it is time to stop playing and put the toys away.

Tariq learned to control his flapping on a cue to fold his hands.

GIVING CHOICES

Giving children choices helps them learn to be responsible for their own behavior. This strategy also helps children learn how to cooperate with adults as well as siblings and other peers. Simple choices allow a child to have an element of independence and control. When children can control aspects of their lives appropriate for their level of development, they are more likely to cooperate when they are not allowed to do something. Parents, however, have control over what choices are given and can thereby enforce the limits that they want to set.

A skillful parent will learn how to structure choices that are appealing to the child and simultaneously acceptable to the parent. For example, if a child wants to take several toys in the car for a short trip to the mall, the parent may say, "Pick two of them; that will be enough." Similarly, to make dressing in the morning go more smoothly, a child can be given two choices of outfits the night before. Even children with very limited language may have strong preferences. Another time that this strategy might be useful is snack time, when a child might be given healthy, desirable choices.

NATURAL AND LOGICAL CONSEQUENCES

Giving consequences that are natural and logical is a way to correct a child's undesirable behavior. *Natural consequences* come from the laws of nature. For example, a child who refuses to eat a meal will get hungry, and it will usually occur before the next scheduled meal if the child is not allowed to eat until then. *Logical consequences* result from going against the rules of social cooperation. In the instance where Rachel won't share her toys with Melissa, Melissa might not want to play anymore or refuse to share her toys with Rachel at a later date.

Natural consequences do not require any intervention by adults. The child who refuses to eat would automatically get hungry and ask for food. Learning will occur when the child is told to wait. When danger is involved, parents must intervene decisively. We wouldn't let a 3-year-old run into the street to learn about how badly a car could injure him or her. Parents in this kind of situation need to set up a logical consequence. It could go like this:

"The street is not for playing—you could get hurt by a car. You can choose to play in the yard or inside. If you go near the street, that's deciding to come in. What do you want to do?"

Then, if the child goes toward the street, the limits have been violated and he or she has to come inside for a while. Choices may be given again later. A child who doesn't understand danger, obviously, cannot be given this choice. Sometimes parents want to believe that the child understands even when professionals have doubts, and this can be extremely dangerous. If there is any doubt or controversy over how much the child understands, it is advisable to err on the side of safety.

Many situations don't have natural consequences, so logical consequences have to be set up by the adults in charge. Logical consequences fit the need of a particular situation and guide the child toward socially appropriate behavior. They are given in a firm, friendly way. Sometimes it's hard to figure out in the heat of the moment. Let's take the example of a 3-year-old who is riding her tricycle too close to the street. Commonly, a parent might tell her that if she doesn't stay on the driveway and away from the street that she will have to go to bed early. Going to bed early and riding a tricycle have no connection. A logical consequence, however, would be that if the child does not ride in the driveway, then the tricycle will be put away until another time.

GIVING BREATHERS (TIME-OUT)

Giving a child time to calm down is an extremely effective strategy to help a child regain control of him- or herself. It is best when used as a last resort when other methods of discipline do not work. Time-out is appropriate for disruptive behaviors such as tantrums that can't be ignored, constant interference such as interrupting, or aggressive behavior such as hitting or biting. Time-out can be offered as a choice or can be a logical consequence. A child can be offered the choice of calming down or taking some time out.

In my experience, I have noticed that this technique is the most frequently used and misused strategy for problem behaviors by adults who are overwhelmed and frustrated. Often, it takes the place of yelling, screaming, or spanking, but this is not the purpose. Children will not learn how to behave differently if they are merely excluded in an angry exchange with a parent or caregiver. As much as possible, this technique should be used calmly, firmly, and with empathy. Not only can the child learn that he or she has to control his or her behavior if he or she wants to be around others, but the parents also can simultaneously get a chance to cool off and control their negative emotions toward the child.

The breather should generally last until the child has calmed down. A rule of thumb is that the length of a time-out should be 1 minute for each year of age. The idea here is not to use this technique to reject and isolate the child but rather to teach self-control. Eventually, the child may decide when he or she is ready to come out. The parent may say, "You can come out when you are calm and ready to play." This approach will help the child to develop internal controls. For parents who are unsure of how much their child understands, it would be wise to consult with the classroom teacher or another professional. The location for the time-out needs to be away from people. Simply put, the child needs a quiet space. When the time-out is over, don't discuss it—just go on with the activities of the day. Talking about the time-out calls attention to the behavior you are trying to stop.

Although guiding the behavior of a child with a disability is full of difficulties, there are also many windows of opportunity to explore and understand every facet of your child's development. Simultaneously, as parents, we can look into ourselves, our expectations, and our sorrows as our children struggle to grow and meet their needs. In these everyday routine behavioral events, there are countless learning opportunities present for children.

The everyday hassling, limit setting, negotiating, and problem solving are all attempts at finding the right kind of connection between parent and child. All of the ideas and techniques described in this chapter are ways of helping to tune into your child and guide his or her development despite the limitations imposed by disability.

Children go through stages; parents go through stages; and we are in stages together. Although parents need to be in charge and children need to follow, the reality is that we shape each other every step of the way. Basically, regardless of our limitations, children and parents all want the same thing—firm, loving parents who know how to handle problems.

6

A Circle of Fathers

Big Boys Don't Cry

*H*e had been talking freely about himself, his child, and the demands of everyday life, and then he stopped and looked up at the ceiling. The 10 other men in the room, seated in a circle with me as the leader, all waited patiently and curiously for Ted to continue. We had gathered in Columbus, Ohio, to discuss the challenges for fathers of children with disabilities. Before long, the waiting became uneasy, so I asked Ted if there was anything else he wanted to share.

Still looking at the ceiling, he answered hesitantly, "There's so much I want to say, but if I say any more, I'll cry . . . and I don't think I'll be able to stop."

It then became obvious that he was looking up in order to keep the tears in his eyes from overflowing. As he slowly lowered his head and faced the other men, a tear rolled slowly down his left cheek. What had just occurred was such an awkward but tender expression of male emotion. The man who was sitting on Ted's right reached over and put his arm around his comrade. This incident was the catalyst for the other men to open up and many did so with tears in their eyes and deep feeling in their voices.

Ted had unconsciously been speaking for more than himself in his comments; his openness had released the other men from the taboo against expressing their depth of feeling. Is it because we have held it in for so long that men believe that if we cry then the tears won't stop?

REFLECTIONS ON MALE EMOTIONS

I awoke to the sounds of jazz from our clock radio on a Saturday morning—the day before Mother's Day. It was a work day for me; I was scheduled to lead a men's group at a weekend gathering of parents of children with multiple disabilities. I had led several sessions for this group of parents in past years but never a men's group, so today would be different, a challenge of a special sort because the emotions of men are so routinely cloaked. (We men are often a mystery to ourselves and each other as well as to the women and children in our lives.)

As I showered and shaved, the apprehensions that I had contemplated the day before returned. What would this be like? Would the group see me as a real man, a man among men, or as a "wimpy shrink type?" I laughed to myself, for thoughts like these had begun when I was 5 or 6 years old. All boys want desperately to fit in and are terrified of being called a sissy. Well, here was that fear again—for that was what these particular apprehensions boiled down to—proof of how powerful those early and universal experiences and their memories really are. Even real men worry, I reminded myself—this wasn't an episode of *Father Knows Best*.

Would the competition among us keep us from accomplishing anything? Would male aggression hurt any of us? Despite these lingering questions, I felt ready for the challenge. This particular blend of confidence and uneasiness reminded me of my inner self, the angst or the slight edge that I needed to do my best work.

I wished that I could be there with my family, who were planning to work in the yard. The forecast called for a warm and sunny day. Kara would be pointing at the flowers and smelling them. I wondered if the sunflower seeds that I had planted with Antoinette had sprouted yet. I realized that these thoughts were another form of ambivalence about this particular day's work. I wanted to go, and yet I wanted to stay. Although I have often felt this way, the feelings today were intensified because I'd be doing no ordinary day's work. Men's groups require a special effort; getting men to open up isn't easy.

I reminded myself that I would be home for dinner and there would be plenty of daylight left to enjoy the flowers of spring in the company of my family. Finishing my orange juice, I put my notes in my briefcase and headed for the car. The morning air was fragrant from the variety of flowers and shrubs that were in bloom in our suburban neighborhood. I stopped for a cup of coffee to sip in the car along the 80-mile ride west on the Pennsylvania Turnpike.

Before I started the car again, I took a few minutes to review my notes for the day's workshop and some of my recent journal entries. I reflected on some of the concepts expounded on in *Finding Our Fathers: The Unfinished Business of Manhood* by psychologist Sam Osherson—in particular, how fathers have such an enduring impact on the lives of their children and play such a key role in their sense of identity. How men deal with women, other men, and children can often be linked to unresolved matters that existed with their fathers. In the world of work, men are also influenced strongly by their fathers. Many men, as well as women, struggle alone, sometimes throughout their lives, with their fathers in order to arrive at some clue for a sense of completion in one of the central relationships in life.

THE TRACKS OF MY TEARS

I got back into the car and continued my trip. Yellow and white wildflowers were in bloom along the side of the road. My car radio was tuned to a jazz station. I thought about the first time that I had seen my father cry. It was also the first time that I was flooded by my emotions; it was when my brother Don died.

Although it is still difficult to recall, I feel the only way I can explain my journey through a lost dream from a male point of view is to include my brother's death and what I learned about my father, my grandfather, and myself from that experience.

I had just turned 29 years old and had recently married for the first time; my brother was almost 23 years old. I was the oldest of my parents' eight children; Don was the fourth and was still living with my parents at the time. It was a cold, windy December night in 1977. I was careful to avoid the patches of ice on the road as I drove home from a party.

I went to sleep expecting to hear from Don early in the morning because he and I had spoken that previous afternoon and had planned to meet and go jogging. He had told me that he was not planning to go out that night. So, when I woke up to the telephone ringing early that Sunday morning, I expected it to be him. Instead, it was my mother telling me the news—that my brother had been in a head-on crash with a pickup truck. Someone had skidded on the ice. The other driver was in critical condition. Don was gone.

"He was going to call me this morning," I kept repeating to her. He wasn't supposed to have gone out. She asked me to come right away. My head stopped spinning just long enough for me to tell her that I would be there right away.

As I dressed hurriedly, I kept thinking that it just could not be. That telephone call was supposed to be him. He was supposed to wake me up . . . I would see him when I got there. The frigid December air filled my lungs as I started my old 1971 Volkswagen bug. The ride, which routinely took 20 minutes, went quickly. I needed more time with my thoughts but there was none. The house where I had once lived loomed before me.

When I pulled into my parents' driveway, my father came out to meet me. He had been waiting by the window, something he had never done before. He ran across the frost-covered grass to me and hugged me, weeping profusely. I could feel his chest heaving next to mine and his whole body shaking.

This was the first time he had hugged me since I was a little boy and he would call me over to him when he got home from work. It was the first time that I had ever seen him cry. I'd seen him mad and sad and more often grumpy, but never in tears; I didn't know how to take it. It was my first hint of confirmation that Don's death was real—I would never see my brother alive again. In that outpouring of male emotion, there was the gravest of seriousness. I had, of course, grown up with the adage that big boys don't cry, but now I was released from that—if my daddy could cry, then so could I.

My memories of my mother that morning are not as clear, probably because I had seen her cry before and knew what her sobs sounded like. It didn't take a death to release her tears, and her normal mood usually returned in a relatively short time. This time, though, she was devastated. She would become physically sick with her grief for many months.

A little later, my grandfather called, "Hello, Robert . . ." His voice broke down, and he just sobbed uncontrollably. The other man in my life who never cried was in tears. I wanted to console him but I didn't know how. Later that day when I saw him, he managed to hold it in, yet in his eyes I could detect a pain that I had never seen before in this kind man, the patriarch of my mother's family.

I was kept busy that morning calling relatives and friends of the family and asking them to pass the word along. I was upset; my voice shook, but I didn't cry. I felt that I had to be strong and help my parents get through that day. As the oldest, this was my station in life, and I wanted to do a good job.

In the afternoon I went home, got in the shower, and turned on the warm water . . . and then the tears came. My whole body shook as my tears mingled with the warm water and washed over me. I had not willed them to start, and I could not will them to stop. After what seemed like a long time, my body slowly stopped shaking. My mind, my heart, my whole being was inundated with grief. All of my muscles had been heavy, but now they were relaxed.

The days that followed blur in my memory, but my images of Don's funeral are crystal clear. I can still see the sadness and the tears and hear the sobs and consolations of my grandparents, my aunts and uncles, my cousins and friends,

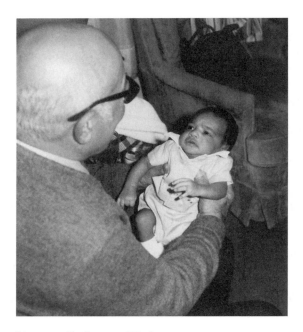

My grandfather and Tariq.

and Don's many friends. The church was filled with people in shock—there is something unusually compelling about the sudden death of a healthy young person with his life in front of him. Add to that Don's naturally pleasant disposition and engaging smile and the dimensions of the loss become more defined.

People kept asking me how my parents were doing. Nobody asked me how I was doing. I imagine my brothers and sisters had similar experiences. Actually, it was a question that I didn't know to ask myself—I didn't know how I was doing. My surviving brothers and I were the pallbearers, and my sisters were with my parents and grandparents. They were crying, and we brothers were "sucking it up" and acting brave.

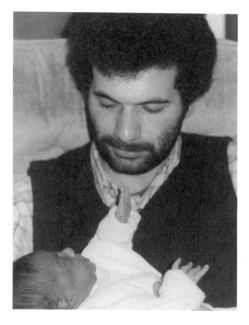

My brother Al and Tariq.

The casket was heavy with our family's grief. When we put it down at the grave site, my sobs burst out despite my will to hold them in and to silence myself. I can still feel my insides shuddering when I call this scene to mind. Then, I recall my brother Rich putting his arm around me in a firm yet gentle way, and gradually I regained my composure. I can still feel his arm there when Rich greets me at a family gathering.

As I reminisce now, that outpouring of feelings by my father, my grandfather, and my brothers was the beginning of the growth of my emotional life as a man—as a more full and complete person. I wish that there had been an easier way, but this was the path that my life took. Then Tariq, by his very existence, would challenge me to grow further.

This quest that was inspired by my son led me to explore the unfinished relationship with my own father. For all of us, our fathers are the most powerful and influential men in our lives.

On the way to the fathers' workshop, I was nervous about how anger, shame, and love for our fathers would play out in the group. Would our competitive fires lead us to fight and inflict new wounds or re-open old ones as so often happens among men?

I had met many of these men before, and we held each other in mutual respect—especially because we bore the common wound of having a child who wasn't "normal." I thought that most of us could connect without taking out our swords. We were knights in the same army—at least the way I looked at it—and that helped me to prepare myself. I hoped that the walls would come down and no one would be hurt because the common needs were so important.

Sam Osherson presented this dilemma as a normal and natural, albeit unpleasant, tension between unrelated males as well as between father and son. We both have a desire to connect with our fathers and to each other, yet we also have opposing impulses that shun intimacy. This may help to explain why men tend to be more comfortable expressing their feelings indirectly through telling stories about their struggles rather than stating straight out how they feel.

I remembered how excited I got when my father came home from work when I was a little boy—how little and insignificant I felt when he was mad at me, yet how warm and wonderful it was when he would put me on his knee and say, "How's Daddy's little boy?" I remembered the many conflicts with my father over politics and lifestyle when I was in college and as a young adult. Over time we had eventually reconciled many of our differences and learned to respect those that remained. Many men recount similar experiences with their fathers yet still find something missing. Maybe this was the "father hunger" described in such well-read books about men as Robert Bly's *Iron John: A Book About Men* and Sam Keen's *Fire in the Belly: On Being a Man.*

We men are supposed to be the "strong, silent" gender and most, if not all, of our previous experiences with intense passions are alone, unspoken, and unshared. What a relief it is, I have found from my own experiences, to tell your story and to feel empathy from other men. So often we just wanted to be heard and appreciated as friends. Now, I hoped to skillfully guide the men in the group today to have an encounter with each other that would be as powerful for them as my experiences in men's groups had been for me.

That power for me is manifest in my ability to relate more quickly and deeply, particularly with men, wherever I encounter them. Perhaps this is a result of listening a little differently, revealing a little more, or asking one more question that makes my interactions richer and fuller. Instead of avoiding what makes me uncomfortable in my everyday personal relationships, I have been more able to wrestle with my difficulties as husband, as son, as brother, as father, or as friend.

In the late 1990s, I counseled the parents of an adult child with mental retardation. When I met the young man's father, a successful businessman, I asked him what it meant to him to have a child who was named after him and who was very limited. "You know; you've been through it," he responded. How often men make comments like this as a way of joining with another man but still avoiding sharing what is really going on for them. Opening up is not considered "manly."

This time I responded, "I know what it's been like for me. Can you tell me a little about what it's been like for you?" Well, that's all it took—that one extra question—for him to open up about his disappointments and his worries about the future. What bothered him the most was that his son could never be fully independent and that his other son and his daughter would feel burdened by looking after their sibling when their parents were no longer alive. These worries about the future are common for fathers in these situations and are reported regularly in the literature. Once he told me these things, I could help him think for himself about the issues that he was consulting me for.

I was easily lost in my thoughts as I continued my journey. I had been that way since I was a little child. My ride through the lush, green Pennsylvania countryside came to an end, and I got off the turnpike and followed the directions to the hotel where the families were staying and the meetings would be held. I had planned to arrive early so that I could join the people already there for breakfast, which would help me get comfortable with people and give me the "feel" of the group. I try to do this whenever I can before leading a workshop or a group. Still, I felt a nervous anticipation and my routine shyness, even though today was special because I could renew friendships and acquaintances that had been developing over several years.

JOINING WITH THE FAMILIES

The sight of children with wheelchairs, walkers, or canes enabled me to quickly locate where the families were having breakfast. Like my own son, these children were growing older and bigger, and both their strengths and limitations were more and more obvious over the years. Some of these children had cerebral palsy and, therefore, had limited use of their arms or legs; some had faces marred by this condition. Some couldn't see or hear. Some had typical mental capabilities, whereas others had mental retardation. All of them had parents and siblings who just looked like regular people.

The children ranged in age from toddlers to young adults. I felt my own sorrow creeping into my chest. What is it about seeing someone who seems to have a worse problem than you that makes you feel a little better? "There but for the grace of God go I," or "Don't complain, there's always somebody worse off." At least my son wasn't physically disabled or disfigured—how weird to take comfort from that! But it is how it feels—odd but human. It was okay to think this or even say this here because these parents have the same experience when they encounter people with more severe problems than themselves. How odd, but how human—this was part of the spoken and unspoken bond that made us comfortable with each other.

The smells in the air led me to a sumptuous breakfast buffet: cereal, fruit, muffins, scrambled eggs, bacon, sausage, and juices. I filled my platter and found a space at a table with two families I knew. I am fundamentally shy, so I was relieved not to have to meet anyone new just yet. We greeted each other, and I just tried to blend in with the conversation. It felt more like home here—I was a fellow traveler, not just a professional "expert." They were comfortable enough with me to call me Bob, yet at the same time my expertise was respected.

George and Isaac were talking about advocacy issues for children with disabilities. Their wives, Sally and Mary, were helping their children to eat. We all exchanged hellos. They asked me about my family because we had all come together to the last gathering. Isaac is an African American man who has been active in civil rights. From this perspective, he seemed very able to identify with his teenage daughter and was very committed to the struggle for her long-term needs. George owns a hardware store in his hometown and is also involved in an advocacy group.

All around the room, men were well represented. This is very rare in my experience—these groups are usually predominantly women and led by women. The fathers of children with disabilities are invisible more times than not and uncovering that mystery was part of my mission today. The fathers of children with more severe disabilities tend, in my observations, to be more actively involved.

THE "NEW" MAN

Men frequently react in extreme ways, and fathers of children with disabilities fit this pattern. They are either very involved or withdrawn and virtually absent with the larger number seemingly uninvolved. From this observation, many professionals assume that fathers do not wish to be involved. Is this really the case, or do men grieve the loss differently and hence react and involve themselves in different ways?

Until the 1970s, the role of the father in child development was largely ignored in the professional literature. Although regarded as providers and protectors, fathers were not expected to be involved in day-to-day parenting activities, with the notable exception of discipline. Who, for example, doesn't remember hearing "Wait until your father gets home?" In emphasizing the undeniable importance of mothers, social scientists lost sight of the father and the larger family context in which children grow and develop. The word *parent* became synonymous with *mother*. This same trend applied to fathers of children with disabilities. Consequently, the literature about these fathers is extremely limited.

By the time fathers were "rediscovered," many men were frustrated with their traditional roles. They found that the "duty" to be a successful breadwinner had sometimes choked the natural instinct to nurture and that they could instead be tender and nurturing with their children and provide discipline, too. And, as more and more women worked outside of the home, fathers, out of necessity, became more involved in the day-to-day care of their children.

Cross-cultural studies reported by anthropologist Wade Mackey showed that when men spent time with children alone, they behaved much like women in their physical interactions, particularly in nurturing. This was true regardless of the gender of the child.

Developmental psychologist Michael Lamb of the National Institute of Child Health and Development, a leading scholar on fathers, reviewed studies that revealed some significant differences between mothers' and fathers' behaviors with their newborn infants. Mothers spend more time attending to the infants' basic needs, whereas fathers tend to play more. Fathers are also observed to be more vigorous and rougher in their play than mothers. Both fathers and mothers adapt their play to the child's developmental level, which implies that fathers as well as mothers are sensitive to child development.

Lamb also found a consensus in the professional literature that mothers and fathers initially respond differently to a child with a disability. Fathers seem less emotional and traditionally focus more on long-term problems such as the financial burden. Mothers respond more openly with their emotions and are more concerned with the burdens of the daily care of the child. Fathers who are less involved in daily interaction with their children tend to have a prolonged period of denial about the disability and its implications. The growing literature about men tells us that men express their feelings differently and use denial more to avoid the direct expression of feelings. I wondered how that would be manifested in the group I was about to meet with.

It has been presumed in the professional literature that fathers have higher expectations for their sons and, therefore, are more disappointed when these sons cannot live up to their dreams. It is a strong blow to the male ego when the father has no heir apparent to his throne. The mother, likewise, has been unable to give the king an heir and both have been deprived of "a chip off the old block."

There is some strong scientific data that shed some light on these generalizations. S. Philip Morgan, a sociologist at the University of Pennsylvania, conducted a study of 15,000 families and concluded that a family constellation with a boy is the likeliest to keep the parents together. Having a son tends to draw the father into a more active parenting role, and having more than one son tends to cement the involvement. In the May 1993 issue of *Child* magazine, Dr. Morgan reported a startling statistic. He estimated that each son reduces the risk of divorce by 9%.

WARMING UP THE GROUP

I needed a few minutes alone, so I excused myself from the table in order to check out the room where we were scheduled to meet. Most of the families were just finishing up their breakfast and taking their children to child care, which had been set up by the conference organizers. The meeting room was next door to the dining room, and just outside was a large window looking onto the golf course and the rolling countryside of Lancaster County. Inside was a circle of 25 chairs as I had requested.

The men gradually began to filter into the room one by one. They stood in small groups near the door exchanging hellos, introducing each other, and talking about what a beautiful day it was. "We'll spend part of our time outside," I promised, having decided on-the-spot that this was the way to join with everyone within my own style of leading a group. It was getting crowded near the door as more and more men came into the room, but no one made a move to sit down. I sensed an awkwardness that tended to occur when men and women had to separate. The women had their own meeting down the hall. There was no companion to shield the entry; the men were on their own but looking to me, I sensed, to help them get comfortable with each other.

They finally had to come in because there was no more room by the door. To get things started, I sat down and then invited everyone to take a seat. I sensed a collective sigh of relief—things would get started; the leader would take over. The men in the group ranged in age from their twenties to their fifties or perhaps sixties. The group was mostly Caucasian with a few African Americans, one Hispanic, and one person from the Middle East.

George introduced me as someone many people there had met before, as the father of a child with special needs and as a psychologist who spoke at many parent and professional conferences. I described some of the problems facing men who are fathers of children with disabilities, noting that men are often poorly represented at meetings for parents of children with disabilities. Where are they? Usually they are at home watching the children so that the women can attend, but the women still feel overburdened and stressed out. The men, at home, think that they are helping out. What a bind for both men and women to be in.

As I looked around the circle of fathers I saw many knowing glances and nods of agreement. I wondered out loud what would be different this particular day while meeting without the women.

I commented that men tended to drift away from their friends after marriage. The trend is to socialize with other couples (as described by Stuart Miller in *Men and Friendship*). Women, however, show a strong tendency to maintain their circles of friends. Having a child with a severe disability, which tends to isolate us even more, makes it even more difficult to maintain and build connections with other men. What do you do when you can't brag about your child's accomplishments in the way that other men do? What do you even say when you're asked how your child is doing? How do you handle that choked up feeling you get when you're searching for the right words? Maybe we could connect with each other today, I added, in a way that we haven't done before.

As a way of warming up, I suggested that we go around the room and introduce ourselves, sharing something about ourselves as fathers as well as our expectations for what we hoped to get out of the group today. There was a brief silence before a gray-haired man to my right began. Ben's child was in her twenties, and he had been coming to these events for years. This was the first time that he knew of that the men had met together as a group. He always got a lot out of these meetings, and he was looking forward to today and hearing what others had to say.

The man to his left, appearing about the same age, introduced himself. Jim's son was 29 years old, and he and his wife had been dealing with disability for quite a while. They were very involved at home together, but she wanted him to be more involved in the meetings and conferences that she attended. He wanted to support her better.

Next came Harry, a salesman who traveled extensively for his work. His child with special needs was 6 years old, and whenever he was home, his wife seemed overwhelmed by the sheer amount of care required. He wanted to help her more and felt bad that he spent many nights away from home, but he, too, seemed overwhelmed and perhaps unsupported, although he was silent about those issues.

Steve, an African American man, talked about how isolated he felt living in a rural area. He said that several times after these weekend gatherings, he had resolved to call Isaac, another African American at the meeting, and stay in touch. But he had never actually connected outside of the meetings. How often had many of us felt that way and not followed through, I wondered. Procrastination, particularly about culti-vating relationships with others, was apparently part of the male mode of being.

Some of the men there were stepfathers. Jack was a house painter whose fiancée had a 3-year-old son who had little sight and no hearing. He spoke simply and very intently, telling about how he was one of six children and how he wanted to be able to give his children more attention than his father was able to give him. He was trying to learn all he could before getting married. He didn't know the best way to help his fiancée—but she wanted him to be with her this weekend.

CONNECTING
THROUGH ANGER AND SORROW

Weren't all of these men displaying typical male responses to loss, to helping their partners, and to denying their own feel-ings? What are men expected to do in the face of loss? As Carol Staudacher, an expert in bereavement, pointed out in *Men & Grief: A Guide for Men Surviving the Death of a Loved One*, keeping the lid on emotions, taking charge of practical details, supporting others, and taking on the loss as a challenge or even a test of traditional masculinity are all part of the script. Yet, men are *not* expected to lose control over their emotions, to openly cry, to worry, or to express overwhelming sadness.

In an essay in *Uncommon Fathers,* Canadian political sci-ence professor Lloyd Robertson worried that his frustration and anger would overpower his love for his daughter, Katie, who was born with severe brain damage. He found himself more cheerful when he was actively involved with his wife in helping to meet Katie's needs and wants. Standing by and watching his child's struggle and his wife's pain was more heartbreaking for him than pitching in and helping with the work. This sort of involvement can break the irresistible pull of grief. Robertson found a parallel in the enduring tale of *Beauty and the Beast,* where the spell is broken when the hero loves another human being as much as he loves himself. In caring for one's child with special needs, a father can learn about unconditional love.

Well here it was; right in this room. It was time for me as the group leader to intervene. Staying strong to support the wife was as far as we had gotten going halfway around the circle. Even though this was just a warm-up, it was too rich an opportunity to miss, so I asked the group to begin to address what this situation meant to them as men as they continued to introduce themselves.

"I'm real mad about being here," said Chuck, a young man wearing a T-shirt from a long-distance race. "My daughter is just 18 months old and I want her to be normal; I resent that I have to be here this weekend, and I resent that my wife has to spend Mother's Day here." There was obvious emotion in his voice, and I could feel the atmosphere getting uncomfortable. What does it mean when men get angry? What is the appropriate response? I felt a little defensive that Chuck didn't want to be a part of this group, but I understood. I didn't want to be here either, and I wouldn't be if my son was normal.

"It'll pass," said Ben. "I remember being angry, but you get over it. It takes time. You'll get through it. My faith really helped me."

"You get a different perspective and then you mellow out," added another middle-age man.

"You just don't get it. I don't want it to pass. I don't want to be here. I'm just trying to hold on to some shred of normalcy in my life," said Chuck emphatically.

Jack rushed to Chuck's support: "You old guys just see things different." His remark provoked laughter, but the tension in the room seemed to grow.

"What do you mean 'old'? We're just mature," remarked Mike, a man who hadn't spoken before. More laughter followed, this time seeming to unite the group, and Mike went on to tell about himself and his situation.

The next participant said, "Maybe Chuck is speaking for all of us when he talks about his anger. We've all felt that in some way." I had been feeling the group tension and through my knowledge and trust in group process knew that something would happen that could draw us back together. Perhaps this group was expecting me to do that job and in some ways

I certainly also expected it of myself. Having a child who was 13 years old at the time placed me in the middle of the group in terms of experience.

I needed to help the younger and the "more mature" to be useful to each other. How could I help them deal with their male anger that often implies rage and destruction? Men tend to use anger to mask other emotions that are much more difficult to express and admit. How about the idea that your child with a disability was a personal failure? My worst nightmare would be to wake up and find that my son was 2 years old again and I had to go through all of this again, which might be more than I could handle. As the leader, my job was to give voice and guidance to these deep passions that had surfaced in the group.

Tony introduced himself as another man who had married into the situation of raising a child with a disability. His daughter's biological father had abandoned and rejected her and her mother. Tony got so attached that he adopted the child when he married. Tears were forming in his eyes. He talked about how bad he felt for his daughter and his wife and how hard it was for everybody. Then Tony began to sob, slowly at first but then more intensely. The man to Tony's left put his arm around him. The rest of us waited, feeling our own wounds, I thought.

Suddenly, Tony's nose began to bleed, the blood flowing freely. Did everyone stop breathing for a moment? Two more men rushed to help by taking Tony over by the door where he could be stretched out on two chairs and lean his head back to stop the bleeding. The tears had stopped by now.

"Does he need a doctor?" someone asked. Tony said that he would be okay—that he wanted the group to go on; he didn't want to miss anything. I asked if he had nose bleeds often and he responded that he had them whenever he got really upset. That let me know that it was okay to continue, but I remained on alert to get help if necessary. I returned to my seat and told the group Tony's wishes. From their reaction, I could tell that it was okay for big boys to cry here. It was safe to continue the process that the group had temporarily suspended.

"Maybe Tony has expressed something for all of us with his tears and his blood, just like Chuck did with anger," I commented before asking the next man to introduce himself.

Harry, a gray-haired man with an adult child spoke next. "I knew what I was going to say before Tony spoke, but now all I want to say is that I'm at a loss for words. I just respect his feelings, and I'm one of the 'mature' guys," he said with a chuckle.

Fred was next: "My 2-year-old son, our only child, sees and hears very little. It's been really hard. I'm used to a lot of excitement and action. I was in the airborne rangers, and my hobby is hang gliding. I did all the things I thought a real man would do, but nothing prepared me for this. Last week I went to a fathers' event at my son's school. There were five of us there. We were each off in a corner playing with our kid. Nobody really talked to each other like we are doing here. It's different here. I need more of this kind of head medicine."

Finally, it was George's turn; he would be the last to introduce himself. "I had two children already, a son and a daughter, when my youngest was born with some problems. He's 3 now. I have my own business, and I've been pretty successful, but nothing prepared me for this. I live in a rural area and to get my son what he needed I had to really fight and push for it. That little guy has really changed my life. I'm home a whole lot more now with my wife and my other children. I never really spent that much time at home before, although it was something I wanted to do. I really enjoy being home more. Sure, I wish my son didn't have these problems—but I'm a better person now, and I wouldn't want that any other way."

The introductions that I had planned 15 or 20 minutes for had taken more than an hour and a half. Tony's bleeding had stopped, and he had rejoined the circle. I had to modify my plan for the morning somewhat. Who says men have nothing to say? This group, as many others I've led, had certainly proved otherwise.

I wanted to keep my promise that we would spend some of this beautiful morning outside. I summarized what we had said and where we were headed. We would use the time outside to reminisce about our own fathers—some of the warm moments and some of the painful ones. There were several questions about my directions. In order to clarify, I shared some of my own experiences including the first time I had seen my dad cry when my brother died. The point was to go into your heart—for the anger, the shame, the grief, and the love—and then to share it with a small group of men. The next portion would present an opportunity to continue the open expression of thoughts and feelings that had just begun.

I had the group "count off" and then form seven groups of three. Forty-five minutes were allotted to walk, talk, get acquainted, and do the assignment. Again, there was some awkwardness and hesitancy getting started, but the warm sunshine helped us all to get moving. In small groups the men filtered out of the room onto the patio overlooking the golf course.

One group stayed on the patio, taking in the sunshine and the view. Another found a park bench near the first tee. Some walked down the "nature trail" that began behind the first tee and led away from the golf course. One group found a picnic table. Another group sat on a grass bank nearby. Wherever they were, they were talking intently.

From my observations, it was easy talking about themselves now, after the tears and the blood, but hard talking about their fathers. When it was time to go back inside, the participants lingered—perhaps wishing to stay in their smaller more intimate group. As we walked back in groups, small circles of fathers continued to talk with each other. It was wonderful to see men being this real and genuine. Something special had happened, and the group had bonded.

WINDING DOWN AND LOOKING FORWARD

No one wanted this experience to end, but when the group had re-assembled in our meeting room, there were only 45 minutes left until lunch. Hearing from each of the groups about what they had discussed and figuring out what we wanted to do in the future remained to be done. There didn't seem to be enough time—as is often the case when a group is going really well.

The task I had given to the groups was more difficult for some than for others. Some had fathers who were dead; others were not in touch with their fathers; and, alcoholism had ruined some father–son relationships. Shame, anger, sadness, and loss were expressed by almost every man reporting from his small group. These were the same emotions that they had described occurring with their children. Some expressed relief to have talked about these things that they had kept bottled up for so long. One man said that he found these more informal contacts with other men invaluable. Something similar had happened once before by accident in a hotel bar one evening during a previous weekend gathering of this parents' group. Wouldn't it be great if the group could communicate this way intentionally from here on?

Gradually, the participants opened up. Jim mentioned that his dad rarely expressed emotion of any kind. He related to my experience when he saw his father cry for the first time when his grandfather died. Jack, a painter, and Barry, a laborer, said that their fathers showed only anger. Jack talked about how his father always seemed so critical of him. The tender moments were harder to verbalize. Jack talked about how his dad would always take him to a special display of Christmas lights every year and about the baseball glove he still used that his dad had given him for his birthday one year. Barry remembered being ashamed of his father's drinking and, sadly, couldn't recall a single moment that he cherished.

The tender moments were often described as going on fishing trips, playing catch in the backyard, learning to ride a bike while dad cheered, sitting on dad's lap on the tractor as he plowed the field—always one-to-one interactions between father and son. No one said that there were too many tender moments. I was reminded of an interview with former president Bill Clinton, who told the reporter that he made time each day when Chelsea got home from school. Clinton was determined not to grow old with the regret that he had not spent enough time with his child.

Disability had taught all of us how time with our families is precious. Work was now seen in a different perspective by many of us, and some were grappling with how to spend more time at home. One man said that he couldn't talk to his wife the way he was talking to us because she expected him "to be strong." (In the course of the morning, several men had remarked that their wives wanted them to talk more.) I questioned how his wife would actually respond. Whether it was true or not that his wife wouldn't be able to handle his passions, he certainly believed she couldn't. I suggested that expressing ourselves with the women in our lives might come easier now that we had begun with each other. Perhaps if we had more continuing support from each other, our wives might then have more support from us. It could even be more like teamwork instead of each partner struggling alone, hoping for a breather from the other.

Each must find his own way through the grief. For me, I couldn't imagine where I would be without having had Cindy to listen to me and to wipe away my tears so many nights. Clarissa Pinkola Estes, a Jungian analyst and storyteller, suggests that by following the pain a man can reach and discover his inner self. Certainly in relation to grief, sharing it with significant other people in your life is crucial. Sometimes, sharing pain is the only way to lessen it.

The discussion turned to how to stay connected and how to get more of what had happened in the group. We talked of meeting again in 6 months and joining other groups in local areas. George invited everyone and their families to an annual summer barbecue at his house. The idea to form local networks emerged from the people present today—one idea was to have the more experienced men act as mentors to the younger men. I doubted that anyone in this group had read *Iron John: A Book About Men,* but the idea of initiation, which is central to Robert Bly and many in the men's movement, was certainly alive here—more "mature" men helping younger men learn the ropes.

It was time for lunch, and because the door to the room had remained open after the break, women and children could be seen walking by on the way to the dining room. They were looking in and wondering, we heard later, what we were still talking about. Even though the meeting was over, no one left his seat. Indeed, it was hard to leave, so I stood up, formally ending the meeting. Others stood and gathered in small circles, and then, after several minutes, the fathers gradually left the room and headed to the dining room to rejoin their families.

The dining room was buzzing with conversation. The women wanted to know what had gone on in the men's group. They were amazed that we had run over time. One woman told me that she and others were surprised that all of the men had shown up. Looking around, seeing families enthusiastically talking about the morning, I was proud of the work that the group had done. Being associated with these men made me feel good to be a man. Although that day's work was done, there was a lot left to accomplish in the struggle for intimacy and connection.

CONTINUING THE JOURNEY

With no time constraints, I took a more local route home through the farmlands. Tomorrow was Mother's Day, so I stopped at a roadside stand to buy a flowering plant in a basket for my mother. She would enjoy the pink blooms on the impatiens. I remembered how she would read to me when I was a child and how she would nurse me when I was sick. She struggled to be "a good mother" for all of us. The women at the weekend gathering could not nurse their child back to health. My mother could not bring my brother back from his accident—sometimes love is not enough.

For the men I had encountered, perhaps the greatest frustration was that they could not fix everything and make it better for their wives or their children. In this respect, too, love is not enough. The pain makes you go places that you never planned to go. Obviously, the 20 or so men gathered for the morning group do not represent all of the fathers of children with disabilities. There are countless individual differences everywhere. The themes expressed by the group are, however, typical of those expressed by the many hundreds of fathers that I have met as a group leader, researcher, and psychotherapist. I decided to write this chapter through the experience of this particular group in order to bring the ideas alive. I can't help but wonder what the future holds for the group of men that met that day.

The group demonstrated a very real and immediate need to connect. There were clumsy but very real attempts at intimacy. One example of this was the attempt to reassure the young father who was expressing an intense anger about the fact that his child was not "normal." It took time and some conflict to acknowledge that anger and let it be heard. Sam Osherson demonstrated in his work how anger is a part of the male style of connecting. Looking at this powerful emotion from this perspective enables us to embrace it instead of retreat from it. Fathers of children with disabilities need the mobilizing effect of anger to pump us up so that eventually we can face the shame and profound, long-lasting sadness that accompanies our situation.

Even though the fathers initially saw themselves primarily as support people to their wives and children, they were able to acknowledge their own needs once they were together with each other. I know of no other way to break through this wall of emotion that keeps fathers from working through and completing their own grief. One man "broke down" and really cried. Once there was permission to feel in the group, there were tears in many others' eyes at various times. The men began to realize that they were not really "losing it" but, rather, they were finding themselves.

The talk about their fathers and themselves as sons led to a longing for mentorship within the group. One man compared it to the sponsor concept in Alcoholics Anonymous. Invoking their experience as sons was important in bringing this out.

For professional people who are not sure what fathers in this situation need, bring them together as a group and ask them. The ideas collected in *Fathers of Children with Special Needs: New Horizons* by James May can be a helpful guide. The fathers can tell you everything that you want and need to know, but you have to question and listen skillfully because the male imperative to be strong in the face of tragedy can be tricky to overcome.

In a males-only meeting, it is more likely that fathers can take off their armor and get to the real stuff inside.

It's obvious that men have a different tone of voice than women. What's not so obvious, but equally true, is that men have a different tone of grieving. Male intimacy is different from women's, but not defective. Connecting with other fathers can have a powerful impact. This was demonstrated by our group of fathers who got acquainted with each other and became linked by common experience—the experience of disability in their offspring. We began as emotional strangers and departed as "blood brothers."

7

Keeping the Boat Afloat

The Couple's Journey

*F*amily life can be a test of love and resilience, so taking good notes and understanding each other's needs and wants are vital to the success and survival of any marriage. After children arrive, there is a balancing act between caring for their needs and putting time and effort into the maintenance and growth of the marriage. This rite of passage in the development of family life is challenged still further by disability or chronic illness.

On the Sunday after my meeting with the fathers in Lancaster, Cindy and I packed a picnic lunch and took Antoinette and Kara along. After about an hour ride, we arrived at Tariq's residential unit at the Devereux Foundation in West Chester, Pennsylvania. I got out of the car and went inside by myself to get him. I had missed Tariq but was apprehensive about seeing him because he was never easy to manage, even for a few hours. I took a deep breath and released it slowly, preparing myself inside to remain calm and focused. Tariq was glad to see me and he showed it by jumping out of his chair, smiling, and immediately pulling me by the hand toward the door, eager to go outside. For an instant he looked so normal that I half expected him to say something to me, and then I remembered, for probably the millionth time, that this kid will never talk to me. For all of the time that has elapsed, for all of my knowledge and experience, here was yet another moment of coming to terms with the loss.

When I put Tariq in the back seat of the car, Kara was glad to see him. She kept saying, "Hi! Hi!," and waiting for a response that never came. He looked away, out the window, while I engaged the child lock on the door beside him so that he couldn't open it from the inside by himself. Although he was a teenager, his behavior was still more like that of a toddler, and danger always lurked nearby. Kara would not turn 2 years old until August, but she was aware in her own way that Tariq was a part of our family and that he was different from other teenagers his age. She was amused by his mannerisms, which were much like her own. This was a two-edged sword. On the one hand, Kara's awareness was a confirmation of her vitality to me and tremendously reassuring. On the other hand, it is but another reminder, like the child lock, of Tariq's disability, which opens a pocket of sadness inside of me.

I reflected on how Antoinette had tried so hard when she was little to talk to her brother and to play with him. Eventually, she gave up trying to relate to him as a normal sibling because he seemed to ignore her. By the time she was 5 years old, she understood in her own way that he could not play with her or relate to her because of his disability. I recalled how saddened I was at the time because Antoinette's realization reinforced my own conclusion that I didn't want to believe. I felt another twinge of sorrow now because I knew that Kara would learn the same thing. On the way to the park, Kara had imitated Tariq by putting her fingers in her mouth as he was doing. Fortunately, I thought, she wasn't smearing the saliva on the inside of the car window as Tariq did.

We drove for about 15 minutes, passing shopping centers and then arriving into the countryside to Marsh Creek State Park, where late spring flowers and trees were in full bloom. The air was perfumed with the scent of honeysuckle. Sailboats and catamarans skimmed the surface of the water and circled the lake with their bright, multicolored sails reflecting on the water. Those in canoes and rowboats were careful to avoid the path of the more graceful but less agile sailboats. It was a perfect day, and I was eager to get out on the water and enjoy it with my family.

We decided to have lunch first, and so after parking the car, we walked up the hill to the picnic area. Tariq held my hand like a little boy, but the top of his head reached over my shoulder, now making it appear strange that he insisted on walking this way. We searched until we found a picnic table in the woods high above the bank of the creek overlooking the water. It was a peaceful view. We had brought food that Tariq liked so we could enjoy a meal together without hassling over things that he wouldn't eat. We ate tuna sandwiches on whole-grain bread, corn chips, and fresh fruit and enjoyed cold sodas with our meal. A pleasant breeze made for some enjoyable moments as we looked out at the sailboats.

Tariq finished first, probably because the meal for him did not involve talking and interacting with the rest of the family. He got up and started to walk away from the table. "Down! Down!" said Kara, her little voice punctuating Tariq's steps. Tariq turned, smiled, and returned temporarily to the table. Cindy commented on how that interchange was just like Kara's interactions with Harry, our family cat. Antoinette and I chuckled. Cindy's remark was both sad and funny, but as a family we held on to the humor of the situation for that is part of how we cope and part of the way most families in this situation learn to cope. We knew that we would have to leave the table soon because Tariq had made his wishes known and would not be content sitting with us for long.

Because I am a faster eater, I finished and got up and took a walk with Tariq so that everyone else could finish eating with a minimum of pressure. Over the years we had developed ways like this to manage these situations. Kara's presence shed a different light on things; her fascination with Tariq helped us all, I thought. Her realization that she was already more advanced than he was gave me another dose of grief,

Rowing with Tariq and Antoinette.

whereas her affection for him warmed me; whenever anyone found value in his existence, I was comforted by a sense of value in my own self as Tariq's father.

After cleaning up, we walked down the hill back to the lake and the dock where boats are rented. We all fit around the picnic table for a family meal, but we could not all fit in one boat. Cindy got a rowboat for herself and Kara; I got a canoe for Tariq, Antoinette, and myself, and we all put on our life jackets. Tariq resisted by twisting and squirming and making vocalizations that signaled his discomfort, but he eventually complied. Kara was proud of her life jacket and kept pointing to it calling it her "boat coat."

Antoinette sat in the front of the canoe, eagerly anticipating helping to propel the boat. I sat in the rear and put Tariq down on the floor of the canoe between my knees. If he were "normal" he would have a paddle, too, and I would be teaching him about steering, but he wasn't, so I would have my hands full just trying to keep him in the boat. I hadn't taken him out since last summer when he was several inches shorter and 10 or 15 pounds lighter. Now, he was 5 feet tall and more than 100 pounds, so I felt some apprehension about the excursion. I had to keep the boat moving; the movement, as in the car, was soothing and peaceful to Tariq. If we stopped and just drifted, I knew from experience that he would try to stand up and get out. He put his hands in the water on each side of the boat and seemed to enjoy the sensation, humming to himself as we moved along.

A vision of the boat tipping over flashed through my mind. I wasn't sure how deep the water was but with life jackets we were safe. There was no way, however, that I could get Tariq back in the canoe after righting it. If he were a typical teen, it would be a father and son adventure to be recalled years later with a chuckle. Alas, it was not to be so, for we would need help, so I was staying within sight of other boats just in case. What would people think? I wondered. Tariq and I with a capsized boat would be a disabled duo, and what about Antoinette? She is an adequate swimmer and would manage, but she would be left out in a way because most of my energy would have to go toward dealing with Tariq. I was sure that people would help, but I didn't want their help because I wanted not to need it. And what about my wallet and some of the things in there that might be ruined? Talk about taking notes—I should have left it in the car.

As I recount this here, I can feel the tension in my chest and wonder how I came across to Cindy that day. I am grateful that I always feel understood by her even when my mind drifts off or I get grumpy, irritable, or short tempered. Not that I make it easy either, for at those times I don't have it in me to give back to her because I want to get away inside of myself. Not wanting to be alone, she pulls on me trying to bring me out of it. (My grumpiness may be an expression of my resistance to being in the situation with these thoughts about my son.) Eventually, I surrender from my withdrawal and am glad to be back with her and not alone with my darkest thoughts and feelings.

Cindy and Kara in the rowboat.

Out on the water, I steered the canoe toward Cindy and Kara, who was excited and pointing in our direction. We got close enough for Cindy and me to take pictures of each other and the children. Kara was having a great time, and she wanted to get out and take a walk on the water. Antoinette, Cindy, and I all chuckled, marveling in the sheer joy and immediacy of Kara's experience. Cindy wouldn't be able to keep her out on the lake much longer. It was getting hard to stay close together and out of the way of the sailboats, so we decided to split up for a while. I steered out across the lake, keeping Tariq balanced between my legs, while talking to Antoinette and trying to teach her a little about canoeing. We reached a tranquil little cove on the other side of the lake. The sailboats avoided that area because it was difficult to catch a breeze there, and people were fishing from their boats and from the rocks on the edge. Sometimes Tariq's babbling kept me from hearing myself think, and today it led me to flash back on all of those sleepless nights when he was little. At other moments I was impatient with Antoinette, and she seemed resentful that my attention was always divided and secondary to the task of keeping the boat balanced and Tariq in it. Who could blame her?

After a while it was time to return, so we headed out of the cove and pointed the canoe toward the flag that marked the dock. It was just a speck on the horizon that got bigger almost imperceptibly as we paddled along. Antoinette really liked this part, and she was feeling more at ease now. She was proud that she had been able to help paddle the boat so far out onto the lake. Tariq dangled his hands contentedly in the water and hummed to himself as we paddled and talked. I explained to Antoinette how we would chart a course through the circling sailboats that were tacking to and fro.

Thank God, I thought, for this moment when everything in the boat was in balance. As we got closer, I could see a woman in a red dress. That was Cindy, I thought; then I could see Kara in her arms; they were waving to us as we approached. I felt excitement in my chest for my beloved and for my baby. It was good to be back—to be reunited in a few minutes. As we approached the shore, I told Antoinette to take her paddle out of the water and to watch how I guided the canoe gently toward the spot on the shore where one of the attendants was awaiting us. The current carried us while I steered and squeezed my knees a little tighter around Tariq. As the bow touched the shore with a light thud, I took another deep breath and reached for Tariq before he would jump out and run away. Having anticipated his movement, all went smoothly.

The canoe hadn't tipped over (not that it wouldn't another time), and all in all, it had been a peaceful day on the lake. I reveled in the moment. It was a day made possible, I thought, by the relationship Cindy and I had cultivated and developed over 8 years. It hadn't been an easy role for Cindy to take on—the role of stepmother in this situation. With Kara, we no longer fit in one boat as we once had. But we had learned how to steer, how to keep things balanced, and how to chart our course among the other boats. Through trial and error and frustrating experiences, we had developed these skills that began with keeping everyone safely in the boat.

We were all pleasantly tired from the exercise as we rode back to Tariq's school and dropped him off. He seemed glad to be back, and he didn't particularly notice me when I left him with his counselor. This bittersweet moment did make the separation easier because on those occasions when he notices my departure, he cries and clings to me like a young child, which makes it hard to leave him. As we drove away, we talked about our pleasant outing, assuming it was so for Tariq also, but there was a lingering question that his enduring silence left imprinted on our experience.

A BIOLOGICAL BACKFIRE

A successful marital relationship is based largely on a basic faith in the relationship or union by both parties. This kind of faith is often what makes it possible to work out problems or get through the tough spots. When a child is born "imperfect" or when a disability or chronic illness is discovered, the resulting evocation of powerful emotions puts the relationship on trial. As Josh Greenfield put it in *A Child Called Noah,* the "defect" can be a demoralizing symbol of a deep and profound biological failure to produce a healthy child. Even when two people share the same sorrow, their individual pain and unhappiness may drive them apart. How can we understand each other in the wake of such devastating pain?

The intense inadequacy, the self-doubt, and the loss of control that are such an integral part of the experience produce powerful reactions. Psychiatrist Donald Nathanson's concept of the *compass of shame,* described in his book, *Shame and Pride: Affect, Sex, and the Birth of the Self,* is manifested as people frequently withdraw, avoid, attack their spouse, or attack themselves. The only way out requires working through the painful feelings with one's partner and arriving at some form of joint acceptance. As marriage expert Harville Hendrix put it, marriage is therapy. And, as therapy, it often involves redefining one's values and relationship with the other.

In *Ordinary Families, Special Children: A Systems Approach to Childhood Disability,* Milton Seligman and Rosalyn Benjamin Darling concluded from their review of the research that there is sparse and contradictory information regarding marital problems and divorce in families of children with disabilities. For a relationship that is fragile or unstable, disability can be "the straw that breaks the camel's back." Yet, couples with strong cohesive marriages may become closer and more loving, and those in relationships that haven't yet been tried by adversity may develop increased closeness and strength.

A 1993 television movie, *Born Too Soon*, based on a true story, showed how one couple survived by learning to understand each other. I include a summary here because the issues that they faced are, at least in my personal and professional experience, typical for most couples in similar situations. In the film, Liz and Fox are a professional couple—both are journalists. When Liz's water broke months early, she was terrified and blamed herself for working too hard. Fox joined her at the hospital and was at her side comforting her and pledging to go through the experience together. Their infant, Emily, was born weighing less than 2 pounds, and the first months of her life were spent in the neonatal intensive care unit.

At first, Fox is right there with Liz struggling to keep hope alive. They worry openly about whether their infant will survive as she sleeps in an incubator with tubes and wires stuck in every opening and all over her. Before long, however, a rift develops between Fox and Liz when one of the doctors advises them not to get "too attached" because that will make losing Emily even harder. Liz continues the natural process of becoming attached to her infant and becoming absorbed in her minute-to-minute care. Fox, however, begins to withdraw by resisting having his picture taken with Liz and the infant in the hospital and returning to work.

After Liz is discharged, she spends all of her time at the hospital with her infant. As the emotional split between her and Fox widens, she finds support from some of the other mothers whose babies are in the hospital. One mother related how she couldn't wait to sleep and dream because "No dream is as bad as not knowing what is going to happen to your baby."

Liz tries to confide in Fox that she is always emotionally drained. She gets upset when people ask her about Emily because she isn't ready to talk about it yet, and she gets upset if they don't ask. Fox advises Liz to think of something else, even to do some work—a typical male response. His attitude leaves Liz alone and desperately overwhelmed with her feelings.

The couple argue over her involvement and his withdrawal. He gets mad at her for not taking care of the house, and she is furious at him for listening to the doctors about not getting too attached. Because she can't feed Emily or hold her, the only thing that she can do for her daughter is to be there in the hospital by her side every day. Liz is in anguish because it feels to her that Fox wants to take that tiny vestige of motherhood from her by asking her to deal with this crisis his way.

Fox, like many men, uses his anger to connect and tell of his pain. He admits to Liz only in the heat of an argument that he wanted a healthy infant and that he can't just sit there and watch their infant die. Liz is understandably too angry to accept this explanation for his abandonment of her and Emily, but Fox eventually has a change of heart and begins to take care of things around the house and to visit Emily more. Only then does the couple begin to understand and help each other through the grief.

When Emily needs another surgery, Fox and Liz wait through it together, but the infant does not survive. Fox and Liz are able to have a healthy infant a few years later. They had learned to understand each other, and fortunately biology cooperated the second time.

DO YOU READ ME?
TODD AND BETH'S DILEMMA

Even a child's mild learning differences or disabilities can confuse and divide a couple. In general, more severe disabilities are diagnosed earlier—at birth in the hospital or a little later when something is obviously wrong and professional help is sought early—and couples get the news together. A child with a mild disability, such as attention-deficit/hyperactivity disorder or a learning disability, provides a different sort of challenge. One parent may notice problems and tend to worry, whereas the other parent may be a container for the hope that everything will work out. The overall balance may work in the sense that the family keeps functioning, but it is very uncomfortable for both partners, each locked into his or her role.

A couple consulted me for help with their problems dealing with their son's reading difficulties. Beth came in first by herself—as is often the case in my practice. Her son, Phillip, was now 7 years old and more than 2 years behind in reading. He was regressing emotionally—whining and clinging to his mother. Beth had recognized that there was a problem long before it was pinpointed in the reading process but she wasn't sure what it was and doubted herself. She had talked to her husband, Todd, about it quite a bit, and he always said that things would work out even though he himself was also concerned when Phillip stopped enjoying school and began crying to stay home in the mornings. Beth felt increasingly desperate and worried about her son.

At his teacher's suggestion, Phillip had been evaluated by a reading specialist. Specific reading weaknesses were found, including difficulties in short vowel sounds and in connecting sounds with symbols. Remedial activities were suggested and some improvement had occurred, but Phillip hated going to the reading tutor. He had refused to go into the tutor's house when his father took him for his lesson, throwing himself on the ground and having a tantrum. Todd picked him up and carried him in, but little was accomplished because he was so upset. When the lesson was over and they went home, Todd punished Phillip because he didn't know what else to do.

At the time of the initial consultation, Beth felt that there was a stalemate. How could they force Phillip to read, an activity that he found extremely difficult? I listened to this mother's anguish. She and Todd were in their late thirties, and Phillip was their firstborn child; they also had a daughter who was still in nursery school. Phillip was very bright and got excellent grades in everything but reading and writing (which depends so directly on reading). In tears, Beth told me of her worries that her son would be unhappy, would not succeed, and would never feel good about himself again.

Because Phillip had become very emotional, his teacher wondered if there was a problem at home that was affecting his school performance. Beth felt that she was being blamed by this suggestion. Todd had trouble understanding how upset his wife was, but he knew that his son's learning difficulties weren't Beth's fault. They had both agreed on disciplining Phillip for his behavior at the tutor's. Nonetheless, they were very uncomfortable with what to do now. Beth said that they both felt badly about punishing their child when they knew learning to read was so difficult for him. All of the relationships in the family were strained. They hadn't had any fun together in months.

Beth said that she and her husband were willing to try whatever I suggested. The tension in this family had to decrease, so I recommended a moratorium on tutoring for the rest of the summer. Beth and Todd could take Phillip to the library, if he wanted to go, and then Phillip could pick a book on a topic that interested him. If he wanted to, he could just look at the pictures. In addition, I suggested that they just have some "family fun" over the weekend by doing something that they always enjoyed together. I insisted on meeting them all together the following week.

Phillip was extremely shy when I met him; on the way to my office from the waiting room he buried his head in his mother's side as would a younger child. He sat on Todd's lap and snuggled up with his dad. While giving him time to "warm up," I talked with Todd and Beth, getting to know them a little better as a couple. What Beth had told me about her husband seemed accurate. He had been concerned for some time, and his son's unhappiness had now motivated him to accept help. He felt bad that he couldn't help Beth enough with this problem.

Gradually I worked their son into the conversation:

"How do you think Phillip is feeling about his difficulties in reading?" I asked them.

"He can tell you that himself," replied Beth.

"I feel stupid, and I hate myself, and I hate when they make me read," explained Phillip. He said all of his friends were reading at a higher level and he had to stay at the same level. I could see a glazed, worried look in Beth and Todd's eyes. I gave Phillip some crayons and paper and asked him to draw a picture of his family doing something together. I showed him to a seat at my desk while I continued to talk with his mom and dad.

"Your son expresses himself so clearly," I said. Hearing a child express such painful feelings can be extremely difficult, and this is a common dilemma for couples like Beth and Todd who have articulate children struggling with a learning difficulty.

"Beth has a great bond with him, and I rely on her to let me know what is really going on," commented Todd, "but lately everybody's been upset and it hasn't been working. I'm not sure why."

I asked Todd to tell me about his frustrations and asked Beth to just listen for a while. He was reluctant at first, but as he warmed up he spoke slowly and clearly with obvious emotion about his feeling of failure that he couldn't help his son with his reading and his growing isolation from Beth. The lines of worry softened in Beth's face as he explained himself.

"What would it be like if Todd talked this way at home?" I wondered out loud.

"I wouldn't know how to act!" remarked Beth emphatically. "I'm usually out in a boat with my emotions, and Todd is always there on the shore to reel me in. I don't know what we would do if he was out there with me."

"Maybe you could learn to row together," I remarked. "And temporarily I'll be there to reel the two of you in, if you need me, until you can do it yourselves." They were skeptical, having been together 10 years and not sure that they could change, but they agreed to try. I asked Phillip to bring his drawing over. He displayed a colorful and carefully conceived drawing of his family at the playground. They were all on the swings, and he was in the middle. I suggested that Todd and Beth give everyone their wish and have some fun together as a family over the weekend. I asked Todd and Beth to come to the next session without Phillip.

When I met them the following week, Todd and Beth were much more at ease. They had gone camping for the weekend, a favorite family activity that they hadn't done while they were "stressed out" over the reading problems. I asked them about their dreams and fantasies for their son's future. Beth spoke about giving him every opportunity and being a good mother and making sure her son was genuinely happy. That seemed to be going out the window now. What would become of the son of a professional couple who couldn't read adequately for his age? Todd had imagined their son becoming a successful professional. Now, he wondered if Phillip would even be able to go to college. Beth and Todd had not previously discussed any of this together.

I told them that a big part of dealing with a child's special needs is learning to separate the problem into manageable pieces rather than carrying around a heavy weight of worry and fear. I suggested a battery of tests by a colleague of mine who was a school psychologist who could make recommendations for Phillip's practical educational needs. At first, they were reluctant to agree, for fear that their son would be labeled negatively, but they eventually agreed because they didn't want to go on living as they had been.

While the diagnostic process was going on, I continued to meet weekly with Beth and Todd, coaching them on how to express themselves and listen to each other, a form of rowing the boat together. I coached them on going back to having fun with Phillip and following his natural sense of wonder about the world. One week Beth told me about Phillip's curiosity about bees. I suggested following up with anything related to bees, including books with lots of pictures so that he could learn something without the pressure to decode the words.

In my sessions with Phillip, I observed how difficult it was for him to decode words and how he shut down entirely when he got frustrated. As Phillip felt less tension within himself and within his family, he was able to apply himself more. His teachers began to notice progress at school.

Fortunately, Phillip's test results were very reassuring. Intellectually, he showed a pattern of average-to-superior abilities overall. Although he needed special attention in reading, there were no indicators of emotional disturbance as the cause. Beth was overjoyed that she was not to blame and she and

Todd were proud of their son's essential brightness. The prognosis was that Phillip could make substantial progress with remedial help, provided that he could continue to express his feelings and ask for help when he needed it. The roof had not caved in on this couple's dreams for their child. Although there were uncertainties about how far and how fast he could progress, they could live with that because they had learned to share the burden.

COUPLES GROUPS

Groups have the power to teach in a special way. I learned one of these special lessons while I was working for the New Jersey State Department of Education as a regional trainer for an agency that serves children with both physical and mental disabilities. For many years, my image of this rural area near the seashore had been that it was a tranquil and fun place where life was simple and close to perfect. That anyone's life there could be disrupted by a disability in the family didn't fit my fantasies. It was the week before Mother's Day, and I had been asked to give an after-dinner talk to a group of mothers. The 25 or so women I met that day expressed fantasies very different from mine about their relationships and their lives.

After dinner, while awaiting dessert and coffee, I talked about some of my experiences with my son and led a discussion about the journey from grief to coping with the day-to-day life of raising a child with a disability. To an outsider, such a topic for an after-dinner talk might seem grim, but for this group it was a lively and animated discussion full of humor and hope. What emerged as the main need was the women's desire to be understood more by the men with whom they shared their lives. Many were extremely frustrated because they felt alone with the emotional burden of their children with special needs. They thought that their husbands were tired of hearing from them and would respond to me as another man. They joked about feeling that they were nagging when they kept trying to get their point across. The social worker, who was present, was asked to set up a fathers-only meeting for me during the week preceding Father's Day.

On the evening before the men's meeting, I arrived early and mingled with the first few men who arrived, getting a feel for what they were expecting. All of them had been told that they really needed to hear what I had to say—that it would be new and different and that they hadn't heard it before. Was I a messenger for the women, I wondered? This felt strange—like I was being set up for something that I didn't quite understand.

When the meeting began after dinner in a restaurant, I talked briefly about my own experiences and then led a discussion about the grief that parents in this situation go through. Before the discussion got too far, one man asked, "So what's new about this? Is this what you talked to our wives about?" I responded that it was.

"Well, this isn't new to us," another father replied. There were nods and agreement around the room. I was taken off guard, but now I knew the nature of the set up. I would handle this right now.

"Why do the women think this is new to you?" I asked.

There was silence, so I waited.

"Well, maybe we don't talk about it," responded another man.

"Can women understand what men don't say?" I asked.

"You've got a point there," a father named Tony replied, "but there's nothing I can do about the situation, so I gave up talking about it a long time ago."

Now the participants began to discuss their frustrations as men and as fathers and the strain that their children's disability placed on their marriages. Several men openly admitted that their wives were dissatisfied with how they were handling their problems and admitted that they worried privately whether their marriages would survive. The romance was long gone for many of them, and none could bring it back. Most of them had never really talked like this before to each other. They commented on how they were more open without any women present. At the end, it was suggested that a meeting be held in the fall with the men and women together.

Now I had the confidence of both groups, and the stage was set. The women felt frustrated, alone, overburdened, and misunderstood. The men, however, felt nagged, frustrated, powerless, and also misunderstood. Here was a challenge! On the feeling level for me, it was like being a kid again—torn between my parents and wanting them to get along better. Then I was powerless, but now I was a mature and seasoned professional with the confidence that I could make a difference.

BRINGING THE MEN
AND WOMEN TOGETHER

According to a Native American proverb, you can only begin to understand a person after you walk a mile in his moccasins. For this reason, during the fall couples' meeting, I decided to use role-reversal exercises in order to help the men and women understand each other. Role reversal would diffuse the tension between the spouses and the groups by allowing each person to experience the problems of the opposite sex.

On the way to the meeting I recalled the healing power that I always felt while sitting on the beach watching and listening to the waves. I visualized the times that I had been there with Tariq, hoping that the waves would heal him somehow. He did seem more peaceful there, I had thought, and I felt more at ease with him. He was with me in spirit as I pictured him playing in the waves and laughing when he ventured out too far and got knocked down.

I imagined that I might be dodging some bullets tonight because I knew the pain of not understanding each other. I knew the death of romance in a relationship, and I knew the long-lasting pain that accompanies divorce. All of these deep emotions were present in this group, so I had to be objective to be effective. Arriving early, I met briefly with the social worker who knew the parents. She was there to facilitate a discussion for the women while I would do the same for the men. Each group would be asked to select a recorder and a spokesperson.

Close to 50 people were in the room, most of whom had come with their spouses. There were some stepparents in remarried family situations and some single parents. I could feel the tension and anticipation. My introduction consisted of reporting on the separate meetings of men and women that had occurred in the spring, and then I asked everyone to form a big circle to play an adaptation of the commercially available product, *Gender Bender,* which utilizes role reversal.

First, the women were asked to answer a series of questions on paper as if they were men. The men answered as themselves, and we compared the results. Here are some examples:

1. You are in a bathroom that has run out of paper towels. How do you dry your hands?
   a. On your pants
   b. Shake them dry
   c. On the curtain
2. Which characteristic shows a woman has a lot of passion?
   a. Red hair
   b. A fiery temper
   c. A wiggle when she walks
3. Do you think the women's liberation movement is
   a. Completely justified
   b. Partly justified
   c. An attack on men

There was laughter and a release of tension while the group wrote down their answers, which were collected and tabulated quickly. The number one answer for the first question by the women answering as men was drying your hands on your pants. The men had the same answer. Number two was evenly divided between b and c; the men answered similarly. Number three was tougher because it was more serious. The women as a group correctly predicted that the men would say that the women's movement was partially justified; three even said that the men felt it was an attack on them. The women were surprised that three men felt the women's movement was completely justified. There was more laughter and relief around the room. Men and women were discussing heavy topics without hurting each other.

Now it was time for the men to answer some questions as if they were women. The women answered as themselves this time. The questions included these examples:

1. You found a *Playboy* under your son's bed; you
   a. Leave it
   b. Talk to him about it
   c. Tell your husband to handle it

2. A man who doesn't talk much has
   a. Inner strength
   b. Good listening skills
   c. Nothing to say

3. The thing men understand least about women is
   a. Fears
   b. Strengths
   c. Needs

For the first question, one third of the men said that they would talk to their sons if they were women, and two thirds said that they would tell the husband to handle it. The women were evenly divided between those answers. Clearly, the modern women present were indicating that they are different from our mothers' generation, and the men certainly had at least a clue as to the women's thinking on the subject.

For the second question, the men's answers were almost evenly divided among inner strength, good listening skills, and nothing to say. The idea of the strong silent type still had a lot of influence. Yet, the majority of the women's answers indicated that the man who didn't talk much had nothing to say. Only a few thought that such a man was a good listener.

The thing that men understand the least about women was evenly divided between fears and needs, according to the men. The women answered that their needs are the least understood. By the end of the game, the group was warmed up and actively involved. It was clear that men and women spend a good deal of time trying to figure out the opposite sex. The last question was crucial, because understanding each other's needs is central to expressing real compassion for each other. It was time to continue the role reversal—but now about the situation of having a child with a disability in the family. Men and women were instructed to form two separate groups. The women were asked to discuss why it is hard to be a father of a child with special needs and what women need from men. The men were to discuss why it is hard to be a mother of a child with special needs and secondly what men need from women. Each group was to pick a spokesperson and a recorder. One gender had to leave and go to another room. The women asked the men to leave. The stage was set for the real dialogue of the evening.

STUMBLING FORWARD—MALE STYLE

Sitting around in a circle spilling your guts isn't exactly a typical male activity, so it was no surprise that this meeting started out awkwardly and went differently from the predominantly female meetings that are typical of parent groups. When I went down the hall to the room assigned for the men's meeting, one man was already there and another followed me in. After a few minutes, no one else had arrived, so I ventured back out into the hall.

The rest of the men were standing around the coffee pot fixing their coffee and munching on cookies. There was awkwardness there—little conversation and many eyes directly and indirectly checking me out. It reminded me of how I felt as a child on my first day in a new school out on the playground, not knowing anyone yet and wanting to feel a part of things. I could lead by asking everyone to come down the hall to the assigned room, but instead I led by joining in, standing around, and getting a cup of coffee. "The women can see us standing around here from where they're sitting. They probably think we're not doing anything," remarked one of the men.

"So what are we going to do?" I asked.

"We need to get started," said Willie, a grandfather in his sixties and the oldest man in the group. He explained that he and his wife had come tonight to support their daughter, who was a single parent of a child with cerebral palsy. They had also raised a child of their own with a physical disability. Instantly he had the group's respect and admiration. Sensing this, I asked Willie if he was willing to speak for us.

"I've never done anything like this before, but I'll try. I've been a truck driver all my life. One of my daughters has a doctorate; she's the director of a state school for children with disabilities." Willie started asking each man what he thought about why it was hard to be a woman with a child with special needs. As the men stood around and sipped on coffee, the ideas flowed about what they thought the women needed.

1. Women have it harder because they need more practical help in the everyday things. It's just too much to handle. A nanny would be ideal, but a teenager to help out for a few hours a day with child care or household chores would be great.

2. Women need more understanding and compassion from their husbands. We need to communicate more and listen to how they feel.

3. Women want to talk about other things, too—not just the child with the disability.

4. Women need more physical help when the man is home; they're worn out from the everyday grind.

5. Women want men to play with the child with special needs more and get to know more about him or her.

6. Women want men to take the children out and give the woman some free time for herself.

7. Women want men to assume more responsibility around the house.

8. Women want men to pay more attention to how the woman is feeling and what she might need or want each day.

Now it was time to talk about what the men wanted from the women in their lives. This was much harder to get started.

I asked how women could be expected to understand what men don't say. Again, in his own simple style, Willie started asking each man what he wanted. Once again we were able to develop a list.

1.　We want the women to understand that we are trying to help in the way we know how and that we're frustrated when we can't make things better.

2.　We need more time as a couple again, to be together without the children.

3.　We want women to be more rational and less emotional so that we can discuss problems and find solutions.

4.　Let us as men take more responsibility with the child with special needs. Sometimes it seems that the women can't let go of doing all of the work and being overwhelmed all of the time. Let's get more organized and distribute the work.

5.　We need more strength and stability in our marriage. It would help if they told us what we are doing right so that we could feel more secure in the relationship.

The women had been done for some time when the men's group finished, and they had been sitting around in their circle chatting informally. Maybe it took longer because men aren't used to conversations about relationships. It's easy to talk about work and sports, but this stuff gets hard. The women were eager to know what the men had been talking about, especially because it appeared that the group had just been standing around drinking coffee.

The men reported first. When Willie was about halfway through reading the list of why it is hard to be a woman, he was interrupted: "This is too good to be true. The doctor (pointing to me) must have been coaching you guys," remarked one of the women. The whole group howled with laughter.

Willie spoke with the wisdom of a grandfather, "He just got us started; we came up with this stuff ourselves." The women were satisfied for the moment, and Willie continued reading.

"This is incredible," remarked Mary, a red-haired woman of 30-some years with an 8-year-old child with a mental and physical disability. "You guys sure have done a good job keeping this a secret; I'm really glad we're finding it out tonight."

Now it was the women's turn to report on why it is hard to be a man. Mary was the spokesperson. She explained that because the women's group did not really expect the men to come up with much, they had developed a much shorter list. Nonetheless, the women did hit the mark as they reported their information.

1. Men have an extremely hard time with all of the intense emotions involved with the child with special needs. They want women to be more rational and more supportive of their style of caring.

2. Men feel unappreciated for their efforts especially for how hard they work to pay the increased medical bills and so forth.

3. Women are so intense that men feel like they're getting nagged all of the time.

When Mary was finished, I intervened, "So how did we do at understanding each other?"

There was laughter and smiles. I pointed out that the differences in the male and female styles of relating that were expressed in the group were similar in most couples, not just those with a child with a disability. As Robert Bly pointed out in his article, "Where Are Men and Women Today?" there is a lot of forgiveness that simply comes from naming these differences between men and women and it doesn't mean that either one is wrong.

I recommended the book, *You Just Don't Understand: Women and Men in Conversation,* by linguist Deborah Tannen, because it explains in detail the different conversational styles of men and women in easy-to-understand language. As Tannen pointed out, men and women have quite different definitions of the comfort of home. The man generally has been using language all day in his struggle to succeed at work. At day's end, at home with the woman he loves, he has nothing to prove at last and wants to be free not to talk. Yet, in a general way, the woman, if she works outside of the home, has been careful not to be too expressive all day in order to avoid being called aggressive or neurotic. If she works at home caring for children full time, she may not have had an adult to talk to. At her day's end, when she is finally with the man she feels close to, she wants to be free to talk.

In the dialogue that evolved out of the role reversal, the men and women presented what they each wanted for themselves. Again, the women were amazed at how specific the men's group had been. "I hope we can be like this one-on-one!" said Sally, a woman in her late twenties with a child in early intervention.

By the time the women's group reported on their wants, the men listened openly. The tension in the room was all gone at that moment. Mary reported that the women wanted the following:

1. The men to be involved in the child's education; they were tired of going to the meetings alone; they wanted the men to try whenever possible to take a few hours off from work to be with them at these times.
2. Some time alone to relax without the children
3. To be able to talk about their feelings without the men getting defensive
4. Time together as a couple
5. Men to develop a better understanding of their child's special needs and not leave it all to the women

By the time Mary finished, it was almost 9:30 P.M. The meeting had lasted 30 minutes longer than planned; baby sitters must have been wondering when parents would return. After a brief summary of the evening's events, the couples were urged to continue the discussion by themselves, with friends, and in their ongoing support groups. Some more involved problems could be untangled best by consulting a professional skilled in counseling couples and sensitive to the issues around having a child with a disability. I asked everyone to find their partner and to end the evening by whispering something special in each other's ear. People began to file out arm in arm, hand in hand.

There was a long way to go, I thought, but there was no doubt that these couples had left understanding more about each other than they did prior to the evening's experience. In that respect, my work was fruitful. On the ride home, I pondered how I was just like the other men there. How many things did I expect Cindy to understand without talking about them? How many times did I expect her not to be upset because it was too frustrating for me to listen about things that I couldn't fix? Each time that I facilitate a group for couples I learn and understand more about what it takes to understand each other better. I bring something new to each group, and each group finds its own unique way of teaching itself.

Although the stories in this chapter cover many of the difficulties encountered by parents of children with special needs, it is wise to remember that every relationship is unique and special and needs to be understood in that way. The vitality of healthy children reinforces parents' efforts and keeps us all going. The joys of watching a child's development can be very exciting, but with a child with special needs these joys may be few and far between.

It is particularly necessary for these parents to have enjoyable time together as well as develop in themselves the ability to enjoy playing with their child with special needs through floor time. Whenever I speak to groups of couples, I ask early on when they had their last date. It is rare in my experience that couples go out together with any regularity due to the often overwhelming demands they face. Yet, those demands make it all the more necessary to find time together for the sake of the marriage, which obviously will benefit the children.

The difficulties can be overcome. One couple that consulted me, for example, told me how afraid they were to leave their child with a chronic illness even with a trained respite worker. They realized that they were having a hard time letting go and trusting. They thought that no one else could comfort their child when ill or get emergency medical help if needed. The solution that they eventually found was to carry a beeper, and now they can go out with regularity and peace of mind.

IMPERFECT RELATIONSHIPS

Just as parenting even a typical child requires giving up the dream of the perfect child, a rewarding and enduring marriage calls on us to abandon our longing for the perfect union in which all of our needs are met and our partner is also totally satisfied. Relationships can be incredibly complex and seldom are quite what we expect. My own daily experiences remind me of my trials and frailties, and as Helen Featherstone observed in *A Difference in the Family: Life with a Disabled Child,* insight cannot solve every problem that comes up. It is, however, an important tool to maintain the love between a couple when the very fabric and meaning of life is challenged by disability in the family. For some people, a child's disability may reveal problems in a marriage that no amount of understanding and insight can repair or pave over, and divorce may ensue. For others, a child's special needs can be a red herring that distracts a couple from fundamental issues about their relationship. Problematic relationships can become considerably worse. Because 47% of first marriages fail, and 57% of all marriages end in divorce, according to the U.S. Census Bureau, none of us can afford to be smug.

Hope for relationships can, however, spring from the crises that couples experience when their child has a disability. "Normal" crises such as childbirth, moving, loss of a job, financial problems, and trials in parenting can all strain a relationship in parallel ways. Many have observed that ordinary trouble differs only in degree from the strain caused by disability. In my view, however, having a child with a disability is a quantum leap away from everyday problems, but it is nevertheless an experience that prepares us to learn from life.

The stereotypes of female and male suggest a splitting of love and work. According to psychologist Carol Gilligan in *In a Different Voice: Psychological Theory and Women's Development*, expressive capacities are delegated to women through communication in relationships, whereas instrumental or problem-solving tasks are regarded as logical and masculine. This neat but outmoded model collapses under the weight of a shared sorrow that neither love nor logic alone can heal. The stage is then set for a far deeper connection and relationship, perhaps even more intimate than would have been possible with an easier life. The many voices that have been incorporated in this chapter illuminate, I believe, these essential themes.

8

Differing Views
of the Mountain

*Understanding How Siblings
Respond to Disability*

*J*effrey's younger brother, Peter, had been silent for 39
years. Then, through the sometimes controversial technique of facilitated communication, a breakthrough occurred:
    Jeffrey, I'm not stupid, he typed with the aid of his facilita-
tor. *Jeffrey, I love you so much sometimes it hurts.*

These were Peter's first words to his brother Jeffrey Lurie,
who is the current owner of the Philadelphia Eagles. For hours
on that day in January 1992, Peter "talked" to his brother
about their family life together. He remembered being at a residential school at the time of their father's death 30 years before, when Jeffrey, the oldest of three, was 9 years old. Peter
said that he had wanted to share his grief with the rest of the
family and now finally he could.

Jeffrey related his family's story to a spellbound audience
of several hundred people at the Small Miracles Award Dinner
sponsored yearly by the Center for Autistic Children in Philadelphia. Jeffrey Lurie's grandfather, father, and uncle had built
a $4 billion movie house, General Cinema, and publishing
company, Harcourt Brace. And, although Jeffrey had all of the

comforts of life, his brother's silence and his father's death had taught him how fragile life can be. Jeffrey told Sal Paolantonio, a sports writer for the *Philadelphia Inquirer,*

> *Every day, it's like having a friend inside your head . . . It makes me want to really make the most of every day, month and year, in terms of the people I am with. The relationships. The family that you have. The work that you do. It makes you want it to be the most intense experience possible, eliminate all kinds of mediocrity. If I'm going to have a relationship with my daughter, let's say, I want it to be as great a relationship as I can make it, because I don't know how long it's going to last.*

THE IMPRINTS OF
BIRTH ORDER AND GENDER

We are not only parents; most of us are also siblings with one foot back in the world of our own childhood and one foot in the world of adulthood and parenting. Having a disability in the family heightens a parent's challenge to be fair to all. In this quest—grasping the lessons of our family of origin—can help us understand the dilemmas of the family that we procreate.

Historically, primogeniture meant that the firstborn son received the inheritance as well as a key position. At times, the "natural" order was reversed in religion and mythology when a later-born son overtook the elder. When reversal occurs, it threatens the self-concept of the older child and can leave the younger one feeling chronically guilty. Even today, most parents long for a son to carry on the family name. Despite recent social advances in the realm of gender equality, a son born after a daughter represents a reversal of the traditional social order, and daughters are not valued equally. On the positive side, having a sibling of the opposite sex, when both are valued equally, can be a great advantage throughout life in learning how to get along with the opposite gender.

Same-sex siblings have a special kind of identification with each other. Because they are so alike, they have a special challenge to establish individuality. Two women who grew up together tend to be more intimate and sometimes more jealous. Two male siblings tend to be more competitive. The greatest power struggles are between siblings of the same sex. This is especially true when there are only two children and thus no one else to dilute or buffer the struggle.

BREAKFAST WITH MY BROTHER

I had known him all of his life, and if nature is kind to us, I will know him for the rest of my life. I got a warm feeling going to meet him for breakfast. He is one of my younger brothers, and on this brisk October morning, fallen leaves crackled under my feet as I walked to the train station. It was still dark as I waited for the 6:05 train. I was leaving early to meet Paul before I started seeing my patients at the office. The Phillies had just won the National League Championship Series. As the train rumbled along the tracks, I read the sports page and thought of my grandfather and how he would have enjoyed this time if he was alive because the Phillies of 1993 had gone from last to first. They were the collective Rocky of this town, and with their scruffy image of a band of biker types, some overweight, some chewing tobacco and drinking beer, they had captured the imagination. They had charisma, sex appeal, and watchability.

I remembered all of those summer nights on my grandparents' back porch listening to the Phillies whether they were winning or losing. Pop was a real fan. . . . I wondered if Paul was having the same thoughts. My reminiscences were punctuated as the train lurched to a stop at my station. It was getting lighter outside as I emerged from the underground station. I always enjoyed the walk to my office through the historic section. Passing Independence Hall, I remembered my father taking all of us as children to see the Liberty Bell. We had taken turns putting our fingers in the crack. My brother Don was there with us then, but his image was now frozen in time. His loss was premature. There is always a space for him in those family images stored in my memory.

Recalling those memories brings back a whole world of warm, compassionate, loving feelings mixed with the inevitable rivalry and jealousy that exists among siblings. This morning rendezvous with my brother brings up the complexity and richness of the family life that we share. Because we are 10 years apart, we were not in direct competition with each other, and I reflected on how this has helped our relationship.

As I approached the little deli where we had agreed to meet, I saw my brother's car parked outside on South Street. He's always on time. As I entered the eatery, I saw that he was reading the sports page. He looked up, and our eyes met. It was a little like looking at myself in the mirror. I look more like my mother and he looks more like my father, but everyone always surmises that we are brothers. I like how it feels when people say that. Of course, it is the same feeling that I have with my other siblings and to a lesser extent with my cousins and others in the extended family.

As I sat down across from Paul in the booth, we exchanged greetings, and our talk initially centered on the Phillies. He sat with his head cocked slightly to the right—his good ear pointed toward me. He had lost all of his hearing in one ear after a severe infection damaged his eardrum as a young child. He compensates well, and most of the time I forget about his hearing loss. The server brought us steaming hot coffee, reminding me how much Paul always liked coffee and how as a small boy he would drink what was left in the cups when my mother and father had left the table. Then my mind came back to the present.

"I was thinking of Pop. He would have loved this series."

"Me, too," he responded with a knowing smile. "I remember one time when I took him to a Phillies game at Veterans' Stadium. He wasn't comfortable; he kept asking when we would be leaving. He would have preferred to listen to it on the radio."

We laughed, and it was the special kind of laughter that you can enjoy with a brother or sister. Like this memory of our grandfather who was born in 1902 and grew up in the days of radio, there were so many memories and so many mixed feelings that we shared growing up in the same family. There was the love and loyalty that is easy to talk about. Yet, the darker, more difficult side of our emotional lives is easy to ignore.

Overemphasizing sibling rivalry tends to accentuate the negative, whereas ignoring it denies an integral part of the reality that bonds siblings.

Every time that I have an involved conversation with one of my siblings, it seems that our similarities and differences come up. Fortunately, our differences naturally have a wide span through age, sex, temperament, and abilities. Affirming our differences helps control rivalry and serves as a way of expressing it constructively. Am I as accomplished as a psychologist as my brothers are in their careers? Am I as far along my career path as I am supposed to be by virtue of my age? Have I been a good big brother?

In the Bible, the first murder was a fratricide; Cain killed his brother, Abel. It's a story about that murky area in the consciousness—the wish to get rid of a sibling and be the sole beneficiary of the parents' affection. There is a certain amount of shame in seeing oneself as competitive or as having angry murderous impulses. After all, aren't we supposed to love and respect our brothers and sisters unconditionally? What are we doing comparing achievements? Most people long for a balanced view of these emotions that can emerge in adulthood. In *The Sibling Bond,* Stephen Bank and Michael Kahn discussed the positive aspects of aggression and rivalry. Two brothers wrestling, for example, can represent contact, warmth, and presence.

This point reminds me of the endless wrestling matches between my brother Al and me. Al is 2 years my junior and was my constant companion until I left home for college. In a fight, a child is alive and real and noticed. In these power struggles and interactions, siblings can learn how to resolve conflicts. Yet, I felt some guilt for winning, even though I was supposed to by virtue of being older and was putting myself under tremendous pressure to do so. Certainly, this was the downside of feeling responsible to lead and achieve.

When Al and I discussed this as adults, it was a relief to know that he had not held it against me, but I still could never feel good about so consistently winning. Now, we eat breakfast together on occasion and take a walk in the woods where our grandmother took us as little boys. Sometimes I follow his lead when we climb rocky trails, and I get a hint of the feeling of what it was like for him to follow in my footsteps during those early years. As he has pointed out to me, our roads diverged so long ago that it's very different now as we relate from different vantage points, and each of us has hair that has begun to gray. Our bonds have truly passed the test of time.

For parents, the fantasy of a close, cozy set of siblings is part of the image of a perfect family. Squabbles among brothers and sisters sometimes crush that dream. There can be a dilemma over when to let children work out their differences and when to intervene. Too much intervention keeps children from learning for themselves how to resolve conflict. The key is to be able to express negative feelings without doing damage. The goal is for children to work out their own solutions whenever possible. It takes parental patience and wisdom to give up an element of control and facilitate this process for children. Sometimes it just means waiting a moment or two.

One of the ways that siblings can help each other as children and as adults is to validate their shared reality about parents and relatives. My conversation with my brother Paul about our grandfather did that for us on this particular morning, and it re-affirmed the length and strength of our bond. Sometimes a different perspective can be helpful and comforting. Paul saw my relationship with Al differently because he primarily remembered the closeness of his two oldest brothers. Yet, there may be a difference in perspective that can breed conflict and ill will.

As the oldest in our family, I had grown up always helping my parents take care of the younger ones. The feeling of being so responsible at a young age is very common among eldest children. The pressure to set "a good example" is a burden at times but naturally develops leadership ability. As for most eldest children, my role was always clear and that has been a blessing. Since my teenage years, I have found myself in leadership positions in sports, union activities, professional groups, and now speaking to and for parents of children with disabilities.

My brother Paul was the sixth of eight children. He was a younger brother to three brothers and two sisters and an older brother to two younger ones. In most families, middle children like him tend to have a hazy role and are pressured from all sides. They have no clearly defined place, but their experience tends to produce people who are friendly, diplomatic, and good negotiators. They are usually blessed with a moderate sense of responsibility, are connected strongly with older siblings, and are very protective of younger siblings.

I remember teaching my younger brothers how to play baseball and being proud of their accomplishments in little league. I remember how, at one point, they thought I could do anything. There was a certain competition among the older group of us for the attention and admiration of the younger ones. This is another frequently cited form of rivalry in the literature on this topic. Nonetheless, it is hard to admit and carries a twinge of embarrassment along with it. The oldest is by nature bigger, stronger, and knows more, so he or she is expected to win. There's a lot of pressure, and the oldest may also feel guilty for winning at the expense of a younger sibling who is also loved. No wonder so many siblings report strained relationships in adulthood.

The youngest, like the oldest, has a unique position and is never displaced. The child in this position feels chosen for special protection by older siblings as well as by parents. Yet, the youngest is often regarded as spoiled or as the favorite whether that is true or not. Although the oldest is usually expected to help in parenting, the youngest is often expected to take care of the parents as they age.

In *Mixed Feelings: Love, Hate, Rivalry, and Reconciliation Among Brothers and Sisters*, Francine Klagsburn explored the unique perspective of each position in the birth order. There is such a wide range of factors that make up the building blocks of our personalities that these generalizations about birth order don't always hold up. Nonetheless, many of them can be used to better understand ourselves and others. In every case, sibling bonds leave special imprints that affect the way we parent our children whether our experience fits the "norms."

In a workshop that I conducted, I met a man who was the second child in his family, but he was the first son. He was treated as if he was the oldest child and that always felt weird to him. Of course, it also strained his relationship with his older sister, who was never treated in accord with her natural position. His dilemma is full of meaning in reference to how gender affects the birth order.

BREAKFAST WITH MY BROTHER, REVISITED

Paul asked me how Tariq was doing. It was an uneasy moment. There wasn't much to say, but I wanted to answer because I don't want him to stop asking me. Some people never ask, so it is comforting that he asks me regularly and listens to the answer.

"He's getting whiskers. He'll need to be shaved soon. I doubt he'll ever be able to safely handle a razor."

There was an awkward pause as Paul didn't know what to say. He didn't really want to think about this, and I didn't really blame him, nor did I really want to talk about it. I'd rather avoid the pain of those thoughts, and I didn't want him to feel too uneasy or inadequate, so I shifted the subject.

"How's Sam doing? What's his latest accomplishment?"

My brother's eyes lit up. This was the sort of thing that parents of typical children can easily talk about. Fortunately, I could join him in this. Sam was almost 2 years old, a couple of months younger than my daughter, Kara, and it's always fun to talk about them. There are the inevitable comparisons, and I wonder if this reflects our own rivalry. I'm glad that I have a daughter because the competition will never be as direct as if these toddler cousins were the same sex. They are supposed to be different by virtue of their biology. Yet, I am both glad for him and somewhat jealous that he has a healthy son.

"I've been playing ball with him. He's all boy."

"Kara's having fun playing with an alphabet puzzle. She is starting to recognize some of the letters on her own. I guess she's learning from *Sesame Street*. At the playground, she's climbing all over everything. She might like gymnastics."

Sometimes we talk about the movies that we have seen recently. Our conversation on this particular morning reminded me of the television movie *Family Pictures*. Based on the novel by Sue Miller, it is about a man and a woman struggling to raise five children, including a son with autism. It is about relationships and forgiveness.

The story is told through the eyes of Nina, the oldest child, giving it a different and much needed perspective. Randall, the child with autism, strains everyone's patience, and the viewer can feel the tension. Lainie, the mother, tries to treat him as normally as possible, devotes most of her time to his care, and seems inseparable from Randall. David, the father, and the other children all feel neglected at times. Here is a major dilemma of all families with a child who isn't "normal."

One day, the family receives the devastating news that Randall has wandered away on a field trip at his school and has been killed by a car. I shuddered—for this is still my worst fear for Tariq, and I could imagine a funeral like the one in the movie. What makes this film special to me is the confrontation and the subsequent reconciliation that occurs between Nina and her mother at the end. There had been a lot of friction between mother and daughter. They had argued bitterly for years, and at this point Nina is married and pregnant with her first child.

Nina starts with a shrill voice asking why her mother divorced her father after Randall's death. Lainie explains in a firm tone that they had both worked hard to stay together.

Nina counters from her perspective that it seemed like it was only for Randall's sake that they stayed together because when he died they broke up. She feels that her mother's love is conditional and summarizes it in her tearful statement: "It's be quiet, be good, be happy, be well. Most of all, be well. Be all of those things, and I'll love you. I'll love you, my perfect baby."

Lainie responds by explaining that she wishes that she could have loved Randall the way she loved her other children. She explains that it would have been a gift if she could have asked the same from him as from her other children. She acknowledges that she wasn't a good mother to Nina because she yelled and hit. She makes no excuses as she admits that perhaps Randall did keep the family together. Lainie concludes that her love for Nina and her other typical children held her to the earth.

The reconciliation that results is possible between a parent and an adult child when both can speak honestly and openly from the heart. It takes courage to have this kind of dialogue, but it can liberate its participants from so many dark feelings. In speaking her mind and in hearing her mother's response, Nina begins to make sense out of her life. As the film ends, Nina reflects on a portrait of a large extended family and sees it as a portrait of courage. From this perspective, every child that is born represents an immense risk on the part of the parents. There is so much potential for pain and tragedy that any child's existence is a miracle.

I reflected on the risks that my parents had taken to have and raise eight children—only to lose one of us in a car accident. I thought of my grandparents and their courage. My grandfather came over alone on a boat from Italy when he was 12 years old to meet his father who was already here in America. He never knew his mother, who had died when he was only 2 years old. During the Depression, my grandparents raised five children to adulthood. They lost a 2-year-old daughter to illness, which wasn't uncommon in those days. In fact, around the turn of the century as many as 20% of all children died before their first birthday.

I wasn't the only or the first in my family tree who had rolled the dice and lost. I thought of Cindy and her parents because she, too, had lost a brother—he was only 17 years old—in a bus accident in Israel. He was buried on the kibbutz while her family sat *shiva* half a world away in Philadelphia. Every family has its share of tragedy. Nina's words from the movie keep echoing inside of me. Love is such a risk, but who would want to live without love, without a connection to others?

I wondered what Antoinette would make of Tariq when she was grown. All parents want to be fair, and we want our healthy children to grow up loving us as parents and loving

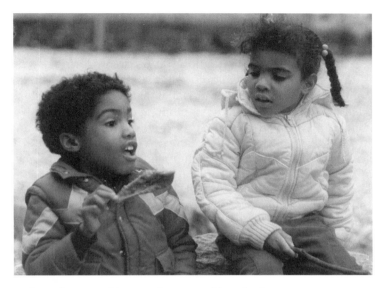

Tariq at 6 years old—very interested in a leaf.

their siblings who are less fortunate in some ways. In 1995, one night when everyone else was out, Antoinette and I were having dinner together, and she asked me if I would rather have one healthy son than three daughters. What a heavy question for her! But I was glad for her sake that she was able to ask it. I told her that I would be overjoyed for Tariq to be healthy, but not in place of any of my daughters. She seemed relieved by my answer.

VETERAN PARENTS SPEAK OUT

In 1996, I addressed a unique group of parents—Vietnam veterans who had been exposed to Agent Orange. One of the tragic consequences of their exposure to that chemical compound was that their children had a much higher incidence of all sorts of disabilities, especially neurological disabilities. The class action court case that had awarded damages to these veterans and their families also established funds for parent training for those whose children had a disability.

The topic of my presentation was the issues facing parents in raising siblings of children with disabilities. The timing seemed perfect. Because I had videotaped *Family Pictures,* I decided to show the ending to stimulate a discussion. There was some risk involved because the movie was so intense, and these fathers' genes had been damaged by chemicals in southeast Asia. Did I dare uncover that pain? I knew that the parents who had come had difficult lives and wanted all of the help that they could get. About 50 people were present—two thirds were women. So, after a brief introduction about myself and the movie, I showed the last 10 minutes, which began with Nina confronting her mother.

There was a heavy silence when I turned off the VCR. I asked if anyone would start the group off for the evening by sharing what had opened inside of them as they watched the film clip. Almost instantly a woman in the front row spoke up. "I felt very sad," she said, "I'm always yelling at my child who doesn't have the problem. I expect so much from her, and she's not even 4. I know I have to change."

Another woman in the front said, "I'm always running around trying to keep up with my son who has ADHD [attention-deficit/hyperactivity disorder]. I'm never sure what I'll find around the next corner. My nerves are shot. My other children are really on their own. I don't know what to do."

Another woman said, "My child just developed juvenile diabetes. Now that he's insulin dependent, it's like his whole personality is changing. He feels so different. My daughter is losing the healthy brother she used to have. I'm not sure how to help her. I'm a school social worker, but I'm at a loss for how to handle this."

"My 2½-year-old has a hearing impairment and neurological damage," said a woman in the back. "My 4-year-old looked at her the other day and said, 'Why won't you talk to me? Why?' I don't know what to tell her. I told her that her sister's ears were broken, and she will have to learn to talk with her hands. Did I do the right thing?"

Of course, it was right—for information liberates us all—parents and children—from some of our darkest worries. Getting reliable information can be like having your electricity restored after a storm has knocked out your power. The pain is still there, however, and that is one thing that makes it so difficult to know if we are doing the right thing as parents.

In 1972, Frances Grossman reported on the first large-scale study involving college-age siblings in *Brothers and Sisters of Retarded Children*. These brothers and sisters reported that talking to their parents about the disabilities of their brothers and sisters was as difficult as talking to them about sex. One of Grossman's conclusions was that the feelings and attitudes of the brothers and sisters to a large extent mirrored the way that the parents had handled the disability. Parents who can speak freely help their children understand their own emotions.

A hand went up right in front of me. There was an urgency to the gesture and the woman's voice trembled as she spoke. "I think I talk to my healthy daughter too much. My husband doesn't want to talk about our child's problems. For years I've confided in my other daughter, who is now a teenager. I know this isn't right, and I feel horrible about it, but I haven't known where to turn."

We all need to share with other adults. It doesn't make things "all better," but it helps. Sometimes we get isolated from other people, but this meeting was an opportunity for participants to connect and maybe go back refreshed to the important people in their lives.

So far none of the men had spoken, which was not unusual in these meetings. A simple intervention often can change that. I opened the door by asking if any of the men wanted to share.

After an awkward pause, a man seated near the center of the room with his arms crossed came through. "Our 3-year-old has just been diagnosed with PDD [pervasive developmental disorder]," he said clearly and directly. "We don't know what to think. My wife is really worried about the effect on our two older children, and I am, too. That's why I'm here tonight."

He had no sooner finished when another man raised his hand. He was a slightly built man with glasses and spoke timidly. "My wife tells me I don't talk about this enough, but I don't know what to do and that's why I have nothing to say. It really makes me feel like a nothing as a father. I want to go home with something to say."

The man seated beside him patted him on the back to comfort him. Many men and women were nodding around the room. It was a signal to move on. Stressing how many of the answers to these questions were already within the group, I asked everyone to imagine that they had a sibling with a disability or chronic illness. What would they want from their parents?

WHAT SIBLINGS WANT

There is the clear, simple voice of a child in all of us. Everyone who grew up with siblings can gain access to these deep feelings. Children who have a sibling with special needs unavoidably wonder about and miss the brother or sister that they might have had, as Mary McHugh described in her compelling personal account and from her extensive research in *Special Siblings: Growing Up with Someone with a Disability.*

The first thing that came up at the Agent Orange gathering was that siblings would want a fair distribution of attention from their parents. This could be in the form of taking their problems just as seriously as those of the child with special needs. Recognition of the positive in each child without having the pressure of being "the star" of the family was mentioned.

"So much gets taken for granted when you're normal," said another speaker. "As parents, we make such a big deal out of the accomplishments of our special child. If I was a sibling, I would really resent it if my parents didn't notice my struggles and accomplishments."

That comment, like Nina's in *Family Pictures,* reflected the reality that the child with the disability does not have to compete for the parents' attention. From the siblings' perspective that child always wins.

"I'd want my own life!" said the man who had been the first male to speak up earlier.

Other parents followed up talking about time alone without any responsibilities and time with their friends. Because they are always expected to help out their exhausted, bereaved parents, siblings often feel like junior parents and, yet, find it hard to express their negative feelings about this role. They may feel inconsiderate or disloyal to their struggling parents.

Looking for solutions within the group made ideas flow freely; I wrote them on a newsprint tablet in the front of the room. The mood of the group was shifting. Energy was beginning to flow out of the heavy thoughts that had dominated the evening so far. People were eagerly copying down the ideas.

"I would want to be treated as an individual, and I would absolutely hate it if my parents always reminded me how lucky I was. That would drive me up the wall," added a woman who hadn't spoken previously.

A man who had listened intently so far spoke next. "I would want information about the disability," he said. "I'm sure I would have a lot of questions, and I would want answers."

Just as parents need information, so do siblings on their level. Information helps siblings to answer the questions that come from their peers or even from adults who are too uncomfortable to ask the parents directly.

The woman whose child had ADHD shared next, "That makes me think that I would want my parents to be concerned about my feelings. I would want them to ask me how I felt."

Like their parents, brothers and sisters have a host of feelings that run the gamut from confusion to fear, anger, sadness, and embarrassment. Sometimes their shame is so acute that siblings wish that they didn't even know their brother or sister who acts or looks unusual. This can be especially true if there is a strong physical resemblance between the two. Although it may be hard to express these thoughts, most siblings long to have their feelings described or confirmed in some way. It helps to relieve their guilt about having negative feelings toward a brother or sister.

Let's take the anger that a sibling might feel toward a sister who keeps messing up his things like his video games, for example, including pulling out the plug when he is playing with it and forcing him to start over again. The anger makes him want to get rid of or even beat up his sister, who is being a pest. Then there is the guilt that may be felt when he thinks it over and remembers that she just wants to play, doesn't understand how to play that game, and wants him to do something different. Surely this is an understandable cycle of emotions but very difficult to deal with internally.

Parents who have come to terms with the darker side of their feelings about their child's disability and their own feelings as siblings themselves are in the best position to help their other children feel whole and lovable. Research on the adjustment of siblings of children with disabilities consistently shows this.

"I would want a normal family life," commented the man whose child has PDD. "That would mean doing things together as a family as well as time alone with my parents to do things or just talk."

"Privacy would really matter to me; I'd be sick of a kid who didn't understand any better and was constantly getting into my things," declared the woman whose child was deaf.

A man who had listened with a somber expression all night stated firmly, "I would want a break once in a while from all the worries and responsibilities. It would be great if there was a sense of humor in the family."

Another woman who had listened intently so far spoke up next. "My 9-year-old daughter has a learning disability. The other day when I was serving breakfast, I spilled some orange juice. I started joking that I had a spilling disability."

She was interrupted by a hearty round of laughter, and then she told us that her pun had caught on with the whole family. There were many nods and smiles around the room. There was a resurgence of hope following the open expression of the group's feelings. They had captured the essence of what siblings themselves say in interviews and what is recommended by professionals. It was time to move the group for-

ward another step. Given that everyone wants to be good parents to all of their children, and we get a sense of their needs
when we meet together and talk, why is it hard to do?

The room got quiet briefly, and then the woman whose
child had ADHD spoke up. "So much of the time I'm out of
breath chasing the special one—watching out for what might
happen next. I find myself calling my daughter for help when
my husband isn't home. It's hard for me to hear my daughter's
concerns. I feel like a broken record. I'm so wound up."

It got quiet again. It can be really, really hard, and sometimes we run out of gas. People always tell me, and I'm sure
other parents get this a lot, that they don't know how I've survived. Sometimes that makes people angry, but I think people
are saying that they admire the strength, courage, and love
exhibited in such quantity by the parents of children with special needs.

As Shakespeare wrote in *Hamlet,* "There is nothing either
good or bad, but thinking makes it so." Talking about these
things is one way that parents can find the good side, take care
of themselves, and replenish their energy. They can take better care of their children by learning to take care of themselves. That sounds simple but there's something more to take
into account. Disability can disrupt normal occurrences in the
family life of brothers and sisters.

I met a man who was very concerned about the unsettling
outlook of his 3-year-old daughter. She kept calling her older
sister who was 6 years old "the baby." The 6-year-old had a visual impairment and a developmental disability. Although it
seemed weird to this father, in this case, the younger daughter functioned at a much higher level than her older sister. Her
way of looking at things was in accordance with the reality
that she experienced.

Disability had reversed the natural order. Her father had
explained the disability to his younger daughter, but she still
called her older sister the baby. That will stop when the
younger girl develops the capacity to understand the abstract
concepts involved. She will, nevertheless, be uncomfortable at
times. This younger child, like my own daughter, Antoinette,

feels like she is the oldest child. In a functional way, what is historically false is actually true in terms of the role that children play in the family. The younger, "normal" child loses both a "normal" playmate and a role model and, moreover, the attention that she would have naturally gotten as the baby of the family. When parents are sensitive to this, they can help their children understand.

When the typical child is born second, parents are quite naturally thrilled with the healthy child's development. However, this is a two-edged sword. Every achievement can remind parents of the limits of their child with special needs. Without warning, the inner confusion and turmoil may be re-ignited. In this way, chronic grief can reverberate through a family.

Physical resemblance is another tricky area. As Antoinette moved toward adolescence, I noticed that she got uncomfortable when people commented on her resemblance to Tariq. That bothered me at first. I wanted her to have the warm feeling that I had when people told me that I looked like my siblings.

Indeed, I still want that for her. I realize that Antoinette was responding partly from her own fear that something might be wrong with her—a fear revealed by every sibling of a child with a disability when I have interviewed them. When the disability is invisible, such as with a learning disability, autism, and a mental disorder or impairment, this worry seems even more prominent.

THE MEANING OF *RAIN MAN*

A certain level of mystery shrouds sibling bonds. The 1988 movie *Rain Man* provided a compelling illustration of this theme. Dustin Hoffman's masterful portrayal of Raymond, an autistic savant, focused attention on children with autism. At the time the movie was released, I was asked to be interviewed about autism from a parent's perspective about *Rain Man* for a local television station. Tariq had just turned 9 years old and was home for the holidays. We didn't own a VCR at the time, so I asked my sister Marilyn to tape it for us. When you are lucky, siblings are always there for you as Marilyn showed time and again, calling me regularly to ask about Tariq's progress and always making Tariq welcome in her home.

My son and I appeared on the evening news together. Antoinette was only 7 years old at the time and she was too shy to be interviewed, but she showed up in the background. At the end of the interview, Tariq hugged me and then gave the reporter a "high five." It was a warm and memorable moment that I am happy to have preserved on tape as one of our "family pictures."

Unlike Raymond, Tariq and most children with autism cannot read or write or memorize the telephone book. Nonetheless, this movie depicts a character transformation in Raymond's brother that has meaning and relevance for siblings of children with various kinds of disabilities. Raymond's brother, Charlie, is an angry hustler who is calloused and self-centered. His mother died when he was 2 years old. He is estranged from his father, and at first he does not know that he has a brother.

"My father has stuck it to me all my life," he complained. He feels that nothing he does is good enough. When his father dies, Charlie discovers that he has been excluded from a $3 million inheritance. In his quest to find out about it, Charlie discovers that he has a brother in an institution. He kidnaps his own brother in order to bargain for his fair share of the inheritance. As a result of his disability, Raymond lives in a world without normal perception and human relationships, and he unwittingly provides his brother with someone he cannot con. Charlie is forced to confront his own stunted emotional development.

Ironically, Charlie begins to find himself and his feelings as he struggles to relate to Raymond, who cannot connect emotionally with another person. Because Raymond doesn't crave or accept attention or affection, he is not inherently lovable. On their long trip together by car from the Midwest to Los Angeles, Charlie begins to appreciate his brother.

When Charlie was little and got scared, he thought someone called the *rain man* could save him. During the trip, Charlie calls Raymond *Rain Man* and inadvertently discovers that the *rain man* in his fantasy was his brother *Raymond*, who remembers singing to Charlie. Eventually, Charlie comes to love Raymond for the unique person he is, and then he wants the best for him. As he told Raymond's guardian, "I'm not pissed off at my dad anymore. It's not about the money anymore. Why didn't he tell me? Why didn't you tell me? It would have been nice to know him for more than the past 6 days." By making a genuine connection with his brother, Charlie is transformed. Raymond cannot be normal, but Charlie proves to himself that he could have genuine relationships.

I hope that someday my daughters will find a meaning for themselves in Tariq's existence, and I trust that they will. Sometimes when we confront our own limitations, we realize just how fragile life can be. This can lead to a deeper appreciation of our own talents and abilities and a fuller sense of self.

ALL OF US ARE FRAGILE

Tragedy can visit any family. In 1987, I was teaching a graduate seminar in special education at Antioch University in Philadelphia. One night after class, one of my students approached me. Emily was always serious and intense about her studies and her job teaching students with hearing impairments. When everyone else had left the room, she shared with me that her younger brother had died from leukemia several years before. Her parents wanted to be interviewed for my research.

I was invited to spend a day with the family, who lived in a fashionable neighborhood in Delaware. Emily's dad was a physician in general practice; her mother was a physical therapist. Her brother, Brad, was an undergraduate student in the field of special education. They were a family of survivors. Emily admired the way that her parents had handled their situation, and I hoped that this family could tell me something about how they coped. As I pulled into the driveway, I noticed a basketball backboard and imagined how the boys in the neighborhood must have gathered here. Part of me wished that I could play ball today instead of talk to a family about death, but I was honored that they trusted me enough to share their deepest emotions.

As I rang the doorbell, I hoped that I could avoid any mistakes—asking uncomfortable questions or probing too far. Emily's mother, Helen, offered me tea and invited me to sit in the living room to talk. Helen began her story in a slow, deliberate voice. Pictures of the family were all around and from them I could see that Danny was a very attractive child. She explained that Danny had leukemia since he was 3 years old and was constantly in and out of hospitals, but in every possible respect, he was treated the same as her other children. His IQ score was in the normal range, although his development had been somewhat slow. He was small for his age and couldn't keep up physically with his classmates, but he enjoyed school and socializing with other children. He needed special education classes because of a mild learning problem, and a tutor was necessary when he had to be hospitalized or stay home for extended periods of time.

The Simons believed that life was lived one day at a time and, although they worried about how long Danny would live, they treated their son as normally as possible. I was drawn in as I listened to Helen's account. She told her story with flair, a sense of drama, and suspense. I shared the hope that this family had for the survival of their infant.

Brad and Emily always watched out for their younger brother. When the neighborhood children were playing baseball or kickball, his big brother or sister made sure that Danny was on their team. People in the neighborhood knew Danny and were very kind to him. If he began to feel dizzy or weak while riding his bike, he could always rest at someone's house or use the telephone to call home.

Unexpectedly, when he was 9 years old, Danny died in his sleep. Emily got the telephone call while away at college. As she told me, my mother's telephone call to me about my own brother ran through my mind as I pictured the telephone in Emily's dorm. I recollected going to the hospital with my dad to see my brother's body—but there was no way I could imagine the horror of parents finding a child of theirs in bed, never to wake up again.

It was time for a break, so Helen invited me into the kitchen and began to put out a spread of cold cuts on the table for David who would soon be home from the office for lunch. He greeted me warmly with a firm handshake, and once we began to talk, he reflected on how hard it must have been for his son and daughter to live with bereaved parents. I thought that this was his way of saying he wasn't the perfect dad. Helen excused herself, leaving David and me alone. He encouraged my questions as he prepared a sandwich.

I asked how he and his wife had treated Brad and Emily throughout the period of Danny's illness. He said that they had tried to keep family life as normal as they could. For example, they always vacationed together even though the uncertainties of Danny's illness made planning difficult. They all helped in his care, but Brad and Emily were always encouraged to maintain their usual activities.

David believed that Danny's illness had not disrupted the family from functioning. In fact, he said, "We rallied around him when he was ill." David had to spend extra time with Danny, attending him right in the home with intravenous fluids and other medical necessities. Still, he always found time for Brad and Emily. In commenting on what his painful experiences have taught him, he said, "Everyone's mortality became much more on my mind. I thank God every day that my surviving children are alive and healthy, but I now realize how quickly that can change. Life is truly fragile, and health is something I give thanks for every day."

ANOTHER VIEW OF THE MOUNTAIN

A mountain looks different from every direction. It could be a slow-rising chain of hills from the north and a granite wall from the south. There might be a creek on the east. The rocks, the trees, and the soil may be different depending on the approach. None of the views may match, yet they are all views of the same mountain. The same is true of families; what any member sees is determined by his or her vantage point. The challenge of disability or chronic illness fits this metaphor that was originally developed by Temple University Professor Vytautus Cernius to describe how groups appear to their members. Age, place in the birth order, gender, native abilities, emotional temperament, parents' attitudes, and individual history all make each person's perspective unique.

After lunch, I spent the rest of the day talking to Brad and Emily. From her vantage as the oldest, Emily had not at first been aware that there was anything radically different about her little brother other than his frequent hospitalizations— although she knew he didn't run as fast as the other children his age and his coordination was not as good. She and Brad were athletic and Danny wanted to participate in athletics at their level, but he couldn't. When she entered high school, she began to worry more about Danny.

Emily was always encouraged to ask questions, and there was open discussion about whatever issues she raised. She recalled how everything always led her to one question, "As Danny gets older, will he get better?" Her parents only said that they hoped so. Her best friends had known Danny since birth and accepted him, but sometimes Emily was embarrassed to tell other people about Danny's condition. She didn't tell anyone she didn't have to. When necessary, she would just explain what had been explained to her.

As far as discipline was concerned, both Brad and Emily told me that their parents were very fair. They had been praised for everything that they accomplished and had been disciplined when they did something wrong. Danny had been encouraged to do everything he could "until the last day of his life," and his accomplishments were considered as praiseworthy as were Emily and Brad's. The virulent resentment depicted in *Family Pictures* was not present in this family.

At the end of our conversation, I asked Emily if there was anything else that was important about being a sibling of a child with a disability. She told me something that virtually every sibling I have met since has confirmed. She knows that other people her age rarely think about it, but she wonders about having a child with a disability. Her worry will not stop her from having children, but it is a heavy weight to carry.

Brad told me his first memories of Danny were of medical problems. He recalled beginning to ask his parents questions when he was about 5 years old. At first, his parents explained that his brother was not as strong as other children. As he got older and asked more detailed questions, he got more detailed answers. Brad would get annoyed when other children at school would ask, "Is he bald or something?" He became embarrassed when people asked too many questions. When he got older and could verbalize his answers better, it was easier for him to deal with the questions.

Brad did not feel that he missed out on anything because of his brother. He never had to stay home when Danny was sick. He realized that other children his age didn't have the same experiences. At first, Danny was like two different people to him. He was loud and noisy and wanted his way when he was healthy, and yet he could be very sick at times. Like his sister, Brad wondered whether his brother would get better.

Emily and Brad both believed that Danny had brought their family closer together—he had been a part of the bond of love and compassion that linked them. Having a physician for a father had made Brad feel secure—as a child, he thought his father could fix anything. If anything seemed wrong, Brad thought, "Call dad at work—he'll know whether to worry or not." He knows now that his father did not feel that way about his own abilities.

As Brad spoke, it struck me that he was describing the parents' task, disability or not, to carry the brunt of the worries and the responsibility. Parents lead the way up the rocky mountain trail. That's the only fair way—as hard as it might be. When there is a disability in the family, the trail is steeper and more treacherous. More than ever, the children in the family look to their mother and father for direction in how to handle the practical obstacles as well as their mixed emotions.

What sustains parents as well as siblings is a special kind of pride that develops. Brad and Emily had that special pride in

Tariq enjoying pizza with Kara and Zoë.

their younger brother. They knew how much effort it took for him to accomplish some things that others take for granted—such as riding a bike or learning long division. They were proud of their parents for how they handled the problems and made each of them feel special. They were proud of their own accomplishments and grateful for their health—both physical and mental.

For myself, I hope and trust that my daughters will be able to look back as young women and feel the same way—love and hate, rivalry and reconciliation, grief and joy, and embarrassment and pride. We are really all in this together—parents and siblings of children with special needs—it is only our views of the mountain that differ.

9

The Trouble
with Elephants

Finding and Building
Circles of Support

*A friend is one to
whom one may pour out
all the contents of one's
heart, chaff and grain
together, knowing that
the gentlest of hands
will take and sift it,
keep what is worth keeping
     and
with the breath of kindness
blow the rest away.*
          —Arabian proverb

Although sorrow sends us inward to be alone and lick our wounds, we can usually heal those hurts by opening up and confiding in others. True friendship, as the Arabian proverb states, divides the grief and makes it more bearable. It is indeed a special friend to whom we can turn in our darkest moments for solace.

When someone you are close to dies, relatives, friends, and even acquaintances rally around to offer help. But after a short time, perhaps not knowing what to say or how to respond to the bereaved person, people seem to avoid broaching the subject of death. The same is true when you are worried that something is wrong with your child's development or after your child has been diagnosed with a disability or chronic illness. The topic may be horrifying or psychologically threatening to talk about.

One of the things that we are the least prepared for is the kind of social isolation that comes with grief. It is as if there were a giant elephant in the living room. It fills the room, and it is hard to get around. Yet, we find ourselves avoiding it, pretending it isn't there or doesn't exist. It is difficult to communicate honestly when you are bereaved. People say, "How are you?" and we respond, "I'm fine." We talk about work, the weather, the news, the economy, and everything else but the obvious—the elephant in the room that is unavoidably on our minds. Maybe the trivial chatter is just a way of saying that no one wants to be alone with the elephant and an attempt, however awkward, to acknowledge connection and express concern about a shared sorrow. As John Donne wrote:

> *No man is an island entire of itself; every man*
> *is a piece of the continent, a part of the main. . .*
> *. . . any man's death*
> *diminishes me, because I am involved in mankind; and*
> *therefore never send to know for whom the bell tolls;*
> *It tolls for thee.* (From Coffin, C.M. [1994]. *The*
> *Complete poetry and selected prose of John Donne.*
> New York: Random House; reprinted by permission.)

When I look back over my own experiences of searching for help and support in the early days of worrying about Tariq, I see that much of what I went through was fairly typical. At first, I believed that if he could just start talking again then everything would work out from there. When something is

My grandmother and Tariq.

wrong with your child, you often feel like a little child your-self, and you want your mom and dad to help you—to rescue you and protect you from the hurt that you are feeling.

My mother and father would counsel me to be patient and tell me that things would work out. My mother would tell me that she was praying. They would ask me how Tariq was doing, as if he had the flu and was expected to get better each day. I would describe any little changes that I had noticed. Our con-versations lessened the tension I felt, helped me to get through another day, and kept me working with Tariq to help him de-velop. They couldn't, however, wipe away the tears or bandage the wounds; that has been hard for them as well as for me.

My grandparents, who were still alive when Tariq was younger, would reassure me, too. I have a cousin my own age who has mild mental retardation and whose speech came late, and my grandparents helped my aunt and uncle a lot when Gregory was a little boy. They reassured me, based on how my cousin had developed. Even though he still stutters, he learned to read and write a little bit. He has a driver's license and holds a civil service job as a janitor. All in all, he has done very well for someone with his ability. My grandparents seemed confident that Tariq would be like Gregory. Because of their direct experience and their love for me, I trusted their wisdom and hoped desperately that they were right.

I remember how my grandfather would put Tariq on his lap and recite Italian nursery rhymes, the same ones that he had recited to me when I was a small boy. He would take Tariq's hands within his strong palms, as he had taken mine, and rub them on his coarse beard until it tickled. Tariq would smile and then squirm to get away because he didn't like to be held for long. My grandmother, too, would try to hold him, and she would sing the lullabies that she had sung to me, my siblings, and my cousins when we were little.

So many people never tried to hold my son, perhaps shying away from what they could not understand and what was uncomfortable. They would just make small talk, and I would withdraw in the embarrassment of the moment, always remaining outwardly calm. That's why I get such a warm feeling recalling those moments that my grandparents tried to hold Tariq, despite his squirming and wriggling. Of course, I wished that he would sit still and cuddle with them, but nonetheless, I felt myself held by them because they never stopped trying with him.

No parent wants his or her child to be noticed as different from the norm. You want a healthy, happy child who fits in and makes you proud. But what do you do when your child is different? Speaking for myself, I had a hard time when my son was diagnosed with autism. I walked around looking out of the corner of my eye ready to pounce on people for their reactions. Actually, it was more my perceptions of their reactions, not to mention the perpetual knot in the pit of my stomach. Like many parents whose children are different, it felt to me that I was battling the whole world.

I wish we had *Everybody's Different: Understanding and Changing Our Reactions to Disabilities* by Nancy Miller and Catherine Sammons much sooner. These authors give us an enlightening look at the many differences that exist among people in every walk of life and explain that these differences need not divide us socially. Life is definitely easier when you understand your own reactions, as well as those of others, while realizing that you are not alone—not by a long stretch. The authors help us understand our internal emotional reactions to disabilities and the differences that result from those conditions. They teach us strategies to build our lives, our families, and our communities in a way that is inclusive and respectful of our differences.

When Tariq starts "stimming" (i.e., repetitive behavior patterns that are a prominent characteristic of children and adults with an autistic spectrum disorder) or flapping, especially now that he is full grown, I automatically want him to stop and act "normal." Internally, my reaction can be rather desperate because I don't want him *and* me to be noticed as different. I also still find myself trying to avoid taking photographs when he is not behaving "normally." There is a certain image that I prefer of him in my head, as much as I hate to admit that. But his behaviors are, after all, a part of him.

Even though I would consider myself a veteran parent, I have struggled to understand and own up to these reactions. It has taken me some time, but eventually I am learning to love my son not despite his differences—but rather because of them. The knot in my gut is long gone. Now, for the most part, I can look comfortably around me. I can notice what must have been there before—the friendly faces and kind eyes of compassionate folks.

I know I am not alone. Many parents have told me how isolated and abandoned they have felt in their hour of greatest need. There is a longing for someone to reach out and take a special interest in your child and therefore in you. When you finally do find that kind of support—a gentle hand to touch you and your child and a kind heart to ask how things are— that's when you know for sure that you are not alone.

INTERGENERATIONAL GRIEF

A young father who had come to me for help with his grief told the familiar story of looking to his parents for help. His father had died when he was 7 years old, and he had rarely visited the gravesite. When his son was diagnosed as profoundly deaf, he went to the cemetery, stood by the grave, and told his dad what was going on with his grandson. He cried and asked for help and for strength to carry on. He cried as he told me about this, saying that he had found an emotional relief and that he has thought about his father and missed him more ever since that day in the cemetery. Certainly my own father must have missed his parents as he went through the normal trials and tribulations of child rearing; who else would you naturally turn to for guidance—whether your child was "normal" or not.

As time passed and Tariq didn't speak, my parents and grandparents, my siblings, and my other relatives all kept saying basically the same thing—that Tariq would outgrow this. Instead of being comforted, I felt frustrated and terrified to think about how I would handle it if he never spoke again. Tariq was different from what they expected, so when he was eventually diagnosed with autism, they didn't know what else to say—understandable enough, but it made me feel very alone, and I just wanted time to myself to withdraw.

I believed that I was the only person who had ever felt this way. No one could help me, I thought, because no one else had ever experienced what I was going through. I believed that it was all my responsibility, and that I should be able to handle it. I didn't want to burden others, but sometimes I felt like I was in a land beyond tears and beyond comfort. Everything—toys, playgrounds, clothes, and healthy children—reminded me of the little boy that I had dreamed of and the sorrow that Tariq's silence presented to me. I thought I would never again experience happiness or peace of mind.

There's still more to this set of beliefs that many parents of children with disabilities get into. You start to think that others don't want to hear about your problems because they have enough of their own. It's easy to get tangled in a web of distorted beliefs as you grieve the loss of your "normal" child. You might even believe that it's too hard to find support and that it takes too much energy to explain your situation, so therefore it will be easier to just hold it in and do everything yourself.

Many parents report that their relatives keep bringing up the same thing. The grandparents of one child with a rare terminal illness, for example, kept bringing up their idea that perhaps the illness had been caused by Agent Orange because their son had served in Vietnam. The disease was, in fact, genetic and could not have been caused by Agent Orange, so the grandparents' response brought their son and his wife frustration and provided no comfort. Perhaps it was just too painful for these grandparents to face the idea that they might have transmitted the deadly gene that skipped their generation.

Fortunately, in most cases, the passage of time brings a gift of perspective. It becomes clear that grandparents can have as hard of a time accepting a disability as parents do, or even harder, and their acceptance can take longer. They face the double grief of their grandchild's disability and their own child's pain. The grandmother of a child who was killed in the bombing of the federal office building in Oklahoma City put it this way, "I've lost my grandchild, and I have to watch my baby suffer for the rest of my life."

This second level of grief often renders the grandparents powerless to offer the support that their son or daughter longs for. They may despair that they could not protect their child from this fate; they may worry that they have passed on a defective gene and that it could appear again in another grandchild. They may also feel overwhelmed and guilty that they cannot help more.

Another couple whom I counseled had a problem with their child's grandparents. Jennifer's parents could not grasp why their grandson had so many peculiar repetitive behaviors and why his speech was so limited. They had never heard that neurological damage could cause such problems. They kept asking Jennifer if she had Tommy tested for lead poisoning. No matter how much Jennifer, who is a registered nurse, disclaimed the possibility of lead poisoning, her parents wouldn't give up. She was close to her parents, who watched Tommy when she was at work, so she really wanted them to understand and agree with her. There was a lot of friction between them.

I suggested that more direct information and involvement in Tommy's professional care might be helpful for his grandparents, and I asked Jennifer to bring them to her next therapy session. After introductions and explaining my role with the family, I asked Jennifer's parents if they had any questions about Tommy. Of course, they brought up lead poisoning right away, and Jennifer sighed. Jennifer's mom commented that it was getting hard to talk about this issue. It was clear, nonetheless, that these grandparents wanted to help and that their help was needed and wanted.

In my most dignified and authoritative manner, I explained that the cause of Tommy's limitations was unknown. From reviewing his records, I knew that he had received excellent care at some of the best medical facilities in our area and that there were no indications of lead poisoning. I patiently explained that bringing this up repeatedly was frustrating Jennifer and recommended that they avoid that. Knowing that they were trying in their own way to understand, I suggested that they visit their grandson's classroom and meet and talk to his teachers. I also recommended that they take a look at the books and articles that their daughter had collected related to Tommy's speech and language development.

Hearing this firsthand from a doctor made a difference. I wasn't a part of their family system and was considered an objective source of information and guidance. They could tell that I cared about their grandson and, therefore, couldn't write off my comments as they did their daughter's. Jennifer told me at her next session that her parents had stopped talking about lead poisoning. She felt relieved and was much more comfortable when she was around them. They were reading and getting a better understanding of Tommy's condition.

Looking forward to a warm, indulging role with their grandchildren, grandparents may naturally expect to have pleasure without the responsibilities of being an authority figure that they had with their own children. Being involved with the new generation can be a source of special pride and satisfaction but when confronted by disability, their role is not what they expected. And if they are in some form of denial, they can add to the parents' burden.

The grandparents lose their dreamed-for grandchild who was to be their legacy to future generations just as the parents have lost their dream child. Getting to know their actual grandchild can be more difficult because they are often removed from the child's everyday life and because they may face the dual challenge of supporting their adult child in a time of tremendous need. In these ways, grandparents are affected by what happens in the nuclear family and they also affect those family members. Because they see and hold the child less often, it takes proportionately longer to bond with that child. They actually need help from their children to understand their grandchild's disability, but it takes time for parents to be ready to lead the way.

Once grandparents understand the problem, they can be a great asset. With the experience and wisdom gained from raising their own children, they may have much to offer in sharing coping strategies and in discerning which issues are linked to the disability and which ones are the typical challenges of child rearing. They may also have time to help with many of the practical demands of caring for a grandchild with special needs.

THE MIND–BODY CONNECTION

Although many people temporarily conclude that it is easier to hold in their feelings and do everything themselves, in reality, nothing could be further from the truth. In ancient Greece, Hippocrates, the father of medicine, stressed that emotional factors could be a contributing cause in disease as well as in recovery. In more recent times, research psychologist James Pennebaker and his students have found a mountain of evidence that demonstrates that disclosing our pain when we're suffering through a major upheaval can greatly improve our physical and mental health. Conversely, holding it in can lead to recurrent health problems including colds, the flu, high blood pressure, ulcers, and even cancer.

Having a child with a disability certainly qualifies as a "major upheaval." The inhibition of our upsetting thoughts and feelings is physical work, the burden of which can lead to long-term health problems. People who can open up in a group generally report that they enjoy it and learn from it. In addition, their health notably improves—which incidentally provides the scientific basis for the rapid increase of self-help groups for all sorts of problems.

In *Healing and the Mind*, Bill Moyers interviewed psychiatrist David Speigel of Stanford University Medical School about a groundbreaking study on the mind–body connection. His patients were women with metastatic breast cancer, which kills most women within 2 years. Speigel set out to test the hypothesis that women who received group therapy in addition to standard medical care show an improved quality of life, and they did. The women in the group reported less anxiety, depression, and pain than those who did not take part in group psychotherapy. What startled Speigel some years later when he was reviewing the data was the discovery that those who took part in the group psychotherapy had lived *twice as long* after they entered the study as those who had received only standard medical care. Social isolation is painful and dangerous to physical and mental health, whereas connection and support is healing and promotes physical and mental health. The group therapy was indeed powerful medicine.

According to Pennebaker, writing about our inner turmoil can also be therapeutic. Writing helps us organize and understand our thoughts and feelings. Keeping a journal that we write in with some regularity can, thus, be extremely helpful for our physical and emotional well-being. By translating the feelings about the events into words, we can gain perspective and understanding about ourselves and what has happened.

When you confront upsetting circumstances by talking or in writing, you are often relieved when you find out that you are not alone, and this helps you gain insight into how you feel. Because the federal government estimates that there are as many as 45–50 million people with a disability or chronic illness, there must logically be others not far from you who could view you with empathy and understanding. You need a place to connect and talk freely. With this kind of support, you can see yourself as just an ordinary person who happens to be going through a difficult ordeal, and this may be a great consolation.

Part of the journey to get to the other side of sorrow is to find the people, whether related to us by blood or not, who really want to listen. As Brett Webb-Mitchell pointed out in *God Plays Piano, Too: The Spiritual Lives of Disabled Children,* when someone listens to your story, it is the essential first step in acknowledging your existence. Through telling our stories, we make meaning out of what may seem chaotic. The power in storytelling is that life is an ongoing narrative and can be best understood in this way. It is clear that telling and listening to stories is crucial to human caring and interconnection.

Alas, telling and listening is not always easy. Some people want to avoid adversity and those who are going through it. They may not want to be reminded of how fragile life and health can be, or they may not have enough physical or emotional resources to share. There is a true burden in listening to other people's pain and even a possible health risk, as Pennebaker documented, because the listener may not know how to handle internally what he or she is hearing. One place to find people who can listen is in support groups. These groups are often organized in local school districts to include interested parties of children with various disabilities or they may cover larger geographical areas while limited to specific conditions such as learning disabilities, autism, attention-deficit/hyperactivity disorder, or Down syndrome.

FINDING SUPPORT IN GROUPS

A special kind of camaraderie exists among parents of children with disabilities. Although not related by blood, we are deeply related by our circumstances and can offer each other much comfort and understanding. There is one such group near the central New Jersey shore that usually asks me to facilitate a meeting each spring. In 1996, many in the group had children who were graduating from a half-day preschool program and moving into a full-day kindergarten program. The subject of this particular meeting was the parents' worries and concerns about their young children moving on to another educational setting.

The meeting was held in the morning, so I expected mostly mothers, but a fair number of fathers came and partic-ipated actively. The group had agreed to videotape the session for some people who couldn't attend. The description that fol-lows is based on the complete video record of what happened. What transpired in 90 minutes illustrates the power and po-tential of parent groups to provide a type of support available nowhere else. When the meeting began, I asked people to speak out about their worries. What part of those worries did they think would be the same for any young child, with or without a disability? What part of the worries had to do with special needs? I knew that thinking about these questions and sorting them out has a calming effect. Isolation can be very painful, and connecting with others in a similar situation pro-vides a soothing antidote.

A young mother in her mid-twenties, her red hair pulled back in a ponytail, spoke first. "My child started a full-time program this past fall. I was so worried. I didn't think anyone else could care for her properly. I remember standing with my husband and looking in the one-way window of her classroom and crying. I knew I would miss her, and I did. She's my first child, so I didn't know what to expect. What really helped though was that she came home happy every day. That told me she was well cared for. I felt truly liberated. That feeling washed over the whole house."

With that comment, the meeting was off to a good start. People know that they are cared for when their stories are ap-preciated and taken seriously. The next person to speak was a mother who was about 30 years old or so, obviously more ex-perienced but no less expressive. She recounted, "This little one in special education was the hardest for me to let go of; I think because he is my youngest. I'm not sure what life holds for me now without a child home all day. I'm not sure I can be as free as I could if he was 'normal.' Is this the beginning of the empty nest?"

A mother who worked outside of the home spoke next, adding a somewhat different perspective. "What's really hard for me," she explained, "is how my children have their alert, fun time with another person. My time is caregiving like fixing breakfast and dinner, giving baths, and getting them dressed. There's not much play. I mostly get to discipline them. That hurts. There's more hassles over behavior with the 'special' one, and that pains me even more."

A burly man spoke next. He had been staring so blankly that I had the impression that his eyes were turned inward. "We're glad to be here," he began, apparently speaking also for his wife seated beside him. "When our baby turned 1, he showed us how really far behind our 3-year-old was. I'm really broken up inside."

As his last words trailed off, his wife continued, taking up where he had left off explaining, "He was really slow speaking, and we were devastated, but it's picking up now that he's in a special class. His teacher thinks he's doing really well."

It sounded like her husband was still reeling from his broken dreams. Somehow this man's expression of emotion seemed like the "go ahead" signal for the group to start talking about the harder, darker side of their experiences. The open and direct male expression of emotion often has that effect in a group. Perhaps the women hold back, fearing that the men may shut down and withdraw, leaving them alone to do the group's work. Next, the mother of a child born prematurely told some of her story.

"My child was a preemie—only 3 pounds. I knew right away there were problems. It was difficult for her to see. The doctors in the hospital thought she was mentally retarded. She wasn't just behind because she was born too soon. She developed very slowly. She got all of the early intervention therapies. Still, she didn't walk until 2 months after her second birthday.

Even that was sooner than expected. It's been so hard; I never thought I would make it this far. Now she's 5, and she's not mentally retarded. She won't always be a child as I was told when she was born. It's a great relief; sometimes I cry over it. I'm glad she survived those first months in the intensive care nursery. I'm ready for her to go to school full time. I need a break."

Her voice trailed off; there were tears in her eyes, so she reached for a tissue and looked away from the many eyes looking tenderly on her. At this point, I asked to hear from some more of the men who had been quiet up until now. It was quiet until some laughter broke the silence. A man who identified himself as a carpenter who had been home for the winter because work was slow spoke: "I didn't know how hard it was day in and day out until now. My son is a real handful. Every time it seems that we have things figured out, he goes to the next stage. He doesn't wait for us to catch our breath or anything. It hasn't been easy being out of work, but I am glad that I've gotten to learn all about him at this early age. I never really imagined that. I had thought I would get more involved as he got older, and we would play ball, and go fishing, and work on little projects around the house—you know, the typical father and son stuff. I think this has made me a better father and a better husband. I understand first-hand what my wife goes through. Right now she's at work, and I'm bringing home the information from school. She's bringing home the bread. What a switch!"

"I wish I was in her shoes," said Julie, who'd been the first speaker during the meeting. "Sometimes as soon as my husband gets home, I say 'I'm outta here,' and I'm off to the mall. He's not thrilled, but I just need a break."

Mary, a single mom with frosted hair and a somber expression, said she had twins with attention-deficit/hyperactivity disorder and language delays. She sounded overwhelmed and her voice was pained: "When we are all home together, I can never sit down. I can't get baby sitters. I'm almost 40; my mother is in her seventies, so she can't keep up with them even though she wants to help out. Other people just see my

little boys as wild. It's so sad. That's where my frustrations are
. . . it's a luxury just to sit and read the paper for 10 minutes
when you're a single parent. I'm worn out all the time, so I
don't feel guilty sending them to school for a longer day."

Another father told his story: "There's some kind of miracle happening to my daughter," he began. As people looked
more intensely in response to the idea of a miracle, he explained that his daughter had congenital heart problems and
had needed three major surgeries in her first 3 years. She had
learned to walk at 2 years old and had begun to talk at 3 years
old. "She still has speech problems, but now we can understand her. My wife is her stepmom; I couldn't have done it
without her. We're a real team. I'm a happy man now—I'm no
longer discouraged. We're having a baby."

Several people smiled, sharing his elation. Others looked
rather sober—perhaps contemplating the risks of having another child.

The oldest woman in the room spoke next: "I thought I
was done raising children, but now I'm starting all over again.
My son's wife had multiple sclerosis, and when she passed
away, he and my grandson came to live with us. Fortunately,
my husband is retired and he's home now, so he can help out.
He's amazed. He keeps asking me, 'Was it this hard to raise the
children?' And for the most part, as I tell him each time he
asks, 'Yes, it was.' Their speech was normal, but everything
else was the same."

The wisdom implicit in this woman's experience lent a
helpful perspective to the group. Many different living situations were represented in the room; the group was a micro-
cosm for the outside world. After the grandmother spoke, I intervened to ask what was going on in the room and what
direction the group wanted the rest of the meeting to take.

Julie spoke again: "It has been so good hearing from others, especially about the normal parts of this kind of life with
a special child. This helps me to feel more normal."

"Let's start a list with our names and numbers," suggested
a woman who had been silent up until now.

"What will we do with the list?" I asked.

"My son doesn't have any friends in our neighborhood," answered the woman who had suggested the list. "I wouldn't mind taking him over and being with the twins for a few hours, so Mary can get a break. I know her children from school, and I can relate to them. If they run around with my Billie and scream and play, that would be fine with me, and Billie would love it."

"What else do we want for ourselves from each other?" I inquired, to keep this trend going.

"Just a couple of hours for ourselves once in a while, maybe at someone's home with coffee and doughnuts. I'll volunteer my house," said Sallie, the grandmother who spoke earlier.

"That would be great to do without the kids," said Julie. "We could also have a playgroup at my house with the kids. I have a big fenced-in backyard with swings and a sandbox. We could drink lemonade and relax a little on a nice day while the kids have fun."

"Some of us guys might want to get together and do something like hit a few golf balls or shoot a few baskets," added Dan, the carpenter. His suggestion reflected the typically male mode of being together in an activity as opposed to just getting together to talk and share experiences, a more female style.

With time running out, I asked for someone to sum up the meeting. Sallie took the floor, commenting, "When we can get together and talk like this, it's pretty clear that we're just ordinary people. That feels really, really good."

Many parents don't find their way to a group like this until it seems that there is no place to go. When relatives and friends don't know what to say, other parents of children with disabilities provide a perspective and support that is available nowhere else. It is calming to share your fears and insecurities without having to do a lot of explaining. You don't have to worry about appearing weak or asking for pity.

There is also the practical benefit of learning from each other's experience. Talking to people with older children who have survived shows that having a child with a disability is not the end of the world. Parents of children even a year or two older can give a preview of what lies ahead. You can get positive but realistic ideas about what the future holds. It can also be easier to talk to a fellow parent than to a professional who, while knowledgeable, has not lived with a child with special needs and has not experienced the emotional roller coaster of everyday life with such a child.

Another wonderful aspect of participating in a parent support group is being able to experience giving as well as receiving help. There are moments when you need help and moments when you may be the person with the answer or a helpful comment. A parent who can give as well as receive is stronger and more self-confident. He or she can reach out to others in a way that was not possible before. It used to be commonly accepted that the blind couldn't lead the blind, but the self-help movement has taught us otherwise.

SUPPORT IN CYBERSPACE

The current explosion of on-line services has exponentially increased the possibilities for connecting with other parents of children with special needs. Computer prices have come down, making it easier to "surf the net." Unfortunately, we still live in a society where equal access to resources of all sorts is very much an issue. The Internet has the ability, however, to be an equalizer. Although many parents don't have the ability to spend the time or money to utilize this service, it only takes one interested person to share information with a group. As more and more public libraries and schools provide access to the Internet, more and more communities will be able to take full advantage of what it can offer.

A woman I know through my local chapter of the Autism Society has made me more aware of just how dynamic the Internet can be. She asked her friends in cyberspace to comment for this book on how the Internet has been helpful in their role as parents. Here is a sampling of their e-mail responses:

Emily wrote that the Internet disabilities lists have been great for her because they are available when she needs them,

24 hours a day, 7 days a week. She doesn't have to find a baby sitter in order to attend her support group meeting because her meeting is at home. She can use those precious hours when a baby sitter is available to go out with her husband. Because up-to-date information is not available in her local library, and a majority of what is available is written for a professional audience, the Internet is beneficial to Emily. The information on the Internet lists is by parents for parents on "the real nuts and bolts of dealing with a child with special needs that is often not an area that schools or doctors are much help with." Emily also felt a large part of her frustration and anger diminishing as she realized how many other people were in the same boat. As she put it, "I stopped feeling as weird, or as if I was to blame, and became empowered to try things that worked for other kids. Even if the tips don't work (they don't always work, darn it), the helpless feelings I used to be plagued by have largely gone away." The Internet provided Emily with the kind of information and support that she needed most. She is now more self-confident because she knows more about her son's disability than many of the professionals she deals with. She reports that she is far less depressed and has even stopped taking Prozac, replacing it with a "holistic antidepressant—getting and giving help on the Internet."

Janette responded from a fairly remote part of the English speaking world—Perth, Australia. Computer-aided communication has helped her learn about the alternative therapies for children with autism that professionals in her area were reluctant to suggest or even tell her about, such as auditory training, epsom salts, special diets, and so forth. Janette also commented that the Internet "is also a place to make friends through the shared common thread of autism. . . What else are friendships made from if not common beliefs, common ideas, shared experiences."

In this vein, Tammy noted that when her child shows some improvement, she can share it with all of her friends on the Internet who get really excited at the news, unlike others who may not understand her joy in seeing even the smallest steps forward by her child as a miracle.

Rosita wrote about how much brighter and more meaningful her son's future looks thanks to the Internet. Through the real, caring friends that she met in cyberspace, she learned everything from how to stand up to her school system to how to enjoy her child and get him to hug her. With this confidence, she became the best advocate for her son and spoke effectively for him because he couldn't do it for himself.

GETTING HELP FROM OTHERS

You get more support when you are strong enough to ask for it and when you can make the first move. Although most parents feel abandoned when they are isolated from others by the wall of their sorrow, more often than not, there are kind people nearby waiting for a cue as to how to help. In *The Lost Art of Listening*, Michael Nichols explored how to listen and be listened to. The heart of the problem, according to Nichols, is reactive emotions that trigger hurt, anger, or fear in the listener, which in turn triggers defensiveness and blocks understanding and concern. Furthermore, when we talk to people we are close to about what upsets us, they may feel implicated and tell us not to feel that way, thus prompting misunderstanding and conflict. An empathic, accepting response, however, would be to say, "Tell me more about how you feel," or "What's that like for you?"

Once we understand our own grief and our child's disability, then we can explain it to others. This frequently ends the awkwardness described previously, particularly when we are at a loss for words about our child's problem.

We can often get what we want by asking for it. We can tell people, for example, that we just need to talk and need them to just listen. Likewise, we could explain that we have a problem that we need to discuss but that we're not expecting them to come up with a solution. This approach releases the listener from the responsibility for solving the problem or making the pain go away.

Support groups, as well as professional guidance, can help us learn how to reach out to others. A therapist or fellow par-

ent isn't responsible for your problems and therefore is unlikely to get defensive when told of them. After you learn to
listen and be listened to, you can practice these skills almost
anywhere with great results.

For example, the parents of a child with a disability often
have friends with children of the same age. It may become difficult to ask them how their little boy or girl is doing because
it brings up your pain. Friends, in turn, may back off a little,
worrying that hearing about their child's accomplishments
may make the parents of a child with special needs feel worse.
Bridging these gaps whenever possible is a hurdle to get over
in regaining normalcy for parents.

After Tariq was diagnosed and was attending the Center
for Autistic Children, I came across old pictures of Tariq and
Leo, my friend Charley's son. I realized what had held me back
from calling my friend, so I picked up the telephone, somewhat unsure of what response I would get. My ambivalence
subsided when I heard Charley's voice. It was as if he had been
there all along, just waiting. Resuming our friendship, we
caught up on each other's lives: Tariq's diagnosis, Leo's interests, Antoinette's development, my divorce, his two other sons
born in the interim, our careers, and the infant born too soon
that he and Michelle had lost. Grief had divided us and now
sharing it had reunited us.

My friend Dave, however, who I met in graduate school,
does not have children and perhaps that made it easier for me
to maintain our friendship throughout the years since Tariq was
born. Dave has a wonderful ability to listen and reflect without
backing off. (As David Speigel told his medical students at Stanford: *"If you see someone crying, don't just do something, stand there.*
Be with them a few minutes and let them know that you're
open to their discomfort. It doesn't take a lot of sophistication.
It just takes knowing what to do in a difficult situation.")

Dave was always just there when I called. When Tariq was
4 years old, Dave helped me make a video of me working with
Tariq to use as a baseline to measure Tariq's progress. Dave's
keen memory for the sequence of events also served as a point
of reference for me over the years. When he called, he was
never intrusive. Several years ago, when his mother died un-

expectedly, he sent word to me through a mutual friend. I was glad that he had remembered me in his hour of grief. I had learned by then that there was nothing better than just being there for a friend. Sharing our losses cemented the bond of our friendship.

When *Family Pictures* was on television, Dave called to tell me about it. "I'm not sure if you'll be into watching it," he said, "but I thought you would want to know about it." The door was always open, and he was very perceptive—for there were times that I wouldn't have been up for watching a movie about a family with a child with autism.

The passing of time and contact with Tariq helped my family understand how they could help. I remember vividly getting a telephone call from my youngest brother, Greg, who wanted to meet me for dinner and offer whatever help he could for Tariq. We shared dinner in a Chinese restaurant where he insisted that I accept his financial help to get Tariq to the Option Institute. What a reversal of roles that was—Greg is 15 years my junior and I was used to looking out for him. When I went out with him while I was in college, people sometimes took him for my son. The money that he had offered was sorely needed, but his sentiment was the invaluable jewel of that occasion that will always glisten in my memory.

My sister Luci also made a perceptive overture that stands out in my memory. When Tariq was little, and I was exhausted and beat up from living in the survival mode from day to day, she offered to watch him and Antoinette for an afternoon or an evening so that I could get a break and just do something that I wanted. What a welcome respite that was! It was one of the most thoughtful gifts that I have ever received.

When Tariq entered the residential program at Devereux, my grandfather asked if we could visit so that he could see what it was like. This was how I discovered firsthand how seeing a child's school can help relatives to understand. Pop was old and frail. We sat on a picnic bench in the fenced-in yard behind Tariq's unit. My grandfather watched the other children intensely; many looked outwardly more impaired than Tariq.

Pop turned, looked at me intently, and stated his conclusion of many years of observation: "Robert, you have had a hard life." I nodded, feeling a lump in my throat and a twitch in my eyes. From that day forward, my grandfather never talked about Tariq outgrowing his condition. He understood something at Devereux that words could never have accomplished. I realized that I should take my parents to see Tariq there. When the next Family Day was held, they came to the picnic with the other families and children at Devereux. That encounter helped them, too, to understand in a way that they hadn't previously. Being able to bring my family to Devereux and benefiting from the experience showed that I was getting stronger.

CONNECTING WITH LAUGHTER

In their camaraderie, parents of children with special needs can share a special kind of laughter. It is an antidote to the sorrow sometimes caused by everyday events. Those who can relate to your sorrow can understand your laughter. Over the years, many parents have told me that developing a sense of humor about their situation has been a key to finding the strength to get through the hard times.

R. Wayne Gilpin, the father of a child with autism and the former president of the Autism Society of America, has collected a volume of stories titled *Laughing & Loving with Autism: A Collection of "Real Life" Warm and Humorous Stories*. The stories are about his son, Alex, as well as about many other children and adults with autism. These accounts are based on the literal interpretations of things that children with autism make. They see things exactly as they are presented and, in so doing, highlight the humor in how seriously "normal" people often view the same words or deeds. The incidents described, like real life, are simultaneously funny and touching.

The logic of a child with a mental disability, such as autism, may be hard to refute. One example in Gilpin's book involved his son coming to dinner with no socks on. When asked to put on some socks before dinner, Alex responded, "But, Dad, if I drop food, I'll get my socks dirty!" Another instance was described by the parent of a young boy struggling to find the right word to express himself. When his dad told him, "Spit it out, son!" the boy stopped talking and spit. Then he continued trying to find the right word.

In my own life, even the lack of speech did not stop Tariq from developing a sense of humor. Soon after he was toilet trained around 4 years of age, he began to signal that he needed to use the bathroom by tugging at his pants and sometimes pulling them part or all of the way down. I would rush him to the bathroom before he could have an "accident." Sometimes, while trying to get him to bed, he would do the same thing. When we got to the bathroom, he didn't have to go. He would laugh—deep and hearty from the belly—the joke was on me.

Often, I have heard parents spontaneously sharing funny stories or situations at meetings and conferences. One woman I know always gets a kick out of telling how she finds time to vacuum. Parents of young children can't do this when the children are napping because it will wake them up and when they are awake it will scare them. Her son has a severe hearing loss, so she runs the vacuum while he is napping. "I have the cleanest floors of any of my friends," she always likes to remark with a smile. What she seems to enjoy even more is how much other parents in similar situations understand and enjoy her sense of humor.

Another mother told me about how she was rushing one evening to get her family ready to go to the movies together. "Hurry up," she told them, "so that we can get good seats." Her 9-year-old-son, who needed a wheelchair because he had cerebral palsy, spoke up, "That doesn't bother me, Mom; I'm bringing my own seat."

Laughter like this in your everyday life has a practical value. In *Head First: The Biology of Hope*, Norman Cousins described how 10 minutes of solid belly laughter would give him 2 hours of pain-free sleep while he was suffering from severe inflammation of the spine and joints that caused great difficulty in sleeping. Cousins's experience has been corroborated by medical research that shows that laughter helps the body to produce brain chemicals called *endorphins*—with benefits including lower blood pressure, enhanced respiration, relaxed muscles, and increased numbers of disease-fighting immune cells.

Cousins regarded laughter as a metaphor for the full range of positive emotions including hope, love, determination, purpose, and a strong will to live. These promote physiological well-being as much as the negative inhibited emotions can damage our health. I highly recommend this book, which also includes a list of humorous books and movies used as a resource by the Duke University Comprehensive Cancer Center.

Donald Nathanson suggests that the pain associated with withdrawing from distressing or embarrassing situations can be relieved by comedy. According to the affect theory of Silvan Tomkins, anything that causes a rapid reduction in whatever is going on in the central nervous system will stimulate laughter. Comedian Buddy Hackett said in an interview reported in Nathanson's book, *Shame and Pride: Affect, Sex, and the Birth of the Self,* that whenever he creates laughter, he releases people from pain. In the joy of the moment, whatever is causing physical or emotional pain is released. What a blessing of our inborn human nature!

As attested by famous examples such as Christy Brown and Helen Keller, a positive outlook can help a child develop as fully as possible. Even if a child doesn't accomplish as much as these role models, the quality of family life is always greatly improved through a hearty sense of the comedy in everyday life. In fact, this was one of the common characteristics that I found in my doctoral study of families who had coped successfully with disability. Each and every family told me that a sense of humor had helped them survive and even prevail through the problems they faced. As Johann Wolfgang von Goethe observed long ago, a person's joy is doubled when it is shared with others.

There are many lessons on this journey of connection and support as we are drawn together by our similarities—meeting through tears and laughter. It takes courage to acknowledge the hurt of grief and loneliness and to thereby risk being hurt again. But that risk is necessary to get to the other side of sorrow. Whether we are related by chance or choice, we must learn to accept and honor our differences. When we do this, we can then divide our sorrow, multiply our joys, and make connections to support us through a lifetime.

10

A Perilous Partnership

Parents and Professionals

*W*hat we really need from professionals is empathy for our situation and good services for our children. When we don't get one or the other, we tend to doubt them and ourselves and usually get angry in the process. From my own experience, as well as the testimonies of countless other parents, professionals lacking in feeling and hope and who seem to be just doing their jobs provoke sharp resentment. It is rare to meet a parent who doesn't have a horror story or two about a doctor or the educational system. Yet, professionals who are compassionate and hopeful and who take a special interest in the family are kindly remembered and effusively praised.

The anger and anxiety experienced when parents seek help can be simultaneously intense, confusing, and energizing. As many parents can testify, it would be next to impossible to get over the hurdles and through the maze of obtaining the proper services for their child without the tremendous energy and determination that derives from uncomfortable but motivating feelings.

Anger is difficult to decipher and doing so is part of "emotional intelligence." Daniel Goleman quoted no older an authority than Aristotle on this subject: "Anyone can become angry—that is easy. But to be angry with the right person, to the right degree, at the right time, for the right purpose, and in the right way—this is not easy." Although Aristotle understood the dilemma, modern mandated policies on children with disabilities and their parents' rights, along with the psychological concept of assertiveness, give us the tools to be angry in the "right way."

The best outcomes for children and families happen when parents and professionals work as partners with mutual respect and shared decision-making power. Parents, by virtue of their bond with their child, are true authorities in their own right, with information to contribute that no one else has access to. Professionals, however, through training and experience, can offer expertise and a broad perspective that parents alone don't have. Each has only partial knowledge, with complete expertise only possible in the partnership. Their combined viewpoint should be the basis for decisions, plans, and goals.

Parents' relationships with professionals are born out of necessity and desperation during a time of grief and are therefore rife with opportunities for misunderstanding and conflict. You don't want to be there in the first place. No one wants to spend countless hours having his or her infant diagnosed and treated in offices, clinics, hospitals, and special schools by doctors, therapists, psychologists, teachers, social workers, and so forth. You simply want someone to fix your child and your dream—to take your pain away.

The denial, anxiety, guilt, shame, depression, and anger of the grief process (as discussed in previous chapters) occur repeatedly, and sometimes several of these feelings arise simultaneously. You don't want teams of professionals peeking over your shoulder asking questions. After all, parenting is very personal and many of the questions may lead parents to doubt themselves and wonder whether they are to blame for their child's problem. These are understandably difficult waters to navigate, and parents are understandably impatient with professionals who don't seem to grasp the intricacies of the situation.

Professionals, however, have their own stresses in handling administrative pressures, paperwork, large caseloads, upset parents, and their own professional goals and ideals. Professionals are human, too, and they have emotional reactions of their own while diagnosing and treating children that they care about. As they bond with the children in their care and work for their development, they experience many of the same emotions as the parents—from excitement with a child's new achievement to discouragement at a child's lack of progress to anger when they are powerless to provide services that they really want to.

Unfortunately, most professionals who work with children have had little formal training in how to understand parents' natural reactions to disability and are unsure about how to work with the parents and the child as a unit. When a parent is visibly anxious or depressed, professional observers quite naturally speculate about what effect this might have on the child's development and want the parent to "calm down" and "cheer up." What is often missing is the realization that accepting those feelings helps to facilitate the parents' grief and therefore also helps the child as the parent learns how to face the future with hope and enjoys being with his or her child.

As the parent of a child with spina bifida, professional writer Gilbert Gaul, in *Giant Steps: The Story of One Boy's Struggle to Walk,* helped us understand why these early experiences with professionals are so intense. Gaul wrote about how parents don't readily give up the heroic image of the physician. We want to believe that doctors are next to God and can make our children whole and healed. If our expectations weren't so high, it might be easier to change them and there might be less anger, which routinely accompanies unmet expectations. Although easier said than done, we have no choice but to accept the limitations of medical science and its practitioners in order to function as partners over the long haul for our children.

As we try to implement this principle, we discover the barriers on both sides of the partnership when dealing with today's dominant medical model of providing services in many public and private agencies. In this system, services are provided from the top down and primary expertise and decision-making power is squarely with the professional partner. Some parents have had negative experiences with professionals or authority figures. These can be carried over to the new situation, contributing to parents' justifiable anger and making trust and collaboration difficult. Parents who are also professionals have a special view of this dilemma that can be helpful for others on both sides of it.

A UNIQUE PERSPECTIVE

No matter who you are before your child is diagnosed with a disability or chronic illness, you can never be prepared for what is to come. It can help to hear from people you think know how to handle things—perhaps with less anger, worry, and frustration than you. In 1992, at a family conference for parents and professionals, Paul and Penny LeBuffe collaborated in a presentation titled *From Mental Health Professionals to Special Needs Parents,* about their personal experience as parents.

Paul and Penny worked at the Devereux Foundation, a residential facility in West Chester, Pennsylvania, for children with severe disabilities who could not be cared for at home and educated in public schools. (Tariq was a student there from 1988 to 2001.) Penny had been a residential counselor and supervisor and then served as an admissions representative. Paul had been a research psychologist. They found that they were not as prepared as they had imagined for parenting a child with special needs, but having hundreds of people listen to their story had helped them find meaning and purpose in their family life. Penny credited Ann Turnbull, a well-known parent/professional from the Beach Center on Families and Disability at The University of Kansas, for pointing out that academic degrees can sometimes be a hindrance.

Penny's first conversation with a caseworker about her daughter, Katy, was seared into her memory, and like so many parents, myself included, she could recall exactly what was said. "It was like being run over by a truck," Penny said.

Me with the Devereux staff who have worked with Tariq over many years.

Until Katy's 16th month, Paul and Penny thought that they had a Gerber baby, but then her vocabulary stopped developing. Katy kept using the same five or six words and was still cruising around holding on to the furniture without walking independently. In their search for confirmation that something was wrong, Paul and Penny were told that they were overanxious. Although this was not unusual, these parents in particular *knew* that something was wrong. Katy's pediatrician had guaranteed that she would walk and was alarmed when she didn't because he had predicted it.

After 2 years of tests, Katy was found to have a rare, progressive, degenerative neurological disorder. It was likely to be a terminal condition, and she was losing the skills that she had developed prior to 16 months of age. The people in the audience gasped when they heard this. "I didn't know what to say to make Penny feel better," Paul commented. The grief had to take its course and wash over them as they contemplated whether their daughter would be happy, whether she would have friends, and whether she would ever live outside of their home. These concerns are common to parents and come with them to every interaction with professionals, and in the short run, there are no answers that make you feel better.

Geneticists told Paul and Penny that there was a one in four chance that they would have another child with the same disorder. In a stroke of good fortune, the couple had already conceived their second child, Denise, by the time that they found out what was wrong with Katy. Paul told the audience that day that the new infant kept them "sane." Many couples, such as the Greens described in a previous chapter, have had similar experiences that heal their pain and anguish when they conceive a typical child. Unfortunately, others in similar situations are terrified, with good reason, to try again for a typical child because they are tempting fate and could lose the genetic lottery for a second time, having a second child with special needs.

It's a shame that so many professionals seem to be un-aware of the intensity of the emotions that parents feel despite the fact that the couple may be holding hands and wiping tears as they sit through a meeting. Perhaps the couple is being asked for the tenth or twentieth time to recount their child's early development. Although professionals may indeed be so overloaded and swamped with paperwork that they cannot read every report, this all too common experience is infuriatingly unacceptable. Penny and Paul had to reiterate the same information three times during the same visit to a well-known medical center for an operation for their child. No matter what your education or prior experience, there is no way to bypass the pain. It can even be harder for professionals who may expect to have an easier time getting through it because of their education and experience.

Paul and Penny concluded by challenging a current prac-tice of "professionalizing" parents by asking them to serve as co-therapists and co-teachers. This approach often leaves par-ents with little time to hold and cuddle their children and each other. It is a part of the parents' job to obtain services for their child but above all to love and nurture that child. This is where floor time described in previous chapters is so valuable in guiding parents into loving, satisfying, growth-inducing rela-tionships with their children whether specially challenged or typically developing. "We're parents and that's enough," as Paul and Penny said in their conclusion.

The story that they told was reminiscent of the collection of essays titled *Parents Speak Out: Then and Now* edited by Rud and Ann Turnbull. It is a unique book about disabilities because the editors and contributors are all professionals in the field and parents or relatives of someone with a disability. Their perspective highlights the tremendous challenges of living normally while relating to and caring for a person with a disability. Even competent, loving, and well-trained parents who work in the field sometimes feel overwhelmed when dealing with the "system."

David, a physician and the father of a boy with leukemia, spoke to me frankly on this theme. As he put it, "When you're dealing with your own child, things suddenly hit home. . . . No matter how much training you have, you don't appreciate what someone else in this circumstance goes through until you experience it yourself. In a way, being a physician was a disadvantage. As a lay person, you tend to attribute more abilities to doctors than they actually have. The limits of medicine are far greater than most people realize. As a doctor, I knew that, and I knew that everything isn't curable. Someone who is not a doctor is better off because it is easier to have faith in the medical establishment when you are not a member of that establishment. As a doctor, I knew the limits all too well."

FROM BIRTH TO DIAGNOSIS: THE MEDICAL PERSPECTIVE

Let's take a closer look at how misunderstandings arise between parents and professionals so that we can explore how to close the gap and develop a working alliance. Many children with special needs present a complex clinical picture for doctors. The obstetrician presides at the birth and the pediatrician is on the front line thereafter as the child is seen for immunizations and checkups throughout the early years. But, unless the child is diagnosed at birth or even before (as in the case of Down syndrome), parents usually suspect a problem before anyone else. Because every child is unique and development is often uneven, the doctor, like the parents, may have no choice but to "wait and see." Likewise, both parent and doctor may unconsciously minimize the problem because neither party wants it to exist.

When there is fear and worry, parents are hungry for reassurance, and doctors may be reluctant to confront them with the possibilities or even the bleak truth. Doctors, like parents, can deny their observations or the implications and conclusions of those observations in order to avoid the pain of the ensuing helplessness if there is no easy cure and the painful obligation to tell the parents. A good physician knows all too well the limits of medical science.

As Norman Cousins pointed out, the physician–patient relationship is a powerful medicine in its own right. Parents worried about disability or chronic illness long for a closer link to their child's doctor, which can help them manage their fears while waiting for answers that only come with time.

Any child's developmental problem and the parents' ensuing pain touches doctors and may provoke anxiety and make communication awkward. Parent and professional Helen Featherstone reported on her interviews of several physicians who clearly saw themselves as lightning rods for parents' denial, anger, and anxiety. Because no one wants to be in this position, this may explain why many parents are referred to specialists and shuffled around until they finally get answers to their hard questions and get a straightforward diagnosis.

Even in the most clear-cut diagnostic workup, some form of parental denial usually arises as part of the spontaneous expression of grief. As psychologist and parent Ken Moses explains, the loss is so personal and elusive that few are aware at the time of what they are experiencing. Physicians, however, may take this denial personally when they have to convince parents of what is best for their child. But along with the doctors' "truth," parents also need validation by those doctors of *their* "truth"—that life at that moment has been changed forever and that the loss of their perfect child is momentarily unacceptable. Imagine being asked to trust and believe someone who is telling you that one of your worst nightmares has come true!

The complexity of many developmental problems requires assessment by various specialists, so evaluation at a children's hospital or university medical center by a multidisciplinary team is the best way to get the expertise needed without minimal frustration. The primary care doctor may be slow to make this kind of referral, believing that the parents aren't ready for it or because of his or her reluctance to relinquish control to specialists.

Doctors are understandably cautious in the diagnostic process and generally would rather go slowly and "wait and see," not wanting to err in such a serious matter. Proper treatment, of course, depends on accurate diagnosis, but parents are eager to find out what's wrong and move on to cure their child. No one enjoys being in the dark, so these two very different perspectives unavoidably generate conflict and uneasiness on both sides.

Parents' anxieties can be further heightened when doctors use medical jargon instead of down-to-earth language to explain their concerns and uncertainties. The jargon can sometimes get in the way of feelings that need to be addressed. Being rushed in and out of the examining room compounds the problem.

Many of the horror stories that parents tell have a recurring theme: an overly negative prognosis. The doctor in the hospital said "that my child would never walk," "that my child would be a vegetable," "that my child would never live independently," "that my child will need to be institutionalized." These statements are commonly heard. Even if a doctor hasn't given such a prognosis, a parent may assume it in the dark, devastating moments first following the horrible news. Pediatrician T. Berry Brazelton recommends that physicians first help the parents find the child's strengths and delay a realistic discussion of prognosis to a postdiagnostic conference, giving parents time to absorb the diagnosis.

I discovered inadvertently how radically my perceptions of professionals changed over time. Readers will recall that when Tariq was finally diagnosed with pervasive developmental disorder at 4 years of age at the hospital where he was born, I was furious with the multidisciplinary team. I vividly remember how I wanted to reach across the table and strangle the people who were telling me that my little boy would never be normal. When I returned with Tariq for a re-evaluation 4 years later, they seemed like kind, caring people. I could see the concern in their eyes as I contemplated why they looked so different from the first time when they had seemed cold, distant, and aloof. The main difference was in me: I was over the shock that came with hearing my son's diagnosis—not to mention that Tariq, the team, and myself were all 4 years older and presumably wiser.

Many of those who tell the angriest stories have never confronted or revisited the personnel who inspired their anger. They may unconsciously need their anger as an exterior focus—a means of protecting their spouse and their child from that anger. In my case, I only revisited the scene because my lawyer recommended a re-evaluation by the same team as evidence for a due process hearing before an impartial arbitrator. The re-evaluation turned out to be serendipitous; it helped me to turn off an angry tape that had been playing in my head. My anger hadn't been wrong or bad, for it was part of my grief, but it wasn't good to displace it onto others or to hold a grudge. I was relieved when I was able to let it go and breathe normally again.

Some readers may find my outlook on the medical profession too forgiving. It may be true in some cases—but doctors are people, too, and they can be good, bad, or mediocre; moreover, even the best make mistakes and have weaknesses. I recommend that readers who are dissatisfied with their child's doctor discuss their problems with him or her and try to resolve them. You can ask for an "extended consultation" so that your doctor will have plenty of time for your discussion and you won't feel rushed. If discussion does not resolve your problems and the negative feelings that accompany them, then seek another doctor in whom you can trust and rely. You need that kind of relationship with your child's pediatrician for yourself as well as for your child. Other parents of children with disabilities are a fine source of referrals in your search for an understanding physician. The books by pediatrician Mark L. Batshaw listed in the bibliography at the end of this book may also be helpful as a source of medical information about various disabilities. Dr. Batshaw himself had learning disabilities and attention-deficit/hyperactivity disorder. He credits his mother's devotion to his development as the motivation for his eventual success—and he became a developmental pediatrician because of his desire to help other children like him.

EARLY INTERVENTION: THE EDUCATIONAL PERSPECTIVE

Day by day, after diagnosis, parents live with their children and learn to love them as they are. Although grief can be prolonged over a matter of years and through the life cycle, the most intense and immobilizing initial reactions are usually short-lived, lasting at most a few months. After that time, most parents are strongly motivated to find the best programs that they can to maximize their child's achievements. Once goals have been re-adjusted, most parents will find meaning and joy in their child's accomplishments, no matter how small.

Just as parents have no control over the problem, they are also not in control of the services available to resolve it—even though these services have become more accessible since the enactment of the Education for All Handicapped Children Act of 1975, PL 94-142, which was championed by parent organizations such as the Pennsylvania Arc and through subsequent legislation. Many parents report long searches to find information about their child's disability, early intervention, preschool programs, speech and physical therapies, and other community resources, such as respite care. When a child has an uncommon problem, such as pervasive developmental disorder, deaf-blindness, or an even rarer chronic illness, the search for services can be even longer and more torturous, particularly in rural areas where shortages of experienced service professionals are common.

Because early intervention services are federally mandated, fortunately, most parents find adequate services easily; others may still find them only with persistence, advocacy, and sometimes legal representation. Take the example of Cynthia and Eric, whose 3-year-old daughter, Jessica, is deaf and has cerebral palsy. She was assigned by the local school district to a preschool classroom for children with multiple disabilities in a wheelchair-accessible building—which was fine, but there were two major problems. First, every other child in the class had mental retardation, whereas Jessica's intelligence was above average according to specialized testing that she had received. Second, her teacher did not know sign language and had no experience with children with hearing impairments. The school district adamantly refused to change Jessica's placement maintaining that it was "appropriate." Fortunately for Jessica, her parents filed for due process and retained an attorney.

Prior to a hearing, the district conceded and offered a placement in a specialized setting where the teacher was trained in sign language and other techniques for educating children with hearing impairments and in a classroom where there were various I.Q. levels plus accommodations for physical disabilities. Is it any wonder that there are embittered parents?

Mary's 5-year-old son, Pete, who was diagnosed with pervasive developmental disorder, also had a poor initial placement. In her quest for information, Mary had read about the breakthroughs that are sometimes possible through facilitated communication. When she requested this kind of help for her child through her local early intervention program, she was told that it was too expensive and that no one in the region knew how to do it. Unfortunately, Mary hadn't been told the truth. The department of education in her state provided assistive technology and technical assistance to local programs under a federal grant that was well publicized to early intervention programs and schools. Fortunately for Pete, his mom didn't accept what she was first told and called a parent advocate who gave her the information that she needed to get her request taken seriously. Consequently, Pete received specialized help as well as facilitated communication and is benefiting from them.

Although instances such as those cited here are far too common, they are more the exception than the rule. But these injustices should not occur at all, and parent groups can help keep them to a minimum. Exchanging information helps parents to be more assertive in advocating for their children's rights.

The struggle involved is worth it; those who refuse to give up, like Christy Brown's mother, are rewarded. Study after study has shown that when children receive early intervention services, they progress more rapidly and further than children who do not receive such services. Generally, parents can see this progress during the preschool years, prior to age 5, and are heartened and relieved to witness their child's growth.

Once a child has found suitable placement, strong bonds often develop between parents and their child's therapists and teachers. These bonds often are closer than those with the child's physicians. The doctors were the messengers for the bad news and got caught in the cross-fire, and it may have been hard for parents to think of them as kind, caring professionals. Yet, teachers and therapists in early intervention services are usually seen as allies as parents come to a realistic acceptance of their child's disability and limitations. Tariq's primary therapist once arrived on our doorstep on Christmas Eve with a present for him as well as one for my daughter Antoinette—a sensitive gesture that I will never forget.

SCHOOL YEARS: ENTERING THE MAINSTREAM

Most parents have come to terms with their child's disabilities, have realistic goals and expectations, and are attempting to live as normal a life as possible by the beginning of the school years. Our educational system, however, is structured to meet the needs of typical children, and it doesn't always meet the needs of those who are exceptional. Parents and educators often disagree on what is best for the child. When placements are made for the convenience of the school system as opposed to meeting the needs of the child, conflict results. There may also be disagreements over related services, such as speech, occupational, or physical therapies, that the schools must provide.

Another common concern is the inclusion of children with disabilities with their same-age peers as much as possible that is mandated by current federal legislation. It is common to hear educators say that parents are unrealistic while parents, in turn, complain that educators' expectations for their child are too low. These differences in expectations are a frequent sore point in the parent–professional relationship. But, if your child's needs cannot be met in a typical classroom with added special education support staff, he or she may be better served in what is called a *self-contained* special education classroom.

Conflict between parents and educators is common, and I'd like to offer some suggestions on how to bridge the gap. Unfortunately, criticism of parents is common within the culture of schools. Just like parents, however, teachers are rewarded and encouraged by children's successes. Problems in learning and behavior leave them frustrated, sad, and unsure of their competence. Because no one wants to feel inadequate, is it any wonder that parents and teachers spend so much time and energy blaming each other for a child's difficulties? This dynamic is, of course, intensified in special education.

The Feelings Checklist in Chapter 2 has been used in sensitivity training with groups comprised of parents and professionals by the New Jersey Department of Education's Division of Special Education. When responses are compared, parents and educators have remarkably similar responses when asked to check off the feelings that they experienced during a typical day either with their child or one of their students. In the ensuing discussion, the walls came down as each party gained an appreciation for the other's role and perspective. This type of dialogue can facilitate making collaborative decisions.

It is not uncommon to hear professionals say that it is a relief to go home to typical children. One teacher remarked in a group that every afternoon when she picks her children up from child care, she hugs them with tears in her eyes and gives thanks that they are still healthy and growing typically. Parents who hear comments like that are likewise thankful and relieved to lessen the emotional distance between themselves and those who serve their children. Although educators have been trained and are expected to be affectively neutral, that is a myth that undermines partnership. It is not possible to work diligently with a child and not develop an emotional bond, and parents should appreciate this attachment.

Upon hearing how much educators care, parents frequently remark that they are impressed with how many children and their very unique needs are taken care of in an average professional workday along with paperwork and other bureaucratic duties. In addition, they wonder how professionals "have enough left" at home for their own families. Responses such as this in the dialogue that follows the Feelings Checklist encourage professionals to keep on giving because their care is appreciated. "Burnout" is much more common among professionals who are not recognized for their caring.

Likewise, in these discussions, when educators hear about parents' grief and frustrations directly, they are often moved to be more understanding and less concerned with issues such as "realistic goals" and parents' denial. When professionals are contemplating what it would be like to go home to a child who does not sleep through the night, or who is not completely toilet trained, or who is medically fragile, then a different attitude and tone pervade the dialogue. Parents are often impressed with how difficult it would be to deal with so many angry, frustrated, and desperate people who want answers that are beyond the professionals' control and have trouble hearing and understanding the answers that they do get. One lesson of this type of training activity is that professionals as well as parents need to share memories, dilemmas, and insights as they learn to listen better.

Outside of a structured situation with an experienced facilitator, the kind of dialogue described here may be difficult to begin in everyday life. The schools where parents and professionals meet, as Seligman and Darling explained in *Ordinary Families, Special Children: A Systems Approach to Childhood Disability,* are the "turf" of the professionals, and, therefore, parents often find them intimidating. Not to mention the fact that in team meetings to plan a child's program and goals the parent or parents are outnumbered by teachers, psychologists, social workers, learning consultants, and various therapists. Such a setup does not promote equal value for parents' input, and without serious effort the professional views will dominate—not necessarily to the best interests of the child. This is where every parent is called on to develop some skills in advocacy and assertiveness as an extension of his or her role.

DEVELOPING ASSERTIVENESS

Fortunately, modern psychology offers a concept that can give us a handle channeling anger into effective assertiveness in the case of obtaining services for a child with special needs. There is a continuum from passive to assertive to aggressive problem-solving styles. The characteristics of each of various styles are described by Robert Alberti and Michael Emmons in *Your Perfect Right,* a classic self-help book.

Passive problem solving allows other people to treat you, your idea, your feelings, and most important your child in whatever way they think best in the situation when you are trying to obtain services without challenge. You do what others want and not what you think is best. You may avoid the conflict necessary to solve the problem, but you will have given up your rights and established a pattern of allowing others to dominate you. The other person is left to guess how you think and feel, and resentment and anger can accumulate. A person who uses this style talks to others with a great deal of respect, but with little confidence, and, therefore, merely waits and hopes for the best services for his or her child.

Aggressive problem solvers stand up for what they want without regard to the rights, thoughts, or feelings of others. Through aggression, they claim their rights by attacking, viewing their rights as superior, and establishing a pattern of fear and avoidance on the part of their "opponent." Aggressive problem solvers talk to others without respect and often come across as cocky and hostile while demanding what they want. The goal is to be neither passive nor aggressive but, rather, to strongly, clearly, and considerately express your point of view.

Assertive problem solvers, when they are the parents of a child with special needs, think and act in ways that back up the child's legitimate rights. An assertive parent can express strong thoughts and feelings without putting down the thoughts and feelings of another. He or she can attack a problem with respect for a professional's knowledge and establish a pattern of respect, thus avoiding the buildup of anger often caused by miscommunication. The assertive parent is both respectful and self-confident while requesting the services that his or her child needs.

One mother told me how angry she gets when professionals don't hear and understand her. The problem reminds her of difficulties that she had with her mother while she was growing up. Once she can refocus on the love and dedication of the professionals who work with her daughter every day, she is able to calmly and clearly express her thoughts and this usually resolves the problem.

A parent is the most effective case manager for his or her child because he or she knows the child the best. Although it might not seem fair that the parent is thrust into this position, accepting this responsibility is the key to getting the best programs and services possible for your child. A child whose parents are involved in his or her education and treatment every step of the way, despite occasional frustration, generally gets more than the child whose parents get discouraged by the difficulty of navigating the service system. Involved, informed parents who communicate assertively can readily build and maintain good working relationships with professionals. As your child grows and his or her needs evolve over time, these relationships become invaluable.

Unfortunately, there are many occasions in which merely being assertive is not enough, and it becomes necessary to acquire an advocate for your child. Of course, parents must learn as much as possible about their child's disability and how to work through the maze of available services. Here are some tips if you are having trouble resolving a problem with an agency or school system:

Gather information. It is vital to know all that you can about your child's problem as you see it and as others see it. Become familiar with the treatments and educational programs available to children with similar conditions in your area as well as in other geographical areas. It is also wise to learn about your rights and those of your child under federal laws and the laws governing special education in your state. A 1960s slogan "knowledge is freedom" applies here: The more you know, the less likely it is that you or your child will get lost in the shuffle. The appendixes at the back of this book list many sources of information from books, organizations, and the Internet.

Make a plan. When working with the system, keep in mind what you really want to get for your family and any outstanding issues. It is a good idea to prepare notes before a meeting or a telephone call. Think through several options so that you are ready to discuss whatever might work in the event that it is offered to you. Contact parent organizations and advocacy groups for support, and consider the possibility of taking an advocate with you to a meeting to help you stay objective, as well as to let the person you are dealing with know that you are serious.

Take action. Have your notes in front of you when you call schools or service agencies, take additional notes on every contact that you make, and note the date. If you cannot reach the person that you need to talk to, leave a brief message. Do not assume that you will get a call back. Be prepared to call persistently every few days until you get results. When you do reach the person you need to talk to, state your ideas simply, directly, and assertively. If the person needs to get back to you, then ask when you might expect to hear from him or her. If you have not heard by the date that was stated, then call back. The person you talked to may be overworked or may be avoiding you, so be persistent, firm, and assertive for as long as it takes. It is not justifiable, but it is often true that the squeaky wheel gets the oil, so let the individual and the system know that you won't go away until your problem is resolved.

Take it further. If you do not get satisfaction, ask to talk to a supervisor. If that doesn't work, then take your problem to the director of the agency or the school district's director of

Tariq with child psychiatrist Bert Ruttenberg ("Santa").

special education. If that fails, then call a legal rights or advo-cacy group to represent you. Your notes about the problem, including the dates of all contacts, the names of who you spoke to, and what you have been told will be extremely help-ful if you have to go this far. However, most problems can be resolved before legal proceedings are necessary if you follow the steps outlined previously.

Like all long-term relationships, the link between parents of children with special needs and the professionals who serve them as physicians or representatives of agencies and school systems is vital and yet challenging. The anger that can ener-gize you is often as hard to let go of as the dream for the per-fect child, yet carrying it for too long can make one weary. When we first encounter these professionals in the midst of our grief for our child, we are challenged to relive and rework our own childhood experiences with our parents and other authority figures. There is an added benefit to learning to be assertive, knowledgeable authorities. When we do, we can work in partnership with other authorities, which will help to resolve our childhood experiences and carry over into many aspects of life at the same time that it sets the stage for our children with special needs to grow into all that they can be.

11

When the
Miracle Never Comes

*Revisiting the Past
and Looking to the Future*

*P*erseverance in the face of life's obstacles can earn you moments of great serenity. As the world entered the new millennium, my father's death and my son's 21st birthday thrust me, ready or not, into a new chapter of my life as a son and as a father. My concluding reflections to *Special Children, Challenged Parents* began on a winter day as Tariq and I walked hand in hand, silently enjoying the scene. Freshly fallen snow crunched under our feet. Early morning's cool air tingled our cheeks. The trail beneath us wound through the woods. Through an opening in the evergreens, the pure white lake glistened, reflecting the sunlight. People sat on chairs and fished through holes hacked out of the ice. With awe, we stared at the white lake with people on top of it. We had never seen anything like it at Marsh Creek State Park in Chester County, Pennsylvania.

Then, I felt the eyes of another man coming the other way walking his two beagles. There was a look of wonder. For an instant I questioned why. And then I realized the oddness of his view. My 21-year-old son was holding my hand like a little boy. He was looking up at me in the way a toddler adores his father. It's normal between me and my son but an odd sight to others, and today that innocent glance was the punctuation mark at the end of a blissful feeling.

Since the summer of 1988, Tariq has not lived with me. He has resided at the Kanner Center of the Devereux Foundation in nearby West Chester. Because of his disability, he requires 24-hour care. If only he didn't have autism. If only he could speak and read and write. And if only my boy, now a young man, didn't have severe mental retardation. If only he understood danger. If only he slept safely through the night. If only he wasn't a constant threat to run away from everywhere. Then he could live with the rest of my family. I cannot help at times to still wonder what might have been.

LET'S NOT ABANDON THE FAMILY

On the day after Christmas 1999, a couple left their 10-year-old son, who is assisted by medical technology, at the A.I. DuPont Hospital for Children in Wilmington, Delaware. The image of the boy in a wheelchair who needs a respirator to breathe jolted me as I read the article while visiting relatives in Florida. Quickly, it became a national story as the parents were arrested and charged with abandonment. By all accounts, these folks had loved their child dearly. They had 24-hour nursing care in their home for years. His mother had served as an advocate for other children with disabilities and their families. Money was not an issue; his father was the CEO of a Fortune 500 company. The news media and the public were baffled.

For a few moments I thought I had handled things better than those folks. That righteousness was short-lived. The lessons of my life with Tariq flooded into my consciousness. Memories awakened of so many sleepless nights until I had reached the end of my rope. Before reading all of the details, I knew what could drive parents to the brink. I wished that I could be baffled. If only my son was healthy, I would be on that side of the fence. Then, I could be morally offended. Then, I might think it a crime with the parents deserving their mug

shots in the newspaper. Quite the contrary, it seemed to bor-
der on the absurd and the uncivilized to have charged this
couple with these crimes.

Facts can be stubborn things, and the details bore this out.
The boy had 130 major surgeries in his 120 months of life, according to a family member. When his parents gave up on
December 26, they took him to A.I. DuPont Hospital for Children, which had been his medical home in Delaware. The parents had had no help for at least 3 days. The hospital staff
knew and liked the boy, who was reported to be always pleasant and cooperative. His parents had been told recently that
they would have only 50 hours of nursing care for the entire
month of January. This was the result of a nationwide short-
age of pediatric home care nurses that was documented in the
December 31, 1999, issue of the *Wall Street Journal*. Home
health care services were not available at any price even if you
had the means to pay.

When criminal charges were filed against the couple, they
turned themselves in. A condition of their bail was that they
not attempt to visit their son in the hospital. It was not until
January 14, 2000, that the Delaware judge in the case ruled
that the parents could visit their child but only under the supervision of a Pennsylvania child welfare worker. They were
considered to be a threat to their child's safety. They faced
criminal charges of conspiracy and abandonment. The father
was fired from his job, and eventually the couple accepted a
plea bargain and went on with their lives in private, out of the
media's glare.

I understood the rush to judgment all too well. In the re-
cesses of my mind, there was a well-worn path to blaming others for what I cannot understand. My son has taught me how
to look for other paths. Of course, children need strong laws
to protect them from abuse and neglect, and those laws must
be vigilantly enforced. Perhaps our systems of care should be
charged with neglecting and abandoning the physical and
emotional necessities of families who have children with such
complex and involved needs. In my own situation, I had faced
the decision to place Tariq in a residential setting years before,

and many readers of the first edition of *Special Children, Challenged Parents* have written to me wanting to know more about such an extreme situation.

It's not so hard to imagine, however, if you recall how a sick infant will sometimes keep you up all night. You worry and you check to see that your infant is still breathing. What if your child never got better? What if all of the love and the best medical care didn't cure that—but your child lived? Who would you become? I can tell you that it is a grief like no other. It drove me, with my heart in my mouth, to places that I never wanted to go. It felt like my infant died, but the crib was not empty. My dream of a healthy child was certainly shattered, but there was no funeral. Perhaps the dream should be grieved in some sort of ritual, but it isn't, for there is no corpse. Parents are expected to be brave and keep a stiff upper lip. The dream cannot be buried or cremated, and so for a long time most parents would only hold on for dear life.

With love and support you would most likely survive and become a better person. Our life force is strong and resilient. Nonetheless, your longing for the healthy child might last your lifetime. *I have never stopped wanting to hear the sound of my son's voice.* Yet, I love him no less because of that, and perhaps I love him in more ways than I could have ever imagined.

I became totally absorbed, as so many parents do, in caring for my child with special needs. Because of the danger, some nights I kept watch, sleeping outside of his bedroom on the floor. I loved my child passionately and hoped for a cure or a miracle. When none came, in my dark and private moments, I wished to be freed from the burden. I would try to put on a cheery face to hide my guilt and shame. With love and support, most parents survive and become better people, but this is at a price that staggers the mind and heart.

Our children may be happy and content while we still struggle to let go of the dreams we had—whatever they might have been. Often, the grief can be for ourselves—that our lives as parents did not turn out as we expected. We can make new dreams as we learn to accept and enjoy the child that we actually have. I have come to realize that this is the struggle of all parents, even those of typical children, and there has been comfort from that perspective.

Children with special needs are very lovable, but if their challenges are behavioral, as they were with Tariq, we have to chase them around, literally going in circles with our emotions and often swirling out of control. If the challenges are medical, we must care for our children's staggering needs with the fear that every breath could be their last. Simply put, our lovely children are very hard to be with. ***But when you love somebody, you love to be with him or her.*** When you don't feel that and you think you should, the guilt can be unbearable. Your heart cracks open, and it takes time to heal. Let's take a step back and put this whole process and our individual stories in perspective.

THE GENESIS OF PARENTHOOD

Through the entwined mysteries of love and biology, an ordinary man and woman create a child. What is less obvious but no less profound is how a single child gives birth to two parents. For at the moment of birth, a woman becomes a mother, a man becomes a father, and two new fundamental identities begin to emerge. In the typical situation, 9 months of hopes, dreams, and fears reach a crescendo of love that brings with it a powerful drive and near boundless energy to protect and nurture the newborn infant. The woman is changed forever as she becomes a primary caregiver as is the man who has traveled by her side and will continue with new charges.

With *The Birth of a Mother: How the Motherhood Experience Changes You Forever,* psychiatrist Daniel N. Stern and pediatrician and child psychiatrist Nadia Bruschweiler-Stern made an important contribution to the literature about parenthood. How rare and wonderful it is that a book about mothering (and fathering) embraces the challenges of bonding with and raising a child with special needs. The heart of the book is the enchanting description of the psychological birth of the mother in the months that precede and follow the birth of her infant.

Through hundreds of interviews with new mothers and decades of experience, the authors demonstrated conclusively how a woman's mental life changes fundamentally with the arrival of an infant. The striking change in perspective includes the shift from being a daughter to being a mother; becoming a part of the broad community of mothers; seeing one's husband become a father; forming a mother–father–child triangle; and discovering an altered set of sensibilities that are brought to bear on every sight, sound, and smell of the new mother. In today's society, the new mother may balance infant and career as she also finds a new role in her family of origin. A new era begins in the mother's life as she counts time with a private calendar that is marked with her infant's age and developmental milestones.

Next, the birth of the infant spawns the psychological birth of motherhood, as well as fatherhood, and the real infant comes into focus. The mother continues to look at her infant through the lens of her hopes, dreams, and fears. Understandably, any mother may want to repair or redo her own past through her child, but ballet classes or science fairs, for example, are not necessarily the child's wish. So, putting aside these self-fulfilling prophecies and seeing the infant as a unique individual is central in parenthood.

The basics of feeding, nurturing, and caring for the new infant ensure his or her survival and cement the new identity of motherhood. The fundamental questions about loving and being loved are enacted as the mother and infant learn to respond to each other. Mistakes are inevitably made and need to be righted. The mother's unfinished business with her own mother may be elicited in the process and must then be addressed in some fashion. Ultimately, each new mother decides how much of her own relationship with her mother she wants to repeat or reject with her infant—no small dilemma. Each new father goes through a similar passage using his own father as a compass to steer toward or away from at various moments.

But how stunning are the obstacles of new parents who learn that their infant is not completely healthy! With such a dramatic loss, parents also lose their freedom to anticipate the future of their infant, themselves, and their family, for there is no clear picture of their infant as a preschooler, adolescent, or adult in the future. As Stern and Bruschweiler-Stern stated,

> *The birth of a severely developmentally delayed or handicapped baby is a trauma that virtually stops time in its tracks . . . suddenly your future is unpredictable, and emotionally unimaginable. At the same moment, your past, full of hopes and fantasies of pregnancy, is obliterated and becomes too painful to remember. Parents are held prisoner in an enduring present.* (p. 183)

The predictable path through this emotional trauma to an uncertain future involves learning about the infant's problem in intimate detail and learning to see past the disability and bond with the actual infant. If the announcement of the problem occurs before bonding has begun, this is clearly much more difficult and rejection of the infant may occur. Although the birth of a healthy infant empowers the woman as a mother and the man as a father, the birth of a less than perfect infant wounds them in their core.

It can be an agonizing process as many readers can ably attest. Many times the full nature of the problem isn't clear, and no one, including the medical experts, knows how the child will turn out. In a broad sense, the family becomes disabled not being able to predict the future and feels isolated and bewildered. Parents can move forward by exploring these painful experiences, sharing them with others, and seeking psychological counseling when necessary in order to move away from the pain and rejoin the current of their lives. Parents can and usually do learn to grow and love their infant in wonderful ways that are unimaginable in the beginning.

We parents of children with special needs do indeed live within the vast developmental spectrum of the parenting experience. In a broad sense, no child is perfect, and it is the bond that attaches the parent and the child that will sustain families over the long haul. How these passions develop has uniqueness and similarities for parents with children developing typically as well as those with special needs. In all cases, the infant cradled in the parent's arms is different to some degree, small or large, from the child fantasized in the mind. The reconciliation of these images is central in the daily work of all parents—in that sense we are far from an isolated minority.

WHEN THE BOUGH BREAKS

My son's condition continually drove me places that I could never have imagined as an "outsider" to this club of parents who had children like mine. After Tariq's ninth Christmas, I faced the reality that his condition required 24-hour care. That year he knocked down the Christmas tree; there were broken ornaments and shards of glass everywhere. In an instant, the festive mood had been vaporized. We were trying to live like a typical family, but it wasn't possible.

I had thought that I could handle things better than those parents whose children with severe disabilities were placed in residential schools. Now my life was teaching me that was not true. Years of disturbed sleep and around-the-clock vigilance had brought me to the horrible realization that I had reached the end of my rope. Any unsupervised moment could lead to disaster. It could range from Tariq's bolting toward a busy street to smearing his feces all over to climbing out a window. In hindsight, I marvel at how I coped so well for so long. I don't think I could do it again.

Some times are harder than others, and December can be a trying month for many people, as it must have been for those folks in Delaware. The holiday season can bring reminders of the grief for what might have been. There is no holiday for you when you have a child with special needs. Your inner resources for coping are never on a break. Meanwhile, school is closed, and your child's caregivers are with their families, and you are with your child "24/7" (24 hours a day, 7 days a week). If you can't find any support, you feel terribly alone. Your most painful feelings emerge at a time when the world is celebrating and you have no respite.

It used to be the case that the parents of children with such severe disabilities were immediately counseled by their physicians to institutionalize their infants. Often times, they were discouraged from bonding with their child. This approach was later shown to be detrimental to parent and child alike. In those days, it was common for parents to place a child in a state institution and never return. Some families were even advised by professionals not to visit their children because that would make it harder. The child disappeared and the abandonment became a shameful family secret.

Currently, the pendulum has swung the other way. Parents are routinely expected to care for a child at home regardless of the severity of the situation—irrespective of how it affects each family member. The kind of intense stress that many parents of children with special health care needs face daily can stretch you to the breaking point. If a parent in this situation had attempted suicide, that would not have been a national news story. In fact, I was involved in counseling a mother who had attempted suicide twice. She had cared for her son who was technology dependent—he was on a ventilator to breathe. He had not been expected to live past early childhood, but now he had survived to 17—and her will to go on had been broken. As part of a team at the Specare Pediatric Center for Children with Special Needs, we were able to advocate successfully to increase nursing care to around the clock, at least temporarily, for this family.

There is a constant emphasis on doing more for the child, which comes from the professional community as well as from the parents' natural drive to recover a healthy infant. It is not always possible to care for a child with such involved special needs at home, so some families need other ways for their children's needs to be met. It was my experience that it is hard to find support when this is the case because placement is often still seen by many as an unspeakable rejection of the child. Even among parents of children with disabilities, there is opposition to considering such an option for the family. People who keep their children at home are often regarded as better parents. The system and the community tend to tout them as exemplary and look down on those who make other choices. For this combination of reasons, many parents never hear about other ways that their child may be cared for safely and with dignity.

In fact, there are options and I was fortunate to discover them before I broke. My wife, Cindy, had worked at Bancroft's residential program in New Jersey for children and adults with developmental disabilities. She helped me see through the stereotypes that I had read about in the late 1970s. At that time, the horrendous conditions at state institutions such as Pennhurst in Pennsylvania and Willowbrook in New York were exposed. The trend to de-institutionalize children and adults with mental illnesses and mental retardation began— as it should have. Many children and adults with disabilities could, in fact, do better in community settings.

Still, there needed to be humane options for children whose needs could not be met in the home of a typical family. In our area alone, there are several fine private schools with residential facilities such as Bancroft, Devereux, Elwyn, Melmark, the Woods School, and so forth. The children at these schools come from all walks of life. We are fortunate to have so many nationally known schools in the eastern Pennsylvania–New Jersey area. Children come here from many states for the specialized care that is available.

Most children and adults with disabilities do not belong in residential facilities any more than most people who are aging belong in nursing homes. Fern Kupfer, a mother who has been there with her child who is terminally ill, helped the rest of us understand this in *Before and After Zachariah: A Family Story About a Different Kind of Courage*. Perhaps we all share a fear of what may happen to us if or when we can no longer care for ourselves. As a society, we certainly need subsidies and services for families who choose to care for dependent members of any age in their homes. Likewise, we need accessible housing for people with disabilities who can live more independently, as well as good group homes and halfway houses. In addition, we need pediatric child care for children who are assisted by medical technology. Some children require an educational institution with residential facilities, and as Fern Kupfer wrote in the December 13, 1982, issue of *News-*

week, "It [a residential placement] shouldn't have to be a dirty word."

One night early in 1988, I was awake with Tariq in the middle of the night. As I tried to rock him back to sleep, he looked so innocent and peaceful as his eyes finally closed. As I looked at him, I thought that *if he could speak and reason,* he would not want me and the rest of the family to spend the rest of our lives in the way we had been living. He knew that I loved him, and I knew that he loved me back. Everyone who ever sees us together to this day can see that. But he couldn't tell me that it would be okay for him to go to a residential school. I had to wrestle with that alone, and I would have to face myself in the mirror for the rest of my life.

Gradually, with support, I came to understand that a residential program was actually a less restrictive environment for Tariq. There he could and would be more free to run, play, learn, and grow within safe limits. He wouldn't have to be tethered constantly to someone's arm. He wasn't being "put away" and abandoned or forgotten because we could visit him regularly and he could come home for overnight visits. If he made progress in that setting, as some children do, he could come back to live at home. If a child needs this level of care, then the family has a right to it and there is state and federal funding to provide it, so money is not the central issue. Unfortunately, as I was to discover firsthand after reaching this painful conclusion, most people will have to fight a legal battle to get this care for their child and a reasonable life for the rest of their family.

Every tear drained out of my heart for months. Having to prove that my infant was damaged enough to deserve this care seemed like torture. Likewise, the average parent of a child with special needs must often struggle long and hard to get the best possible services for his or her child. Without Cindy by my side, without the Center for Autistic Children to support Tariq's needs, and without an attorney, I could never have done it. When the funding for the Devereux Foundation was approved for Tariq through the due process procedures in June, 1988, I packed his clothes and a few toys. It was the hardest thing that

I have ever had to do. I remember sitting on his bed with my head in my hands. It was not a victory to contemplate the sad reality that my son would not finish growing up under my roof.

Because of his sleep problems, Tariq was assigned to the room right next to the night duty residential counselor. A buzzer would go off if he left his room, and the old converted farmhouse at Devereux's Kanner Center, which housed about 15 other children, was encircled with a 6-foot fence. Now it was someone else's job to be vigilant at 3:00 A.M.—someone who was paid to be awake and who went home to sleep in the morning.

Today, looking back, I have no doubt that it was the best that I could have done for Tariq and for all of us who love him. I know that is all any of us could ever do, whatever our individual circumstances. This confidence helped me face the guilt and get through to the other side. Tariq has gone on year by year and made slow, steady progress within the expected developmental trajectory for a child diagnosed with autism and severe mental retardation. He has grown up in a safe environment. I have seen him regularly and have been involved in all decisions about his care. He remains generally happy and healthy. Not a day goes by that he is not prominent in my thoughts and emotions. He is as much a part of our family as any other member. More than anyone, his life has helped me to understand my father and myself as a father.

THE FATHER–SON CONNECTION

Life is always easier to understand in hindsight. There's a lot that is still blurry to me but it does get clearer as time goes on. In ancient times, Homer wrote that "It is a wise child who knows his own father." Indeed, it is hard to know yourself if you don't know your father. It was true that childhood in our family was far easier than my father's childhood had been. Just as my father always wondered about his father, I have never stopped trying to understand my father.

Being a father myself helped me to understand my own father. As Fred Rogers of *Mr. Rogers' Neighborhood* put it, "When you become a parent, it is your biggest chance to grow again.

You have another crack at yourself." As parents, we weave together the threads of the past from our parents with the threads of the future in our children. It wasn't until I was middle age, after I had been through a messy divorce, had four children of my own, and had struggled for many years with my son's autism and severe mental retardation, that my father made more sense to me. As I came to understand my own grief, I realized that I had grown up in the shadow of his grief.

Many men are not used to talking about their feelings as explained so well in *I Don't Want to Talk About It: Overcoming the Secret Legacy of Male Depression* by psychotherapist Terrence Real. That's why most people didn't know about my grandmother's disability (she was paralyzed on one side of her body following a stroke) until I told them in the eulogy at my father's funeral. Likewise, when a child is diagnosed with a lifelong disability, men tend to inhibit their grief over that loss of a healthy child by withdrawing, isolating, and immersing themselves in work. The way that my father had lived with his grief didn't work for me. I found myself too grumpy, irritable, and withdrawn. I stopped enjoying life, so I had to grow. This helped me understand my father in a new way and how hard it is was for him to grieve his losses—the loss of his parents and the loss of my brother Don in 1978. *For a child, the worst loss imaginable would be the loss of your parents. For a parent, the most feared loss would be the loss of your child.* My father had endured and survived both of these phenomenal tragedies.

My father's death on January 15, 2000, put my life as a son and as a father in perspective. In preparing the eulogy for his funeral, I was able to compose an outlook on my father's life and death. My dad, Albert K. Naseef, was born in 1921. He was the seventh and last child that his mother, Amira, delivered alive. He and four others survived and there were also two stillbirths. When he was 7 years old, his mother died at 38 years of age. Nine months later, in 1929, his father died at 58 years of age. My father grew to adulthood in Girard College— a fine place that we visited often for his class reunions in my childhood years but an institution for poor, fatherless boys nonetheless. He grew up with other bereaved boys, several of whom were at his funeral. They have been friends through all of life's seasons for more than 70 years. Like my dad, now my own son was growing up in an institution, this time with other young people who have rather severe disabilities.

As a child, I often heard my father speak longingly of his father but never of his mother. Often, he told us that he was trying to give us what he never got. Being close to my maternal grandparents, I always wanted to know more about his parents and I felt their absence in our lives. But my dad was quite reserved about himself, as I had been prior to Tariq's diagnosis. Just a few years ago, I asked him about his mother for what seemed like the hundredth time, and finally he told me the rest of the story.

His mother had a stroke when she delivered him in childbirth. She never recovered, just as my infant never recovered. She never cared for him because she needed to be cared for herself. He was nurtured by his sister, Selma, who was only 13 at the time my father was born. So, he was orphaned by the age of 8, and he was never mothered. Then I understood the breadth and depth of his grief—the shadow cast over us, his children.

My dad was determined to give his children a better start in life, as are most parents, and by all accounts he succeeded. He proudly raised eight of us and wished his father had lived to see that feat. No matter how hard and how long I tried, I was forced to accept that I could not give Tariq a better start than I had received, at least in the traditional sense that I had craved. I found a poem by e.e. cummings that captured my feelings toward my dad so well that I read it at his funeral. Cummings wrote that his father was a true father because his dad loved him. So, cummings loved him back. As a child he worshiped his father. In his youth he battled his father, and as men they understood each other. Through it all they loved each other.

Cummings' words certainly rang true for me. As a little boy, I adored my father, as Tariq still adores me. As a teenager and as a young man, we did battle. We butted heads over everything from the Vietnam War to the civil rights movement to religion and even whether marijuana should be legalized. If we agreed on anything, neither one of us would admit it. It was not the kind of battle that I can ever have with Tariq. I can never have the pride of watching my son develop his own mind in this respect and, honestly, that still hurts me deeply at times.

It wasn't until my father was an old man and terminally ill that I think we finally understood each other. I wish that it hadn't taken so long. I wish that we weren't so stubborn with each other. But still, I count myself blessed for I know many men who do not understand or feel understood by their fathers. When he got sick in the summer of 1998, my dad discovered what he had been missing in his life as an orphan. When we all rallied around him, he said that he never felt so loved. Finally, he was convinced that there was a family who loved him and wouldn't leave him. As I still wrestled with my son's extreme and overpowering disability, my father faced the ultimate acceptance of death.

Indeed, his last year was one of his best and that has been a comfort to the rest of the family. His mood was consistently better than ever before. He had decided with my mother's support not to have any more surgical procedures. He wanted to enjoy whatever he could in the time that he had remaining. So, in the end, fate was finally kind to him. He left this life as he wanted to—quietly, at home, in his recliner, with the remote control in his hand. As we gathered in the emergency room around him that night, shortly after he had expired, my brother Al wished my dad a peaceful journey. At the funeral I wished him the same in the language of his parents:

Salaam aleikum

(Shalom alechem)

(Peace be with you)

THE SPIRITUAL PASSAGE

A child's disability or chronic illness changes and transforms us in our core being as men, as fathers, and as sons to our fathers. There are joys as well as sorrows. It helps men who are fathers of children with special needs to connect with other men in similar circumstances. When men sit around and share their experiences of having a child with special needs, invariably I observe a certain pattern. They tell their stories of finding out something is wrong, getting a diagnosis, beginning to get help, struggling to get the best services possible, and learning how to communicate with their wives. They talk about their fears, their anger, and their frustrations. Ultimately, they come to an individual peace of mind, heart, and soul.

Telling our own story and listening to other fathers' stories is one way we learn about fatherhood. The stories of these fathers I know always conclude with how much they have learned and how they have become better men, better husbands, and better fathers. Inside the often tough exterior of these men, they are tender and loving with good humor and insight. For readers who have access to the Internet, you can read the inspiring words of many fathers of children with special needs at http://www.fathersnetwork.org. Let them touch your life through the stories of their struggles and joys.

On my first Father's Day without my father, I appreciated him for butting heads with me. I think that he eventually knew, as I finally do, that we were just trying to connect. It was only when we finally stopped trying to change each other that we understood each other. I am trying to make it a little easier for my children, but I am not sure I always succeed at that. Like fathers everywhere, I want to give them an easier and a better childhood than I had. But if I ever grumble to my beautiful children about how they have it better than I did, I hope someone will just shake me in a firm, loving way.

As difficult as his life has been, Tariq is one of the best things that ever happened to me. I look back and give thanks. As a professional psychologist since 1989, I try to help other people understand what I still sometimes wish I never knew. Yet, there were many gifts that derived from the suffering.

Most striking, in retrospect, is how at first I was so passionately determined to change Tariq and make him the boy that I wanted him to be. Instead, the book I eventually wrote has become the story about how I was forced to change myself, despite my passionate protests to the contrary, and embrace him as he is. It's a book that I wish I had when he was young. He has indeed helped me to become the man that I needed to be. This has helped me to help others, which continually serves to comfort and heal myself and experience value in my life and work. Tariq's gifts to me were not in packages, but, rather, they have continued to unfold and develop over time. Like a tree, they have sunk roots and grown inside me.

Tariq has taught me the meaning of unconditional love. I have learned to honor his sacred right to be loved for who he is. My attachment to his achievements dissolved over time. This was hard to let go in our world driven by appearances and money. Tariq has made very good progress in the past year. He will probably go to a sheltered workshop after his graduation in June 2001. That seemed unlikely for a good while. He is able to sit still and focus long enough to be productive with tasks such as stuffing envelopes or sorting things.

Over the years, I have learned to accept the best he can do and celebrate his achievements. Around the time of his 21st birthday, when I took him to the bathroom, I noticed that he had learned to button the fly on his pants. He didn't need me to do that anymore. My eyes glazed over with joy. A spiritual revelation grows from the intrinsic beauty of each and every child's existence even with, and perhaps because of, such severe limitations in what we have come to expect in life. What a priceless lesson he has taught me without words in his silence!

The inevitable juxtaposition of my son with healthy, typical children used to be so painful. I used to wince every time my friends' kids and my nieces and nephews passed a milestone that Tariq would never achieve—such as riding a bike; learning to swim; graduating from grade school, high school, or college; or getting a job. Now, I can enjoy witnessing their progress, and that's a wonderful gift that has grown out of moments of serenity.

Tariq has taught me how to accept him as well as how to accept myself. I think the challenges in our children radiate inwardly to our own sense of being imperfect. I had to accept my own imperfections, warts and all.

With all children, we have to give up a lot of expectations in order to love our child in the moment. You can't enjoy your life if you don't love them in the moment. Some dreams are deferred and some dreams are remade. Tariq and I do run together, and that is something that I imagined doing with my son. We canoe together, something else I imagined. In those moments, there is nothing wrong with him or me.

A recent gift was learning not to hide differences. For years, I would only keep or put into books the pictures of my son looking normal. Finally, I have gotten to the point of accepting images of Tariq flapping his hands *and* Tariq looking normal. Both images are okay. He is just as lovable either way. I learned this because photographer Tommie Leonardi thought he was a great subject—as he was. What a wonderful revelation! A certain degree of shame was shed, making me feel lighter.

Tariq continues to teach me to live for myself. He needs me, and he counts on me to do that. He cannot help me when I become old and frail. Rather, I must ensure that his needs are met when I am gone. When I understood that my feelings were my own, I could see reality more clearly. He is happy most of the time.

It continues to astound me that my son with no words has helped me to develop my own unique voice. This is even more magical when I recall how shy I was growing up. I was on the edge of the playground throughout my 8 years in elementary school. Today, my voice comes through as I practice my profession in various formats such as writing, public speaking, training, and psychotherapy.

Children with special needs are spiritual catalysts. They challenge and sometimes force us to look at ourselves. They help us accept our own imperfections and the imperfections of others. In that sense, Tariq is not damaged in the least. He is perfect as he is. Along with other children and adults with disabilities, he bears witness to the diversity of the human condition and the resilience of our collective spirit.

I learned that we don't have to lie to ourselves. You can grieve. You can complain. You can mourn. You can go on and enjoy life. You don't have to lie about how hard this can be; that

Our family together in 1999. (Photo by Tommie Leonardi.)

only makes it take longer to get through. If I come back after I die, I won't lie to you, I don't want a kid with autism. I want a son who can talk to me. I have three daughters, and they all talk to me. I love them dearly, and they love Tariq dearly.

In November 1999, when Tariq was 20 years old, we had a big party for him. What was remarkable is that I woke up a few months earlier and said to my wife, Cindy, "It's his 20th birthday. Let's have a party." Cindy threw him a great party attended by family and friends as well as several of his teachers and therapists, past and present. He hadn't had such a big party since he was 1 year old, which is not something I am proud of. But there were so many milestones unmet and so many disappointments to absorb. It took time, and we all just did our best.

I am grateful for the opportunity to tell my story in these pages. This is a charmed part of my existence for there are so many people in every corner of our globe who endure tragedy with no apparent redemption. As professional storyteller Richard Stone noted in *The Healing Art of Storytelling: A Sacred Journey of*

Tariq still puts his head on my shoulder. (Photo by Tommie Leonardi.)

Personal Discovery, the telling of one's story is a vehicle for self-discovery. We can thus come to know ourselves in new and often surprising ways. In the process, we reveal the deepest and most heartfelt sentiments to others and build bonds that endure. The act of telling one's authentic story can be an antidote to the extreme isolation that often characterizes modern life.

Our story helps us make sense of what has happened to us. It is a way of telling time, which stopped for many people when they found out about their child's disability. The story becomes the pathway to finding meaning in our lives. So this is not just a story about me and my son. Everyone can benefit from finding the links to the events in their lives and putting them together with coherence, logic, and emotion.

In the opening lines of *David Copperfield,* Charles Dickens wrote, "Whether I shall turn out to be the hero of my own life, or whether that station will be held by anybody else, these pages must show" (p. 13). At the moment of my son's birth, I had imagined him to be the hero of my life. In the roundabout way that these pages describe, he has helped me to find the hero within me and for that I am appreciative.

Tariq is a young man now. It's hard for me to say that my baby is a young man. I still wonder what his voice would sound like and what he would want to tell me. Tariq is still my little boy. He still puts his head on my shoulder. He has brought so many kind-hearted people into my life. These experiences have made me a better father and a better person. The greatest gift so far is the glimpse that I have into the human heart: where it is not who you know or what you know, but who you are.

Autumn, 1996

Dear Tariq,

After a wet summer, the fall foliage is as brilliant and irides-
cent as ever. As fallen leaves crackle underfoot, the book that
I began writing in the winter of 1990 is finally done. This relationship of ours has truly been "a road less traveled," in the
words of the poet Robert Frost. It wasn't a road I wished for
or chose but rather one I was shoved down by the hand of
fate. Ever since you were a toddler and stopped talking, I, like
many other parents of children with communication disorders, have been having this one-way dialogue inside of my
head with you.

When I first thought about writing this book, I imagined
quite a different ending. I wanted to change you so that you
could talk and do all of the things that I dreamed of for you
and me. I even hoped that someday you would read the book
and be grateful to me for my efforts to rescue you from autism.
It turned out that through the journey, you changed me in a
way that I could never have foreseen.

In order to understand you, I had to tune in to all of the
little clues about your needs and wants and feelings. To do that,
I had to work on understanding myself in order to accept and
love you for who you are—not who I wanted you to be or
what I wanted you to achieve. This whole process chronicled in
these pages is an abridged version of what has made me who I
am today. The truth is, if you were any other way, you wouldn't
be my Tariq, and I wouldn't be the same Bob. I wouldn't want
another son. Even though this didn't turn out to be a book
about a miraculous recovery from autism, it did turn out to be
a story about "the human heart in conflict with itself" (in
William Faulkner's words), surviving, and prevailing.

Our family has grown and changed quite a bit as these
pages were written. Antoinette is in her second year of high
school and is living with your mother now, experiencing the ups
and downs of teen life. Her artwork was displayed last month at

the Please Touch Museum, and she is thinking about college. She will graduate in 1999, the last high school graduating class of this century. When you were a toddler, you had a T-shirt that said "Class of 1997." It brings back a lot of memories when I see a photo of you in that shirt; it was a time of innocence for you as well as me. Now there has been a coming of age.

Kara is 5 years old; she loves art, too, and is talking about opening a bookstore when she is grown up. Zoë will be 3 soon; she follows Kara everywhere she can, carrying her Minnie Mouse dolls, and she wants to be read to all of the time. Both of them enjoy the time that they spend with you (except when you "snatch" their food). In their own way they are gradually learning who you are and what it all means to them.

Antoinette gets tears in her eyes when she reads parts of this—she has missed not having you as "the older brother," although you are no less a brother and no less important to her. Kara is thrilled to see her name in print and has asked whether the book would be in the bookstores that we visit. Zoë can now recognize her name and will be no less excited by the time the book appears on the shelves. I will be glad when they are all older, and I hope the time goes slowly and that they read these pages and know who I am, how much I have loved them, and how Cindy and I have piloted the family boat together.

That road that we were shoved down together, Tariq, diverged so long ago that I have no idea who I would be today if you were a typical child. Frost talked about how "way leads on to way" and doubted if he would ever come back. Our whole experience together transformed me and became a part of me, a part of my character, a part that I hold in high esteem and a part that I wouldn't want to be without. I accept you the way that you are in my heart, but I still wish that we could sit and talk. Although that will never happen, it is just as true that no other son could have done for me what you have. You are in the very fiber of my being, in my every moment, and I wouldn't want to change that.

As I have learned through you, there are many ways to talk, many ways to listen, many ways to see, and many ways to move. The term *differently abled* actually does make sense, and as other parents confirm from their experiences, having a special child can make the parent special too. I am grateful to you for that, and I couldn't have had a better son. In our modern world, many people search for angels. For all that you have shown me, you qualify as my guardian angel, my ever-present spirit guide.

When things are tough, I talk to you more, so it is fitting to begin and end this book with letters to you. It's been a long time since I expected you to talk back, so really I look for the answers in my own head or through other people or in my writing. Still, sometimes I wonder what could have been. Some people say they get over that but so far I have not. Helen Keller wrote an essay called "Three Days to See," in which she described how she would spend her time if she could have but three sighted days. It relieves me to read that from a person who made everything she could have of herself but still wondered what it would be like to have what she was missing. I can see you struggle to make yourself understood at times, so it's not that farfetched to wonder what you would say if you could.

In the past year, your running away from the people who take care of you has become a bigger problem than ever. Sometimes they can't catch you and other times you manage to elude them and get away for a few moments unnoticed. Two of the incidents were very serious; once, you ran out, or "eloped" as the behavioral terminology goes, from the school building. You were found running the water in someone's bathtub about a half mile away. Fortunately, the man who lives there called the police, who knew they should call Devereux right away. A few months later, you eloped around midnight in your pajamas and turned up at the local convenience store about three quarters of a mile away. There was no shoulder or sidewalk on the road that led there, making your journey there even more perilous. Perhaps an angel watched over you.

All of this occurred despite the highest level of supervision; one of your abilities is to take advantage of the slightest distraction. Often I have longed that you could use those powers of observation for a different purpose. After these incidents, concerned and worried staff members informed me of what had occurred. When we met soon after that, their faces televised the gravest worry. Their fears for your life awakened those that I have had since you were very little, with a fury that I'd rather have not recalled. I was visualizing myself at your funeral and feeling the deep hole that your loss would be. This has long been my greatest fear: No parent wants to outlive his or her offspring.

After exploring all of the options, it was decided that no alternative offers more safety than Devereux. Even more precautions were taken to protect you, and the Cheltenham school district provided funds for one-to-one supervision during more dangerous times and hoped to teach you more communication skills to avert the problem. I am relieved because I like having you nearby, yet the worries are never far.

If your disability were less severe and you lived at home, I doubt that I could have mustered the time or the energy to write this book. Although this is but another of those bittersweet realizations, perhaps it is more than that. Maybe the voice developed in these pages can add to the symphony of the voices of parents and professionals that have gone before me in this work.

It is a symphony that represents a host of others who may not have the time or the inclination or the ability to articulate it in written words. Although you, Tariq, will not produce offspring, this book is a living legacy that will touch others. The Talmud speaks of this theme when it states, "Have a child, plant a tree, write a book."

I know a number of fathers of boys with autism, and occasionally we meet over dinner or lunch. When the video of Pinocchio was selling a few years ago, a number of the men mentioned that they identified with Geppetto. I must admit that your disability evoked the same longing in me for "a real boy." Gregory Burns, the father of a child with a rare chromosomal disorder, wrote on the same theme in the October 1995 issue of *Exceptional Parent.* He said that, "knock on wood," his daughter made him real. *The Velveteen Rabbit* also pivots around the idea that living, taking your knocks, and showing the wear makes you real and lovable.

So the lesson, Tariq—I wish that I had learned it sooner— is that I had a real boy all along. The road to this realization has been the "one less traveled by, and that has made all the difference." Your disability deprived us both of a certain "normalcy" but gave us other gifts that are just as valuable and just as natural as the snow. You can read the book, after all, for I know that you can feel the stillness within me as I rest my pen today.

I love you for that,
Dad

Spring, 2001

Dear Tariq,

The past 5 years have been full of changes. The yellow blooms on our forsythia bushes signal that spring is arriving on this raw, drizzly morning. The daffodils will be blooming any day now. It feels colder than it is. This June, you will be graduating from the Devereux Foundation. Since 1988, you have grown and learned and been safe there, and for these reasons this is a day I had not looked forward to. I have been asked to be the parent speaker at your graduation ceremony. When you were a baby, I used to imagine you getting called up at your graduation—now I am getting called up instead.

When Antoinette graduated from high school 2 years ago, she was asked to sing a song. Kara was recently given an award with her "Problem Solving" team at an assembly. Zoë just finished her first season in a basketball league, and she was presented the "Character Development Award" because she tried so hard and supported her teammates so well. It was such a great feeling to watch all of your sisters get recognized. They are all bright and active. I have no doubt that as Kara and Zoë progress through their school years and beyond, they will be recognized many times for their hard work and achievement.

With you, Tariq, it is different more often than not. When you were born, I thought you would speak very articulately and for me. Now, as on many occasions, I have the sense that I will be speaking for you as well as for myself. This time I will be speaking to your classmates and their families. I am not sure what I will say, but I am working on it, son. I am a bit nervous, but I know I will come through when the time is at hand.

When I told a friend that I would be speaking at your graduation, he commented that it would be hard to do that. I actually think it would be harder not to do it. I wouldn't want to sit there with my eyes glazing over without a voice. Graduations are such an intensely emotional time for families. Tears of joy and sorrow commingle during the celebration of accomplishments and the loss of one's family member to an uncertain future beyond the family nest.

I do know that I will tell the folks there about how you helped me to develop my voice. It continues to astound me how you did that without a single word. It's so wonderful to have a voice, for when you have a voice, you have dignity. When you have a voice, you can make yourself understood. When you have a voice, you can connect with others; you can speak and listen patiently with your spouse. With a voice, you are no longer alone. With a voice, you can command respect. You know when you have power, and you can accept when you are powerless. And maybe most of all, when you have a voice, you can begin to soothe and heal the ache in your heart. Although I will always wish you had a voice of your own, I will use mine to advocate for you.

When you were a boy, I despaired of ever getting as far as we are today. It seemed that you could never learn to sit still long enough to accomplish any kind of work. In the last few years, that has come with much satisfaction. I love the look on your face as you complete one task after another. I am grateful to all who have cared and taught and guided you. It is such a relief to me. Now we are waving good-bye to childhood and looking out to adulthood, with wobbly knees, I might add. We don't know yet where you will be living or working, but we do know the transition will be made.

We got here by doing our best. When I look at you, as well as when I look in the mirror, I have no doubt about it.

Running together.

We'll travel the next leg of this journey in the same way and use the tools that got us this far. I've had a lot of practice accepting and loving you as you are. We will continue to face the future with courage while we do our best with what we have. This is so far from what I imagined more than 21 years ago. Nonetheless, through acceptance and courage and endurance, the road through hardship has brought peace and love. Thank you for lighting the way.

Love,
Dad

Bibliography

Alberti, R., & Emmons, M. (1982). *Your perfect right.* San Luis Obispo, CA: Impact.

Bank, S.P., & Kahn, M. (1982). *The sibling bond.* New York: Basic Books.

Batshaw, M.L. (2001). *When your child has a disability: The complete sourcebook of daily and medical care* (Rev. ed.). Baltimore: Paul H. Brookes Publishing Co.

Beck, A.T. (1988). *Love is never enough: How couples can overcome misunderstandings, resolve conflicts, and solve relationship problems through cognitive therapy.* New York: Harper & Row.

Bly, R. (1990). *Iron John: A book about men.* Reading, MA: Addison Wesley Longman.

Bly, R., & Tannen, D. (1992, January/February). Where are men and women today? *New Age Journal,* 28–33, 92–96.

Brazelton, T.B., & Cramer, B.G. (1990). *The earliest relationship: Parents, infants, and the drama of early attachment.* Reading, MA: Addison Wesley Longman.

Brown, C. (1954). *My left foot.* London: Mandarin Paperbacks.

Buck, P. (1992). *The child who never grew.* Bethesda, MD: Woodbine House.

Chess, S., & Alexander, T. (1987). *Know your child: An authoritative guide for today's parents.* New York: Basic Books.

Coffin, C.M. (Ed.). (1994). *The complete poetry and selected prose of John Donne.* New York: Random House. (Originally published in 1952)

Cousins, N. (1989). *Head first: The biology of hope.* New York: E.P. Dutton.

Darling, R.B. (1983). Parent–professional interaction: The roots of misunderstanding. In M. Seligman (Ed.), *The family with a handicapped child: Understanding and treatment* (pp. 95–124). New York: Grune and Stratton.

Dickens, C. (1962). *David Copperfield.* New York: Penguin Putnam.

Dorris, M. (1990). *The broken cord.* New York: HarperCollins.

Faber, A., & Mazlish, E. (1987). *Siblings without rivalry: How to help your children live together.* New York: W.W. Norton & Company.

Featherstone, H. (1980). *A difference in the family: Life with a disabled child.* New York: Basic Books.

Galinsky, E. (1987). *The six stages of parenthood.* Reading, MA: Addison Wesley Longman.

Gaul, G.M. (1993). *Giant steps: The story of one boy's struggle to walk.* New York: St. Martin's Press.

Gibran, K. (1968). *The prophet.* New York: Alfred A. Knopf.

Gilligan, C. (1982). *In a different voice: Psychological theory and women's development.* Cambridge, MA: Harvard University Press.

Gilpin, R.W. (1993). *Laughing & loving with autism: A collection of "real life" warm and humorous stories.* Arlington, TX: Future Education.

Ginott, H. (1969). *Between parent and child.* New York: Avon Books.

Goleman, D. (1995). *Emotional intelligence: Why it can matter more than IQ.* New York: Bantam Dell.

Goodman, J.F. (1992). *When slow is fast enough: Educating the slow preschool child.* New York: The Guilford Press.

Goodman, J.F., & Hoban, S. (1994). *Around the clock: Parenting the delayed ADHD child* (videotape). New York: The Guilford Press.

Greenfield, J. (1970). *A child called Noah.* New York: Washington Square.

Greenspan, S.I. (1996). *The challenging child: Understanding, raising, and enjoying the five "difficult" types of children.* Reading, MA: Addison Wesley Longman.

Greenspan, S.I., & Greenspan, N.T. (1985). *First feelings: Milestones in the emotional development of your baby and child.* New York: Penguin Putnam.

Greenspan, S.I., & Wieder, S. (1998). *The child with special needs: Encouraging intellectual and emotional growth.* Reading, MA: Addison Wesley Longman.

Grossman, F.K. (1972). *Brothers and sisters of retarded children.* New York: Syracuse University Press.

Hendrix, H. (1988). *Getting the love you want: The guide for couples.* New York: Harper & Row.

Keen, S. (1991). *Fire in the belly: On being a man.* New York: Bantam Dell.

Klagsburn, F. (1992). *Mixed feelings: Love, hate, rivalry, and reconciliation among brothers and sisters.* New York: Bantam Dell.

Klein, S., & Schleifer, M. (1993). *It ISN'T fair: Siblings of children with disabilities.* Westport, CT: Bergin and Garvey.

Kranowitz, C.S. (1998). *The out-of-sync child: Recognizing and coping with sensory integration dysfunction.* New York: Berkley Books.

Kübler-Ross, E. (1969). *On death and dying.* New York: Collier.

Kupfer, F. (1998). *Before and after Zachariah: A family story about a different kind of courage.* Chicago: Academy Chicago.

Kushner, H.S. (1981). *When bad things happen to good people.* New York: Avon Books.

Lally, J.R. (Ed.). (1990). *A guide to social-emotional growth and socialization.* Sacramento: California Department of Education.

Lamb, M. (1983). Fathers of exceptional children. In M. Seligman (Ed.), *The family with a handicapped child: Understanding and treatment* (pp. 125–146). New York: Grune and Stratton.

Mackey, W.C. (1985). *Fathering behaviors: The dynamics of the man–child bond.* New York: Kluwer Academic/Plenum.

May, J. (1991). *Fathers of children with special needs: New horizons.* Bethesda, MD: Association for the Care of Children's Health.

McHugh, M. (1999). *Special siblings: Growing up with someone with a disability.* New York: Hyperion.

Mehren, E. (1991). *Born too soon.* New York: Pinnacle.

Meyer, D. (Ed.). (1995). *Uncommon fathers: Reflections on raising a child with a disability.* Bethesda, MD: Woodbine House.

Miller, N.B. (1994). *Nobody's perfect: Living and growing with children who have special needs.* Baltimore: Paul H. Brookes Publishing Co.

Miller, N.B., & Sammons, C.C. (1999). *Everybody's different: Understanding and changing our reactions to disabilities.* Baltimore: Paul H. Brookes Publishing Co.

Miller, S. (1983). *Men and friendship.* San Leandro, CA: Gateway Books.

Miller, S. (1990). *Family pictures.* New York: Harper & Row.

Monette, P. (1988). *Borrowed time: An AIDS memoir.* New York: Avon Books.

Moyers, B. (1993). *Healing and the mind.* New York: Doubleday.

Moses, K.L. (1985). *Not me! Not my child!: Dealing with parental denial and anxiety* (audiotapes). Chicago: Resource Networks.

Moses, K.L. (1989). *Lost dreams and growth* (videotape). Chicago: Resource Networks.

Nathanson, D. (1992). *Shame and pride: Affect, sex, and the birth of the self.* New York: W.W. Norton & Company.

Nichols, M.P. (1995). *The lost art of listening.* New York: The Guilford Press.

Oe, K. (1970). *A personal matter.* New York: Grove Press.

Osherson, S. (1986). *Finding our fathers: The unfinished business of manhood.* New York: The Free Press.

Osherson, S. (1992). *Wrestling with love: How men struggle with intimacy with women, children, parents and each other.* New York: Fawcett Columbine.

Pennebaker, J.W. (1990). *Opening up: The healing power of confiding in others.* New York: Avon Books.

Real, T. (1997). *I don't want to talk about it: Overcoming the secret legacy of male depression.* New York: Scribner.

Schiff, H.S. (1977). *The bereaved parent.* New York: Crown.

Seligman, M. (Ed.). (1983). *The family with a handicapped child: Understanding and treatment.* Orlando, FL: Grune and Stratton.

Seligman, M., & Darling, R.B. (1989). *Ordinary families, special children: A systems approach to childhood disability.* New York: The Guilford Press.

Staudacher, C. (1991). *Men & grief: A guide for men surviving the death of a loved one.* Oakland, CA: New Harbinger.

Stern, D.N. (1985). *The interpersonal world of the infant.* New York: Basic Books.

Stern, D.N. (1990). *Diary of a baby.* New York: Basic Books.

Stern, D.N., & Bruschweiler-Stern, N. (1998). *The birth of a mother: How the motherhood experience changes you forever.* New York: Basic Books.

Stone, R. (1996). *The healing art of storytelling: A sacred journey of personal discovery.* New York: Hyperion.

Styron, W. (1990). *Darkness visible: A memoir of madness.* New York: Random House.

Tannen, D. (1990). *You just don't understand: Women and men in conversation.* New York: Ballantine Books.

Turnbull, H.R., & Turnbull, A.P. (1985). *Parents speak out: Then and now.* Columbus, OH: Charles E. Merrill.

Webb-Mitchell, B. (1993). *God plays piano, too: The spiritual lives of disabled children.* New York: Crossroad.

Worden, J.W. (1982). *Grief counseling and grief therapy: A handbook for the mental health practitioner.* New York: Springer.

Books for Children

Abbott, D., & Kisor, H. (1986). *One TV blasting and a pig outdoors.* Morton Grove, IL: Albert Whitman.

Amenda, C. (1992). *Russell is extra special.* New York: Bruner Mazel.

Asetine, L., Mueller, E., & Tait, N. (1986). *I'm deaf and it's okay.* Morton Grove, IL: Albert Whitman.

Bergman, T. (1989). *Finding common language: Children living with deafness.* Milwaukee, WI: Gareth Stevens.

Bergman, T. (1989). *On our team: Children living with physical disabilities.* Milwaukee, WI: Gareth Stevens.

Bergman, T. (1989). *One day at a time: Children living with leukemia.* Milwaukee, WI: Gareth Stevens.

Bernstein, J., & Fireside, B. (1991). *Special parents, special children.* Morton Grove, IL: Albert Whitman.

Betschart, J. (1995). *A magic ride in foozbah-land: An inside look at diabetes.* Minneapolis, MN: Chronimed.

Brandenburg, A. (1984). *Feelings.* New York: William Morrow & Co.

Brown, T. (1984). *Someone special, just like you.* New York: Henry Holt.

Bunnett, R. (1992). *Friends in the park.* New York: Checkerboard.

Cain, B. (1990). *Double-dip feelings: Stories to help children understand emotions.* New York: Magination Press.

Caseley, J. (1991). *Harry and Willy and Carrothead.* New York: Greenwillow Books.

Corman, C., & Trevino, E. (1994). *Eukee, the jumpy, jumpy elephant.* Plantation, FL: Specialty Press.

Dubuque, N.S. (1996). *Kid power tactics for dealing with depression.* King of Prussia, PA: Center for Applied Psychology.

Duncan, D. (1994). *When Molly was in the hospital: A book for brothers and sisters of hospitalized children.* Windsor, CA: Rayve Productions.

Dwight, L. (1992). *We can do it!* New York: Checkerboard.

Dwyer, K. (1991). *What do you mean I have a learning disability?* New York: Walker and Company.

Elder, V. (1994). *Cardiac kids: A book for families who have a child with heart disease.* Dayton, OH: Dayton Area Heart and Cancer Association.

Fassler, J. (1975). *Howie helps himself.* Morton Grove, IL: Albert Whitman.

Field, M. (1992). *All about divorce.* King of Prussia, PA: Center for Applied Psychology.

Field, M., & Shore, H. (1994). *My life turned upside down, but I turned it right side up.* King of Prussia, PA: Center for Applied Psychology.

Foster, C.H. (1994). *Polly's magic games: A child's view of obsessive-compulsive disorder.* Ellsworth, ME: Dilligaf.

Gehret, J. (1990). *Eagle eyes: A child's guide to paying attention.* Fairport, NY: Verbal Images Press.

Gehret, J. (1990). *The don't give up kid and learning differences.* Fairport, NY: Verbal Images Press.

Girard, L. (1990). *Alex, the kid with AIDS.* Morton Grove, IL: Albert Whitman.

Grollman, E. (1990). *Talking about death: A dialogue between parent and child.* Boston: Beacon Press.

Gross, R.B. (1991). *You don't need words: A book about ways people talk without words.* New York: Scholastic.

Hafer, J., & Wilson, R. *Come sign with us: Sign language activities for children.* Washington, DC: Gallaudet University Press.

Helfman, E. (1993). *On being Sarah.* Morton Grove, IL: Albert Whitman.

Herzig, M. (1982). *A season of secrets.* Boston: Little, Brown and Company.

Holden, L.D. (1989). *Gran-Gran's best trick: A story for children who have lost someone they love.* New York: Magination Press.

Katz, I., & Ritvo, E. (1993). *Joey and Sam.* Northridge, CA: Real Life Story Books.

Koplow, L. (1991). *Tanya and the Tobo man: A story for children entering therapy.* New York: Magination Press.

Kova, S.J. (1993). *My journey of hope: A child's guidebook for living with cancer.* Grand Rapids, MI: Zondervan Publishing House.

Lasker, J. (1974). *He's my brother.* Morton Grove, IL: Albert Whitman.

Litchfield, A. (1976). *A button in her ear.* Morton Grove, IL: Albert Whitman.

Litchfield, A. (1977). *A cane in her hand.* Morton Grove, IL: Albert Whitman.

Lite, L. (1996). *A boy and a bear: The children's relaxation book.* Plantation, FL: Specialty Press.

Lobby, T. (1990). *Jessica and the wolf: A story for children who have bad dreams.* New York: Magination Press.

London, J. (1993). *The lion who had asthma.* Morton Grove, IL: Albert Whitman.

Marcus, I., & Marcus, P. (1990). *Scary night visitors: A story for children with bedtime fears.* New York: Magination Press.

Martin, B., & Martin, A. (1987). *Knots on a counting rope.* New York: Henry Holt.

Mellonie, B., & Ingpen, R. (1983). *Lifetimes: The beautiful way to explain death to children.* New York: Bantam Dell Publishing Group.

Meyer, D. (Ed.). (1997). *Views from our shoes: Growing up with a brother or a sister with special needs.* Bethesda, MD: Woodbine House.

Meyer, D., Vadasy, P., & Fewell, R. (1985). *Living with a brother or sister with special needs: A book for sibs.* Seattle: University of Washington Press.

Moss, D. (1989). *Lee, the rabbit with epilepsy.* Bethesda, MD: Woodbine House.

Muldoon, K. (1989). *Princess Pooh.* Morton Grove, IL: Albert Whitman.

Ostrow, W., & Ostrow, V. (1989). *All about asthma.* Morton Grove, IL: Albert Whitman.

Peacock, C.A., Gregory, A., & Gregory, K.C. (1998). *Sugar was my best food: Diabetes and me.* Morton Grove, IL: Albert Whitman.

Peterson, J. (1997). *I have a sister, my sister is deaf.* New York: Harper-Collins.

Pirner, C.W. (1991). *Even little kids get diabetes.* Morton Grove, IL: Albert Whitman.

Powers, M.E. (1991). *Our teacher's in a wheelchair.* Morton Grove, IL: Albert Whitman.

Quinn, P., & Stern, J. (1991). *Putting on the brakes: Young people's guide to understanding attention deficit hyperactivity disorder.* New York: Magination Press.

Rabe, B. (1988). *Where's Chimpy.* Morton Grove, IL: Albert Whitman.

Reiner, A. (1991). *The potty chronicles: A story to help children adjust to toilet training.* New York: Magination Press.

Sesame Street sign language book. (1990). New York: Random House.

Simon, N. (1974). *I was so mad!* Morton Grove, IL: Albert Whitman.

Simon, N. (1976). *Why am I different?* Morton Grove, IL: Albert Whitman.

Shapiro, L. (1994). *Jumpin Jake settles down: A workbook to help impulsive children think before they act.* King of Prussia, PA: Center for Applied Psychology.

Shapiro, L. (1995). *Sometimes I like to fight, but I don't do it much anymore.* King of Prussia, PA: Center for Applied Psychology.

Sobol, H. (1977). *My brother Steve is retarded.* New York: Macmillan.

Thompson, T. (1996). *Andy and his yellow frisbee.* Bethesda, MD: Woodbine House.

Webster-Doyle, T. (1991). *Why is everybody always picking on me: A guide to handling bullies.* Middlebury: VT: Atrium Society.

This bibliography of children's books was compiled with the assistance of Susan Levine, M.A., Family Resource Associates, 35 Haddon Avenue, Shrewsbury, NJ 07702; telephone: 908-747-5310. Susan also edits two newsletters for siblings: *For Siblings Only,* for young children, and *Sibling Forum,* for pre-teens and teens. Both are available through Family Resource Associates.

Resources for Families

FOUNDATION INFORMATION

AboutFace International   800-665-3223
http://www.aboutfaceinternational.org

AIDS Hotline   800-342-2437
http://www.ashastd.org

Alexander Graham Bell Society   202-337-5220
http://www.agbell.org

American Cancer Society   800-227-2345
http://www.cancer.org

American Council of the Blind   800-424-8666
http://www.acb.org

American Diabetes Association   800-342-2383
http://www.diabetes.org

American Foundation for the Blind   800-232-3044
http://www.afb.org

American Heart Association   800-242-8721
http://www.amhrt.org

American Juvenile Arthritis Foundation   800-283-7800
http://www.arthritis.org

American Society for Deaf Children   800-942-2732
http://www.deafchildren.org
(V/TTY)

Angelman Syndrome Foundation   800-432-6435
http://www.angelman.org

The Arc (formerly Association   800-433-5255
for Retarded Citizens)   http://www.thearc.org

Asthma & Allergy Foundation   800-727-8462
http://www.aafa.org

Attention Deficit Information Network   781-455-9895
http://www.addinfonetwork.com

Autism Research Institute   619-281-7165
http://www.autism.com/ari

Autism Society of America   800-3-AUTISM
http://www.autism-society.org

Brain Injury Association   800-444-6443
http://www.biausa.org

CHADD: Children and Adults with   800-233-4050
with Attention-Deficit/Hyperactivity
Disorder   http://www.chadd.org

Children's Hospice International   800-242-5338
http://www.chionline.org

Cystic Fibrosis Foundation   800-344-4823
http://www.cff.org

Easter Seal Society   416-421-8377
http://www.easterseals.org

Epilepsy Foundation of America   800-332-4050
http://www.efa.org

FACES—The National Craniofacial   800-332-2373
Association   http://www.faces-cranio.org

Fetal Alcohol Syndrome
(National organization)

800-66-NOFAS
http://www.nofas.org

Federation of Families for
Children's Mental Health

703-684-7710
http://www.ffcmh.org

Fragile X Foundation

800-688-8765
http://www.fragilex.org

Human Growth Foundation

800-451-6434
http://www.hgfound.org

Hyperlexia

630-415-2212
http://www.hyperlexia.org

Learning Disabilities Association

412-341-1515
http://www.ldanatl.org

Lupus Foundation of America

800-558-0121
http://www.lupus.org

Muscular Dystrophy Association

800-572-1717
http://www.mdausa.org

National Alliance for the
Mentally Ill

703-524-7600
http://www.nami.org

National Aphasia Association

800-922-4622
http://www.aphasia.org

National Association of
Developmental Disabilities Councils

800-562-6265
http://www.naddc.org

National Association for the Deaf

301-587-1788
http://www.nad.com

National Center for Learning Disabilities

212-687-7211
http://www.ncld.org

National Center for Stuttering   800-221-2483
http://www.stuttering.org

National Down Syndrome Congress   800-232-6372
http://www.ndsccenter.org

National Down Syndrome Society   800-221-4602
http://www.ndss.org

National Family Association for   800-255-0411, ext. 275
Deaf-Blind   http://www.helenkeller.org

National Hemophilia Foundation   800-424-2634
http://www.hemophilia.org

National Multiple Sclerosis Society   800-624-8236
http://www.nmss.org

National Organization for Rare Disorders   800-999-6673
http://www.rarediseases.org

National Pediatric HIV Resource Center   800-362-0071
http://www.pedhivaids.org

National Spinal Cord Injury Association   800-962-9629
http://www.spinalcord.org

Obsessive-Compulsive Foundation   203-878-5669
http://www.ocfoundation.org

Psoriasis Foundation   503-244-7404
http://www.psoriasis.org

Spina Bifida Association   800-526-3456
http://www.sbaa.org

Spinal Muscular Atrophy   800-886-1762
http://www.fsma.org

Stuttering Foundation   800-992-9392
                                http://www.stuttersfa.org

United Cerebral Palsy Association   800-872-5827
                                http://www.ucpa.org

INTERNET RESOURCES

Ability On-Line Support Network
                                http://www.ablelink.org
This site connects young people with special needs to peers and mentors with and without disabilities and encourages humor, respect, and understanding.

ANDI News   http://www.autismndi.com
This site helps parents to understand and implement a gluten- and casein-free diet for children with autism and provides helpful information and child-friendly recipes.

Autism-PDD Resource Network
                                http://www.autism-pdd.net
This site consolidates innumerable Internet resources and includes frank discussion, medical information, and practical advice.

Autism Resources   http://www.autism-resources.com
This site provides an amazing index of autism-related resources and information about hundreds of autism-related books. It also includes recommendations of parents and other readers; books for children, parents, teachers, and professionals; accounts of autistic people; and fiction books.

Autism-Spectrum   http://www.autism-spectrum.com
This site broadcasts radio interviews with people like Temple Grandin, Donna Williams, Tony Atwood, and so forth. It provides a truly international perspective on the disorder.

Beach Center on Families and Disability
http://www.lsi.ukans.edu/BEACH

The Beach Center's primary purpose is to conduct research to enhance the quality of life of families who have a child with a disability. The site addresses many of the questions that families commonly have.

Cerebral Palsy   http://www.aacpdm.org

The American Academy for Cerebral Palsy and Developmental Medicine is a multidisciplinary scientific society that provides information devoted to the treatment of cerebral palsy and to improving the quality of life.

Child and Adolescent Psychiatry   http://www.aacap.org

The American Academy of Child and Adolescent Psychiatry assists parents in understanding developmental, behavioral, emotional, and mental disorders affecting children. The site includes fact sheets on issues such as sleep, depression, bedwetting, and so forth.

Computers for the Handicapped
http://www.wolfe.net/~dr_bill/

This site provides information about software and hardware for people who are quadraplegic, as well as those with visual, hearing, mobility, speech, and language impairments.

Developmental Delay Resources
http://www.devdelay.org

This site is dedicated to meeting the needs of children who have sensorimotor, language, social, and emotional delays. It also publicizes research into determining identifiable factors, such as vaccines, that would put a child at risk and maintains a registry, tracking possible trends.

Disability Resources   http://www.disabilityresources.org

Encyclopedia Britannica Internet Guide calls this site "wonderfully well-organized . . . for cutting through the morass of disability-related material on the Web."

Families for Early Autism Treatment (FEAT)
http://www.feat.org

FEAT is dedicated to providing education, advocacy, and support. This web site includes a daily on-line newsletter about everything that is happening in the field of autism.

Family Village   http://www.familyvillage.wisc.edu

Using a creative small town motif, this site integrates information, resources, and communication opportunities on the Internet for people with cognitive and other disabilities, for their families, and for their service providers and supporters.

Family Voices   http://www.familyvoices.org

Family Voices is a true grass roots advocacy organization with chapters in every state speaking on behalf of children with special health care needs.

Federation of Families   http://www.ffcmh.org

Federation of Families is a national parent-directed organization focused on the needs of children and youth with emotional, behavioral, or mental disorders and their families. Information also is provided in Spanish.

First Signs   http://www.firstsigns.org

The First Signs web site provides parents and physicians with information on healthy and atypical development, screening guidelines, recommended screening tools, insights on how to deliver concerns to parents, and so forth.

Inclusive Education   http://www.uni.edu/coe/inclusion

This site is designed for general education teachers, special education teachers, parents, and school staff to help provide some answers about how inclusive education can be accomplished. It includes resources for making accommodations, as well as links to other web sites.

Interdisciplinary Council   http://www.icdl.com

The Interdisciplinary Council on Developmental and Learning Disorders supports families by providing resource information and opportunities for communication using the Developmental Individual–Difference Relationship-Based (DIR) model (floortime techniques).

National Fathers Network http://www.fathersnetwork.org

National Fathers Network is a national program dedicated to fathers of children with special needs. The site provides articles by fathers, photos, bulletin boards, and publications and connects to many local groups. Information also is provided in Spanish.

National Information Center for Children and Youth with Disabilities   http://www.nichcy.org

This site is a comprehensive federally funded information and referral clearinghouse for families, professionals, and educators. It contains many fact sheets and state-by-state resource lists.

Parents Helping Parents   http://www.php.com

Parents Helping Parents is a parent-directed family resource center that serves families and the professionals who serve them. The information on this site can help other parent-to-parent programs get started.

Parenting Special Needs
http://www.specialchildren.about.com/

This site is moderated by a mother of children with special needs and includes articles, links, chats, and "Parenting from the Heart," a weekly newsletter that keeps you updated on parenting children with special needs.

Pediatric Dentistry   http://www.aapd.org

The American Academy of Pediatric Dentistry provides information about improving and maintaining the oral health of infants, children, and adolescents with special health care needs.

Psych Central   http://www.psychcentral.com

Since 1995, this site has been a one-stop index for psychology, support, mental health issues, resources, and people on the Internet. It has been mentioned in the *Wall Street Journal*, the *Los Angeles Times*, and *Newsweek*.

Respite Care   http://www.chtop.com/locator.htm

National Respite Locator Service maintains a database of respite services for those looking for child care for children with special needs.

Sibling Support Project
http://www.seattlechildrens.org/sibsupp/

Sibling Support Project is a national program, based at Seattle Children's Hospital, dedicated to the interests of brothers and sisters of people with special health and developmental needs.

Special Child Magazine   http://www.specialchild.com

This electronic publication for families, edited by a mother of a child with special needs, includes bulletin boards, articles, information on diagnosis, and a column by Robert Naseef, Ph.D.

Toys and Play   http://www.lekotek.org

Toys and Play is a central source on toys and play for children with special needs; the National Lekotek Center is driven by the philosophy that children learn best when play is a family-centered activity. Through this site, you can gain access to a wealth of resources on opening up the world of play to children with special needs.

**Unicorn Children's
Foundation**   http://www.saveachild.com

Unicorn Children's Foundation supports education, treatment, and research for children with communication and learning disorders. It includes a multidisciplinary directory of professionals by geographic region.

University Affiliated Programs   http://www.aauap.org

University Affiliated Programs engage in activities to support individuals with developmental disabilities and their families with independence, productivity, integration, and inclusion into the community.

Vision Therapy   http://www.covd.org

This site from the College of Optometrists in Vision Development will inform you about how vision therapy can help with visual processing and learning disabilities. It also provides a large selection of links and a list of qualified professionals.

ZERO TO THREE   http://www.zerotothree.org

ZERO TO THREE is a national resource organization focusing on the first 3 years of life that aims to strengthen and support families, practitioners, and communities to promote the healthy development of infants and toddlers.

Index

Page references followed by *t* or *f* indicate tables or figures, respectively.

Other Brookes Books on Parents' Nightstands . . .

Brothers & Sisters
A Special Part of Exceptional Families, *Third Edition*

By Peggy A. Gallagher, Ph.D., Thomas H. Powell, Ed.D., & Cheryl A. Rhodes, M.S.

Filled with illuminating research and ready-to-use strategies, this book helps readers support positive, lifelong bonds between brothers and sisters when one has a disability. The third edition includes more on genetics and heredity, expanded discussion of multicultural issues and financial planning, and a greater focus on the role of extended family members.

2006 • ISBN 978-1-55766-719-9

Special Siblings
Growing up with Someone with a Disability

By Mary McHugh

In this absorbing and candid book, Mary McHugh reveals what she experienced as the sister of a man with cerebral palsy and mental retardation and shares what others have learned about being and having a "special sibling".

2003 • ISBN 978-1-55766-607-9

Steps to Independence

Teaching Everyday Skills to Children with Special Needs, *Fourth Edition*

By Bruce L. Baker, Ph.D., & Alan J. Brightman, Ph.D, with Jan B. Blacher, Ph.D., Louis J. Heifetz, Ph.D., Stephen P. Hinshaw, Ph.D. & Diane M. Murphy, R.N.

This popular book gives parents proven strategies for teaching their children the life skills they'll need to live as independently as possible. Laced with humor, helpful illustrations, and case studies, this is a must-have resource for families and professionals.

2004 • ISBN 978-1-55766-697-0

Third Edition available in Spanish • 2002 • ISBN 978-968426991-0

When Your Child Has a Disability
The Complete Sourcebook of Daily and Medical Care, *Revised Edition*

Edited by Mark L. Batshaw, M.D.

Packed with practical information, this easy-to-read guide gives expert advice on a wide range of medical and educational issues as well as detailed coverage of the daily and long-term care requirements of specific disabilities.

2001 • ISBN 978-1-55766-472-3

To order these invaluable resources stop by your local bookstore, call 1-800-638-3775, or visit www.brookespublishing.com.